THE TAO TE CHING
A NEW TRANSLATION WITH COMMENTARY

The *Tao Te Ching*

A New Translation with Commentary

ELLEN M. CHEN

A NEW ERA BOOK

PARAGON HOUSE
New York

First edition, 1989

Published in the United States by

Paragon House
90 Fifth Avenue
New York, NY 10011

A New Ecumenical Research Association Book

Manufactured in the United States of America

Library of Congress Cataloging-in-Publication Data

Chen, Ellen M., 1933-
The idea of peace in classical Taoism.
"A New ERA Book"
Bibliography: p.
Includes index.
1. Lao Tzu. Tao te ching. 2. Peace.
I. Title.
BL1900.L35C5432   1989   299'.51482   88-22433
ISBN 1-55778-083-8
1-55778-238-5 (pbk.)

The paper used in this publication meets the minimum requirements of
American National Standard for Information Sciences—Permanence of Paper
for Printed Library Materials, ANSI Z39.48-1984.

CONTENTS

Preface   ix

The *Tao Te Ching:* An Introduction   3

1. Date and Authorship of the *Tao Te Ching*   4

   Name, Birthplace, and Occupation of Lao Tzu   6
   Lao Tzu's Meeting with Confucius   6
   How the *Tao Te Ching* Came to Be Written   10
   Other Identities of Lao Tzu and an Account of His Descendants   12
   The Rivalry Between Confucianism and Taoism and Lao Tzu's Central
       Teaching   15
   Conclusion   18

2. The *Tao Te Ching* as a Religious Treatise   22

   The Function and Role of Early Religions   24
   Religions of the Axial Period   27
   Humans Become Gods on Earth   31
   Two Pseudo-Religions of the Twentieth Century   34
   Religion For or Against Life   36
   The Vision of Peace in the *Tao Te Ching*   40

3. Use and Translation of the Text   43

   The Title   43
   The Oldest *Tao Te Ching* Texts   44

v

Division into Parts and Chapters   45
Various Arrangements of the Text   46
The Need for a New Translation   47
On the Transliteration of the Chinese   47

The *Tao Te Ching:* A New Translation and Commentary

The *Tao Te Ching:* A New Translation and
Commentary   49

Chapters 1 through 81   51
Bibliography   233
Chinese Glossary   247
Index   261

To the memory of
My mother
Who bequeathed to me her accumulated *te*

PREFACE

In spite of the more than 400 commentaries (Yen Ling-fen, 1957) and more than forty translations into English, the *Tao Te Ching* is still a closed book to many of its readers. Some sinologists consider it to be a loose collection of seemingly unrelated statements. This is a tragedy. In not grasping its unifying theme, we are deprived of the benefits of a text that bears a particularly appropriate message for our time.

Long years of meditation on the *Tao Te Ching* have revealed to me its highly organic nature, each chapter being connected with others to form an organic whole. In order to lay the foundation for and serve as an introduction to works on Taoism in various stages of progress—on fundamental ontology, cosmology, epistemology, ethics, politics, etc.—I find it necessary first to determine the text itself, examining the philological studies as well as the major commentaries. I am convinced that the time has come for a new commentary on the *Tao Te Ching* that critically incorporates the best insights of important past commentaries, shows the internal consistency of the text and the organic connection of its various chapters, and brings out many passages with deeper and more original meanings, as well as resolves some of the questions posed by its critics, past and present. Above all, my purpose in writing this commentary is to recover the archaic vision of the *Tao Te Ching*, a vision which was already blurred at the time of Confucius (551–479 B.C.).

We are perhaps at the most opportune moment to succeed in this venture. The twentieth century has marked the discovery of the archaic mind. Findings in anthropology, archaeology, depth psychology, and history of religions, as well as the natural sciences have all collaborated to open a horizon of understanding hitherto inaccessible to our predecessors. Standing on the shoulders of giants in these fields, we now see much farther back into the past than Confucius or Plato. At the same time the spectacular findings in archaeological excavations in China in the last thirty or more years, particularly the discovery of the earliest texts of the *Tao Te Ching* in 1973–1974 at Ma-wang Tui of Changsha in Hunan province (Kao & Ch'ih, 1974), have prompted a new assessment of the early development of Chinese civilization. Now one could see that the arrival of Confucianism was a relatively late event on the Chinese scene; thus, identifying Chinese culture with Confucianism represents a shortsighted view (Ping-ti Ho, 1975).

Equating Chinese civilization with Confucianism, which is viewed by many as devoid of deep religious content, entails the corollary that the Chinese are not very religious. Herbert A. Giles says: "Confucianism is therefore entirely a system of morality, and not a religion" (1969: 37). True, Chinese thought and religion are not centered, as are Christian metaphysics and religion, on the nature and worship of the Supreme Being as *ens realissimum,* a Being separate and transcending the physical world of change. Rather, Chinese religious practices revolve around the interrelationship and mutual affectivity of what Heidegger calls the fourfold neighborhood of earth, sky, divinities, and mortals (1977: 327). The absence of a focus on transcendence has been interpreted to mean that the Chinese do not search for or experience the divine. This is another example of Western absolutism at work. Just as there has been the need to destroy Western ontology (W. Marx: 85f), there is also the need to reevaluate the religions of transcendence.

In the years it has taken me to work out this commentary, the *Tao Te Ching* began to strike me more and more as fundamentally a religious text, though it has an altogether different message from those of the religions that supposedly arose in the same epoch. Most high religions worship a warrior-like supreme being. Tao, however, though prior to God (Ti, ch. 4.3) and giving birth to all beings, is a non-being (ch. 40.2). The Taoist is humble and meek, in imitation of Tao whose mode of operation is weakness (*jo,* ch. 40.1) and non-contention (*pu-cheng,* ch. 8.3). Tao is called a valley spirit (ch. 6.1) and is described as subject to the cycle of birth and death (ch. 25.2). Plainly Tao points to an agricultural deity, not a warrior god. While other religions exhort their believers to war against and transcend the earthly conditions, the *Tao Te Ching* regards the earth as the abode of Tao (ch. 25.3). Its central message is the peace of all in the bosom of Tao from which all beings issue and in which all conflicts and struggles dissolve (ch. 4.2). Its vision of peace is grounded in a vision of the ultimate reality as non-being whose passivity and self-abnegation allow all beings to be. The idea of peace *(t'ai p'ing),* central to the text, then becomes the fitting title of this commentary. My aim in writing this commentary is not only to recover the vision of the *Tao Te Ching,* but also to show that this vision, born of a religious experience much earlier than that of the high religions, needs to be reinstated if humans are to find their proper place in the universe.

The second purpose of this commentary arises partly from anxiety about the world's ecology, particularly in the face of possible nuclear conflict. While at times it seems that the momentum of the process has already accelerated beyond control, I am hopeful that the situation still can be reversed. No task today is more urgent than reducing the possibility of nuclear holocaust. We can no longer leave the work of peace in the hands of political leaders alone. These leaders, in order to progress toward peace, must be equipped with the profound religious and intellectual justification for peace. By bringing forth the *Tao Te Ching*'s vision of peace, I hope to help lay the foundation for a new religious-philosophical consciousness conducive to establishing peace on earth among all creatures.

This work had its earliest seed in my college thesis written at the National Taiwan University under the direction of the late Professor Beauson Tseng, who first awakened in me a love for philosophy. I cherish the memory of the many happy hours discussing philosophy in his house during my senior year, while he was busy preparing to assume the presidency of Tunghai University. At Fordham University, Professors Quentin Lauer and W. Norris Clarke taught me how to tread on solid ground of scholarship, the late Robert C. Pollock showed me how to make connections and soar into flights of insight, and Thomas Berry has given me inspiration and encouragement in all my endeavors. Frank Flinn of the New Ecumenical Research Association taught me to be concise. My husband Vincent has been patient, sympathetic, and long-suffering throughout these years of my labor. St. John's University granted me a one-semester leave to prepare the manuscript for publication. The number of scholars and friends who have enlightened me in my intellectual journey far exceeds the few acknowledged in the body of the work and the bibliography. They are the real authors of what is valuable in the work. The inadequacies and errors that exist in this work, however, are wholly my responsibility.

The *Tao Te Ching:*
An Introduction

Part one of this introduction discusses the authorship and dating of the *Tao Te Ching*, which has been a problem ever since the time of Ssu-ma Ch'ien (145?-90? B.C.), the Grand Historian of China. Our treatment is meant not to settle the question but to acquaint the reader of the historical background from which the text arose and the role it has played in the development of Chinese thought.

In part two we address the question, raised by Chinese and Western thinkers alike, of whether and in what sense the *Tao Te Ching* is a religious text. To highlight its religious content we present a history of religions from the perspective of the dialectic between humans and the natural world. We come to the conclusion that those very religious functions which had enhanced human survival in the past have now led us to the precipice of self-destruction. If religion is to be in the service of life today, it needs to radically turn its direction from being the expression of human repudiation of the earth to human appreciation of earth as the cradle of life and the abode of spirit. Here the earth-loving Chinese spirit, in the past judged not very religious by the standards of religions of transcendence, shall stand vindicated in the wake of this new consciousness. As the voice of the primordial Ground providing a theoretical foundation for the new religion of peace on earth, the *Tao Te Ching* is particularly valuable in shaping this new religious consciousness.

The third part is on textual matters. It explains the history and formation of the text, its division into chapters and why in writing this new commentary I find it necessary to render a new translation.

1

Date and Authorship of the
Tao Te Ching

The *Tao Te Ching (The Canon of Tao and Te)* has been called the *Lao Tzu* in China after the person traditionally believed to be its author. Already by the time of Ssu-ma Ch'ien the person of Lao Tzu was enveloped in legend. In his biography of Lao Tzu in the *Shih chi (Records of the Historian, 63: 1a–3b)* Ssu-ma Ch'ien stated that Lao Tzu (the old master) was Lao Tan, a native of Ch'u, who held the official title "keeper of archives" in the imperial court of the Chou Dynasty (1122–249 B.C.). Confucius went to him to inquire about rites. A man of self-effacement, he left the court of Chou as an old man and went into seclusion. Before he crossed the border gate an admirer, Kuan-ling-yin (the keeper of the pass), entreated him to put down his thoughts for posterity. Thus, we are bequeathed with the *Tao Te Ching* in a little more than 5,000 characters.

Having recorded this much of Lao Tzu, Ssu-ma Ch'ien added that he had also been identified with Lao Lai-tzu (old master Lai), also a native of Ch'u and a contemporary of Confucius, who lived to be 160 or 200 years old. Lao Tzu had in addition been identified with a T'ai-shih Tan (grand historian Tan) of the Chou Dynasty who lived 129 years after Confucius's death.

Since Ssu-ma Ch'ien's time the problem of authorship has been raised time and again in the course of Chinese history (Lo Ken-tse: 257–81). There were heated discussions in the Sung (960–1206) and Ch'ing Dynasties (1644–1912). With Ts'ui Shu (1740–1816) and Wang Chung (1744–1794) it was doubted whether such a person as Lao Tzu ever existed.

The traditional belief that Lao Tzu was an older contemporary of Confucius with whom he consulted on rituals would date the author ca. 600 B.C. Hu Shih (1937), Lin Yutang (1942: 8–9), Chiang Hsi-ch'ang (6–10, 476–477), Ma Hsu-lun (7–31), and Kao Heng (1956: 153-187) are among the contemporary Chinese

4

scholars who hold the traditional view. Among Western scholars we may include James Legge (1891: xiv, 9), P. J. Maclagan (70, 88), and Paul Carus (1900).

This date has been challenged by many in the wake of "doubting the tradition movement" at the turn of the century. Since the *Tao Te Ching* is anti-Confucian, the argument goes, it cannot be a work of 600 B.C., before the Confucian school had gained its ground. The question has been asked why, in all the Confucian and Mohist texts belonging to and immediately after Confucius's time, no mention was made of the person Lao Tan. Ts'ui Shu says:

> The literary style of the *Lao Tzu* is close to that of the Warring States Period (300–222 B.C.). It is altogether unlike the writing in the *Analects* or the *Annals of Spring and Autumn*. Confucius praised many ancient sages and his distinguished contemporaries. Why is it that he did not mention a word about Lao Tzu?
>
> (I:12b–13a)

Ts'ui Shu further argues that Mencius (371–289 B.C.), the orthodox representative of the Confucian school, fought vehemently against the influences of Yang Chu (440–360 B.C.) and Mo Ti (Fl. 478–438 B.C.) in his own time (*Mencius* 3B: 9). Yang Chu's thought has traditionally been connected with Taoism and considered a development of the thought contained in the *Tao Te Ching*. Yet Mencius, who attacked the teachings of Yang Chu, never mentioned Lao Tzu in his works.

Ts'ui Shu's position has been criticized as the fallacy of argument by silence (Hsu Hsu-sheng: 24). Yet there is another argument against the theory that the author lived ca. 600 B.C., that military ideas and terms mentioned in the text, like *"p'ien chiang chün"* (second-in-command, ch. 31.5), *"shang chiang chün"* (commander-in-chief, ch. 31.5), "take the empire" (ch. 57.1), *"jen i"* (humanity and righteousness, ch. 18.1), "kings and barons" (chs. 32.1, 37.1, & 39.1), and "kings and dukes" (ch. 42.2), did not become current until ca. 300 B.C. when China entered the Warring States Period (403–222 B.C.) (Ch'en Chu, Preface). It is now generally granted that the text in style and use of terms belongs to the third century B.C. Besides the pioneers Ch'ui Su and Wang Chung, those who date the text to ca. 300 B.C. include Liang Ch'i-Ch'ao (1923), Fung Yu-lan (1952 I: 170), Chien Mu (1957: 119–129), Kuo Mo-jo (26ff), Duyvendak (1954: 6), Kimura Eiichi, Yang Yung-kuo (231–141), and others (Dubs).

Many other theories have been proposed on the date and authorship of the text with few significant results (Ku Chieh-kang, vol. IV. P. II: 303-520; vol. VI. Pt. II; Chan, 1963b: 35–59). While we may not be able to determine with complete certainty who Lao Tzu was and when he lived, how the ancients viewed him or his book can be culled from various classical sources. I propose to sketch a composite image of Lao Tzu in ancient times. This is the more fruitful approach since it bears upon the message and significance of the *Tao Te Ching* to the ancients and hence its message and significance to us today. To accomplish this task I shall use the same method Kao Heng employed (1956: 159–174). I shall present Ssu-Ma Ch'ien's biography of Lao Tzu section by section, then evaluate each section with the help of other classical sources.

Name, Birthplace, and Occupation of Lao Tzu

Ssu-ma Ch'ien's biography begins:

> Lao Tzu was a native of Ch'u-jen hamlet in Li county, in the K'u district of the state of Ch'u. His surname was Li, private name Erh, courtesy name Tan. He was an official of the archives in Chou (the capital).
>
> (*Shih chi* 63: 1a–3b. Cf. Chan, 1963b: 36–37).

In today's version of Ssu-ma Ch'ien's biography of Lao Tzu we also read that Lao Tzu's courtesy name was Po-yang, the name of an immortal of the eighth century B.C. Scholars generally agree that this was a later tampering with the text. Both the private name Erh and courtesy name Tan have the radical for ear, with Tan meaning long earlobes, the sign of longevity. Lao Tan is the name most often mentioned in classical sources. The name Li Erh is not found elsewhere and we do not know the Grand Historian's source. Our question: Is Lao the surname, or does it simply mean old; if it means old, does it refer to the man or the teaching he imparted? It is my view that Lao Tzu stands not so much for the old man as for the old wisdom he perpetuated.

The K'u district of the state of Ch'u is today's Lu I district in Honan province, southwest of the birthplace (Chu Fu) of Confucius in Shantung province. In a later section of this chapter I shall discuss how these two localities gave rise to the traditional view that Confucius was the intellectual leader of the north, while Lao Tan represented the spirit of the south.

Though the *Tao Te Ching* is against the overdevelopment of the mind, its author was said to be an "official of the archives," the equivalent of today's state librarian or historian, with access to the most ancient records. The *Chuang Tzu* (Watson, 1968: 149) also gave the title "official of the archives."

Lao Tzu's Meeting with Confucius

Ssu-Ma Ch'ien's biography continues:

> Confucius went to Chou to consult Lao Tzu on rituals *(li)*. Lao Tzu said, "Those whom you talk about are dead and their bones have

decayed. Only their words have remained. When the time is proper, the superior man rides in a carriage, but when it is not, he covers himself up and staggers away. I have heard that a good merchant hides his treasures as if his store were empty and that a gentleman with full virtue *(te)* appears like a stupid man. Get rid of your proud air and many desires, your overbearing manners and excessive ambitions. None of these are good for you. This is what I want to tell you."

Confucius left and told his pupils, "I know birds can fly, fish can swim, and animals can run. That which runs can be trapped, that which swims can be netted, and that which flies can be shot. As to the dragon, I don't know how it rides on the winds and clouds and ascends to heaven. Lao Tzu, whom I saw today, is indeed like a dragon!"

The meeting of Confucius and Lao Tzu was also recorded by the Grand Historian in the biography of Confucius. There Lao Tzu gave Confucius the following parting words:

"I heard that the rich give gifts of money, the virtuous give gifts of speech. I am not rich. May I be an imposter of virtue to give you some gift of speech: "Those clever with sharp *(ch'a)* observations who yet are fond of criticizing others are courting death. Those with wide *(po)* and discriminating *(pien)* learning who yet expose the evils of others put their own lives in danger. As a son, avoid such pitfalls, as a minister, avoid such pitfalls."

(*Shih chi*, 47: 3a–b. Chavannes, V: 299–300.)

Both speeches are in agreement with the teaching of the *Tao Te Ching*. In both speeches Lao Tzu made it clear that the essence of *li* (ritual) consists not in parading one's own merits or exposing other people's evils, which are the ways to death, but in being humble and yielding, qualities conducive to long life. This is a familiar refrain also in the Bible: Pride is the way to death while humility is the way to life. In both biographies Lao Tzu is portrayed as a kindly old master toward the admiring and respectful Confucius. From Lao Tzu's speech we get the impression that Confucius was an ambitious young man, full of zeal to cultivate virtue, eradicate evil, and above all, to be savior of the world. This moral zeal, fired by the desire for fame and puffed up with pride and self-righteousness, was in need of a dressing down. The encounter with Lao Tzu proved beneficial; afterward Confucius was said to become more reserved and contemplative, while his disciples also made progress.

According to the Grand Historian the meeting took place when Confucius was between the ages of seventeen and thirty. Lao Tzu would be about twenty years his senior. The occasion reminds us of the meeting of Parmenides and

Socrates when Socrates, also as a young man, was eager to exclude all unpleasant things in the realm of change such as "hair, mud, dirt, or anything else which is vile and paltry" (*Parmenides* 130) from the realm of ideas. Parmenides, an old man of wisdom, likewise advised Socrates that he needed to become more mature.

Yang Chia-lo speculated that Confucius and Lao Tzu met more than once (3–8). If they met only once it was unlikely that it happened before Confucius was thirty, since the biographies of both Lao Tzu and Confucius in the *Shih chi* mention that Confucius brought some disciples with him. According to the *Chuang Tzu* Confucius went to see Lao Tzu when he was fifty-one, being at that age still not in possession of Tao (Watson: 161). Scholars have tried to date the meeting by using the key in the *Li chi* that records an eclipse taking place during the meeting. No eclipses were recorded when Confucius was between seventeen and thirty, but there was one when he was fifty-seven. That Confucius did learn from Lao Tan is recorded also in the *Lü-shih ch'un-ch'iu* (*Mr. Lü's Spring and Autumn Annals,* compiled 239 B.C., 2: 10a). Although it does not mention specifically what Confucius learned from Lao Tan, it is assumed that the subject was *li* (rites).

The most authoritative text on the meeting of Confucius and Lao Tzu is the *Li chi,* chapter "Tseng Tzu wen" ("The Questions of Tseng Tzu"), where Confucius himself gives an account of what he learned from Lao Tzu on the subject of rites:

> (Confucius said:) I heard from Lao Tan: When the Son of Heaven or the King of the State dies, the priest fetches the spirit tablets from the many temples and stores them in the temple of the Ancestor. This is rite. When wailing is over and the whole affair is concluded, then each of the spirit tablets is returned to its temple. When the King leaves the State, the Grand Sacrificer accompanies the King with the spirit tablets of the many temples. This is rite. When sacrificing to the Ancestor, the priest comes forward to meet the spirit tablets coming from the four temples. Each time when the spirit tablet leaves its temple or returns to its temple, people must be kept away from its route. So said Lao Tan.
>
> (cf. Legge, 1967, I: 325.)

> (Confucius said:) In the past I assisted Lao Tan in a burial service in the community. When we reached the road, there was an eclipse of the sun. Lao Tan said: "Ch'iu (the given name of Confucius), stop the coffin on the right side of the road. Stop the crying and wait for the change." Then the light returned, so we proceeded. He said this was rite.
>
> (cf. *Ibid.,* I: 339.)

The person Lao Tan in the *Li chi* was without question an expert on rites. It is also without question that the *Tao Te Ching* is critical of the Confucian emphasis on rites (ch. 38). The question is, how can the author of a text holding such a low opinion of rites be the same person to whom the most famous educator of China made one or more pilgrimages precisely to master the subject? To answer this question we must distinguish two meanings of *li*. The *Tao Te Ching* attacks *li* as social decorum in chapter 38, but it respects the deeper sense of *li* in funeral rites in chapter 31. The Lao Tan presented in the *Li chi* as an expert on funeral rites is entirely reconcilable with the author of chapter 31.

The Confucian Han Yü (768–824) in an essay "An Inquiry On the Way" *(Yüan Tao)* repudiated the traditional account that Confucius consulted Lao Tzu on rites (11: 1a–3b; Chan. 1963a: 454–6). Some Confucians have speculated that the account in the *Li chi* in which Confucius speaks of learning rites from Lao Tan was a later Taoist insertion into a Confucian text to exalt their own founder above the founder of the rival school. I disagree. There is no reason for Taoists to claim that Lao Tzu instructed Confucius on a subject which he himself scorned. In the *Chuang Tzu*, which records the meeting of Confucius and Lao Tzu five times (Watson: 132–133, 149–150, 161–162, 224–227, 238–240), no mention is made of Confucius consulting Lao Tzu on rites, but rather on how to acquire Tao. In view of the great veneration of all pre-Ch'in thinkers for Lao Tan, it is equally legitimate to suspect the Confucians of fabricating this story. The reference to Lao Tan in the *Li Chi* could have been written by a pious Confucian to ground the Confucian emphasis on rites upon the ancient tradition represented by Lao Tan. Since Lao Tan was the Wise Old Man who epitomized the ancient Tao, he must have known all the ancient rites held by Confucians to be the culmination of order and civilization. As it turned out, this Wise Old Man taught the virtues of softness and yielding, of ignorance and non-exertion, which did not quite harmonize with the Confucian enthusiasm for knowledge and form, for rites and fame. It would also explain why Ssu-ma Ch'ien, a professed Confucian, fully aware that in his own time Taoism and Confucianism had developed into different, indeed rival, schools, included the meeting of Lao Tzu and Confucius in both biographies. The tradition that Confucius learned rites from Lao Tzu could have been perpetrated by the Confucians. Being historically minded, they had to show that their emphasis on ritual had deep roots in a venerated figure like Lao Tzu, the Old Master. They, not the Taoists, were more likely to be ignorant of the Old Master's negative assessment of rituals.

Hu Shih (1891–1962) thinks there is no inconsistency in being a teacher of rites while holding a rather critical attitude toward the value of such an institution. In his view the meeting between Confucius and Lao Tzu was not at all unlikely (*Shuo ju:* 1–81). Both Lao Tzu and Confucius belonged to the class of *ju* (literati), whose main social function was to perform rites. The *ju* at that time, however, were intellectual skeptics who performed the rites perfunctorily with no commitment to their fundamental meaning. By the time of Hsün Tzu (fl. 298–238 B.C.) the rites were divested of their early religious significance to become a mere civil institution. Even at the time of Lao Tzu, the trend was obvious enough to cause alarm. Thus, Lao Tzu could be both a master on the subject of rites and the author of a text which deprecates the practice of rites devoid of their spiritual commitments. Exactly because he was a man learned in the ways of the past, he was in a position to point out the shallowness of what had developed. Chapter 38.6 calls *li* "the thin edge of loyalty and faithfulness," a mere flowering which departs from the inner core. This was exactly what Lao Tzu counseled Confucius on in the two biographies. *Li,* Lao Tzu told Confucius, was not puffed up with pride, but was rooted in humility and self-effacement; it pertained to the essence, not to external manifestations. *Li* religiously is a reverence for all beings (ch. 31.6), the opposite of elevating oneself at the expense of others. The *Tso Chuan* (Duke Chao, 2nd year), a Confucian text, also says: "Loyalty and faithfulness, these are the vessels of *li;* humility and yielding, these are the principles of *li.*"

How the *Tao Te Ching* Came to Be Written

Ssu-ma Ch'ien continues:

> Lao Tzu practiced Tao and *te.* His teaching aims at self-effacement and namelessness. Having lived in Chou long and seeing its decline, he left Chou. Arriving at the pass, the pass-keeper *(kuan ling),* Yin-hsi, said, "You are about to retire. Please force yourself to write a book for me." Thereupon Lao Tzu wrote a book in two parts, expounding the meaning of Tao and *te* in more than five thousand words and then departed. None knew how he ended.

This passage informs us how the work came to be written. Upon his retirement Lao Tzu left his employ and traveled west. When he reached the border gate, generally believed to be the Han Ku Pass leading to the state of Ch'in, he was entreated by the gate official or pass-keeper to put down his thoughts for posterity. Thus we have the *Tao Te Ching* in two parts.

The story is rather fantastic. The last chapter of the *Chuang Tzu* tells of a philosopher named Kuan Yin who ranked with Lao Tan among "the great and true men of old."

> To regard the Source as minute and the things that emerge from it as big, to look upon accumulation as insufficiency; dwelling alone, peaceful and placid, with the spiritual and illumined—there were those in ancient times whose art of Tao lay in these things. Kuan Yin and Lao

Tan heard of such a teaching and delighted in it. Everlasting *(ch'ang)*, Nonbeing *(wu)* and Being *(yu)* were its building blocks; the Great Unity was its supreme principle. Gentle weakness and humble self-effacement are its outer marks; emptiness, void, and the noninjury of the ten thousand beings are its inner essence.

(Cf. Watson: 371–373)

In the above text Kuan Yin does not have to mean the keeper of the gate *(kuan)* whose surname was Yin, but could be the name of a philosopher whose surname was Kuan and personal name was Yin. The *Chuang Tzu* also records a speech given by Kuan Yin to Lieh Tzu (450–375 B.C.) (Watson: 198–199). The *Lieh-tzu,* a forgery of ca. the third century A.D., attributed one line from chapter 73 of the *Tao Te Ching* to be what Lao Tan said to Kuan Yin: "Lao Tan said to Kuan Yin: 'When heaven hates someone, who knows the reason?' " (Cf. Graham: 129–130).

Kuo Mo-jo proposed that the real author was Huan Yüan, a member of the Huang Lao (Yellow Emperor) school of the third century B.C. (1962: 231–244). According to Kuo, Huan Yüan was the same person, Kuan Yin, supposedly the gatekeeper, but really intended as a hint as to the real author's identity. It was not then uncommon for the master's thoughts to be recorded later by his disciples, the *Analects* of Confucius being a prime example. Since it is recorded in Ssu-ma Ch'ien's *Shih chi* that Huan Yüan wrote a treatise in two parts (prior and posterior) to expound the truth of Tao, and since the *Tao Te Ching* has a prior and a posterior part, Kuo argues that Huan Yüan was the real author.

Kuo's theory is frivolous. If Huan Yüan was indeed Kuan Yin, Ssu-ma Ch'ien, who wrote on both men, would have indicated this. If Kuan Yin was Huan Yüan of the third century B.C., how do we explain that the *Chuang Tzu* (appearing, at the latest, in the third century B.C.) called Kuan Yin and Lao Tan "the great true men of old"? Secondly, the *Lü-shih Ch'un-ch'iu* (compiled in 239 B.C.), in a synopsis of the teachings of various thinkers, ranks Kuan Yin with Lao Tan (b. 570 B.C.?), Confucius (551–479 B.C.), Mo ti (fl. 479–438 B.C.), Lieh Tzu (fifth century B.C.), and Yang Chu (440–360 B.C.?):

Lao Tan values gentleness *(jo)*, Confucius values benevolence *(jen)*, Mo Ti values frugality *(lien)*, Kuan Yin values tranquility *(ch'ing)*, Lieh Tzu values emptiness *(hsu)*, Chen P'ien values equality *(ch'i)*, Yang Chu values the self *(chi)*. . . .

(17: 18a. *SPTK*)

We don't know when Lao Tzu died. The *Chuang Tzu* tells us that after Lao Tan died, Ch'in I went to mourn him (Watson: 52–53). If we follow up the

Grand Historian's account that in old age Lao Tan left Chou for Ch'in, then most probably he died in Ch'in (Kao Heng, 1956: 171). The *Shui ching chu* (*Water Classic,* 19: 1b. SPTK) refers to a tomb of Lao Tzu in Ch'in.

Other Identities of Lao Tzu and an Account of His Descendants

Ssu-ma Ch'ien continues:

> Some say that Lao Lai Tzu was also a native of Ch'u. He wrote a book in fifteen parts on the application of Taoist teaching and was a contemporary of Confucius.
>
> Probably Lao Tzu lived to be more than one hundred and sixty years—some say more than two hundred years—because he practiced Tao and nourished his life.
>
> One hundred and twenty-nine years after the death of Confucius, historians recorded a Grand Historian Tan of Chou who had an audience with Duke Hsien [reigned 384–362 B.C.] of Ch'in, saying, "First Ch'in joined with Chou and then separated. After five hundred years of separation they will be joined again. Then in seventy years a king of the feudal lords will appear." Some say Tan was Lao Tzu while others say no. No one knows who is right.
>
> Lao Tzu was a recluse gentleman. Lao Tzu's son was named Tsung. Tsung became a general in the state of Wei, and was enfeoffed at Tuan-kan. Tsung's son was Chu and Chu's son was Kung. Kung's great-great-grandson was Chia, who was an official under Emperor Hsiao-wen [reigned 179–157 B.C.] of the Han dynasty [206 B.C.–A.D. 220]. Chia's son, Chieh, became grand tutor to Ch'iung, prince of Chiao-hsi, and so made his home in Ch'i.

Having presented what he believed to be the historical facts of Lao Tzu's life and how the book came to be, Ssu-ma Ch'ien from here on incorporates heterogeneous accounts concerning the person Lao Tzu that had sprung up in his time. One theory was that Lao Tzu was Lao Lai Tzu, also Confucius's teacher. To the Grand Historian, Lao Tan and Lao Lai Tzu were two individuals. In his "Biographies of Confucius's Disciples" he wrote: "Confucius studied seriously under Lao Tzu in Chou, . . . under Lao Lai Tzu in Ch'u . . ." (*Shih Chi,* 67: 1b). He also informs us that Lao Lai Tzu wrote a book in fifteen parts on the application of Tao. The *Bibliography* section of the *Han Shu* (History of the Former Han Dynasty, 30/21a) lists Lao Lai Tzu as a Taoist author of a work in sixteen sections, no longer extant. The *Chan-kuo ts'e* (*Strategies of the Warring States,* 17/205/3b), edited by Liu Hsiang, relates Lao Lai Tzu showing Confucius the value of the Taoist teaching on softness in serving a ruler: The soft tongue stays intact when a person reaches sixty, but the teeth, in spite of their hardness, are all gone. In the *Lieh-nü Chuan* (*Biographies of Famous Women*, 2/33b–34a), however, Liu Hsiang presents Lao Lai Tzu as a reclusive religious Taoist who refused office through the good advice of his wife.

The *Chuang Tzu* may be the source of the confusion of Lao Tzu with Lao Lai Tzu. It records a meeting of Lao Lai Tzu and Confucius much like the meeting of Lao Tan and Confucius recorded by the Grand Historian in the Lao Tzu biography:

> A disciple of Lao Lai-tzu was out gathering firewood when he happened to meet Confucius. He returned and reported, "There's a man over there with a long body and short legs, his back a little humped and his ears set way back, who looks as though he were trying to attend to everything within the four seas. I don't know who it can be." Lao Lai-tzu said, "That's K'ung Ch'iu. Tell him to come over here!" When Confucius arrived, Lao Lai-tzu said, "Ch'iu, get rid of your proud bearing and that knowing look on your face and you can become a gentleman!"
>
> (Watson: 297)

The *Chuang Tzu*, however, does not suggest that Lao Tan lived an extraordinarily long life. In one passage (Watson: 52) it records Lao Tan's death. The legend that Lao Tzu lived an extraordinarily long or immortal life arose when the figure of Lao Tzu was fully absorbed into religious Taoism (Seidel, 1969).[1]

1. In recent years we have witnessed a surge of academic interest in religious Taoism—in its contribution to the development of Chinese science (Needham, Sivin), and its rituals and practices (Girardot, Kaltenmark, Lagerwey, Maspero, Robinet, Saso, Schipper, Seidel, Sivin, Strickmann, Welsh, etc.). Though both are rooted in archaic Chinese religion, religious Taoism is a very different phenomenon from philosophical Taoism. Philosophical Taoism raised the ancient Chinese worldview to the level of thought. As a way of thinking it is clearly distinguishable from Confucianism, Mohism, Legalism, and other schools of thought in ancient China. Religious Taoism, on the other hand, is amorphous and syncretic throughout its career. Tracing its roots to the practices of ancient shamans and diviners, as an organized religion it came into existence in the 2nd century A.D. The only indigenous religion of China, in its development it incorporates whatever enters the Chinese religious orbit. It appropriated all the philosophical Taoist texts, including the *Tao Te Ching* and the *Chuang Tzu*, which become its sacred scriptures. But what are poetical musings and metaphysical reflections in these texts now become theurgy and dogma. Its most fervent search and promise is long life and immortality. While it reveres the author of the *Tao Te Ching* as its spiritual founder, it adopts the yin-yang and five-phase theory from the Yin Yang school, believes with Mo Tzu that heaven possesses conscious will (Ch'ing: 48–49), adopts Confucian ethics, and includes many Buddhist teachings and rituals. As a result the religious Taoist canon grew to thousands of volumes (Ch'en Kuo-fu), becoming a treasure trove for the study of all aspects of Chinese culture. My use of the term Taoist is restricted to the philosophical sense.

Indeed, the *Lieh Hsien Chuan* by Liu Hsiang includes both Lao Tzu and Lao Lai Tzu among the immortal. Lao Tzu was exalted to become not only an immortal, but was also identified with Chaos, Tao, or Change, the highest creative principle in Taoism (Fu Ch'in-chia: 99). Kaltenmark says:

> Under the second Han he became a veritable god. In an inscription composed in A.D. 165 on the occasion of a sacrifice held in Po Chou Temple on the orders of Emperor Huan, it is stated that for some followers of the Tao, Lao Tzu is an emanation of primordial Chaos and is coeternal with the Three Luminaries (Sun, Moon, and Stars). He is even compared to P'an Ku, the mythological First Man. When P'an Ku died, "his head became the Four Peaks, his eyes became the sun and moon." Similarly, when Lao Tzu died, he "changed his body," and his left eye became the sun, his right the moon; his head became the Kunlun Mountains. . . .
>
> (1969: 109)

The Grand Historian Tan lived 129 years after the death of Confucius (479 B.C., *Shih-chi*, 4/32a, 5/21a; 28/7b; 63/3b). If Lao Tzu was the same Grand Historian Tan, he would have lived around 350 B.C. (Lo Ken-tse, 1958: 207–278, T'an Chieh-fu, 1924). I reject this view. Even at the time of Ssu-ma Ch'ien (ca. 145 B.C.), Lao Tzu was already enveloped in legend. If the writer of the *Tao Te Ching* belonged to 300 B.C., Ssu-ma Ch'ien lived about 150 years later. In that relatively short period he could not have become so confused with the facts about Lao Tzu that he made Lao Tzu to be some superhuman being who lived 160 or even 200 years. If that were indeed true Lao Tzu would actually have been Ssu-ma Ch'ien's contemporary. Ssu-ma Ch'ien possessed a wide range of sources in writing his *Historical Records.* At the turn of this century skeptics regarded his list of ancient kings and their deeds reaching back as far as the Shang dynasty (1766–1122 B.C.) as legendary accounts. However, excavations of bronze inscriptions from An Yang, many belonging to the Shang dynasty, have verified most of the names he gave and proved his remarkable accuracy. If the author of the *Tao Te Ching* lived so close to the time of Ssu-ma Ch'ien, even if he were a self-effacing man, it would not have been so difficult for Ssu-ma Ch'ien to identify him.

Given these diverse accounts Lao Tzu's persona became confused within a few centuries. In order to anchor him in real history, the Grand Historian listed the names, occupations, and domiciles of generations of Lao Tzu's descendants. Unfortunately, this information did not help to clarify the historical circumstances of Lao Tzu one way or another. Scholars have spilled much ink without arriving at a generally acceptable conclusion.

The Rivalry Between Confucianism and Taoism and Lao Tzu's Central Teaching

Ssu-ma Ch'ien concludes:

> Today followers of Lao Tzu repudiate Confucianism and followers of Confucius also repudiate Lao Tzu's teaching. Is this not what is meant by "People with different taos (ways) do not counsel one another"?
>
> Li Erh taught non-action, to make room for self-transformation; he abided in clarity and tranquillity, to allow for the process of self-equilibrium *(tzu-cheng)*.
>
> *(Shih chi, 63: 3b)*

The direct relationship between the founders of Taoism and Confucianism was a cordial one, if we may trust the classical texts. In Lao Tan's advice to Confucius, however, we can already detect the different orientations toward thinking and living between these two masters. Since then the two schools have had their parting of the ways, and as a result the relationship between their followers deteriorated to one of rivalry and harsh criticisms.

Liang Ch'i-ch'ao (1873–1929) attributes the different ideals in Taoism and Confucianism to different regional spirits (n.d.: 15ff). Confucius represented the spirit of the north, action and reform, while Lao Tzu represented the spirit of the south, which sought to transcend politics and morals to metaphysical and mystical insights *(Ibid.: 31)*. The difference between the spirit of the north and the spirit of the south was stated by Confucius himself in the *Doctrine of the Mean*, a Confucian text with a strong metaphysical leaning:

> Tzu-lu asked about strength. Confucius said, "Do you mean the strength of the south, the strength of the north, or the strength you should cultivate yourself? To be genial and gentle in teaching others and not to revenge unreasonable conduct—this is the strength of the people of the south. The superior man lives by it. To lie under arms and meet death without regret—this is the strength of the people of the north. The strong man lives by it. . . ."
>
> (Cf. Chan, 1963a: 99–100)

In the above quote Confucius obviously identifies with the spirit of the south. In many classical texts, however, Confucius is recognized as the intellectual leader of the north, while Lao Tzu was his counterpart in the south. Someone who desired to study Confucianism would travel north, as we read in the *Mencius* (IIIA: 4): "Ch'en Liang was a native of Ch'u. Being delighted with the way of the Duke of Chou and Confucius, he came north to study in the Central Kingdoms. Even the scholars in the north could not surpass him in any way" (Lau, 1970: 103). On the other hand, those who wanted to learn from Lao Tan were advised to go south or actually undertook a journey to the south (Watson 1968: 251, 307). The *Chuang Tzu* informs us that Confucius himself, after traveling south, met Lao Tan, who addressed him: "I've heard that you are a worthy man of the northern region" (*Ibid.:* 161).

The identity of Taoism and Confucianism with the south and the north is called the local cult theory in the works of Marcel Granet (1957) and Wolfram Eberhard (1968). Liu I-cheng, however, pointed out that the birthplaces of Confucius and Lao Tzu were not so far apart as to account for the wide differences in their thinking (1961, I: 293–294). The main difficulty with the local cult theory is that it could not very well accommodate the mobile factors in cultures, such as migrations, conquests, retreats, changes of capitals, and forced evacuations. Proponents of local cults try to determine differences in thought patterns geographically. This is a static approach to cultures. Since the stable elements have to be weighed against the mobile elements, the identification of a cult with a certain locality is probably arbitrary and tentative at best. This is the built-in limitation of ethnography. To give one example: What had been regarded as the southern culture of Ch'u originated in the north. The Ch'u people were forced to move south under the pressure of the newly powerful Chou tribe. Thus, the *Ch'u Tz'u* preserved not merely the ancient southern lore in China, but also the culture of the Shang originally from the north (Ho Ping-ti: 316).

I believe that we shall miss the heart of the matter if we consider the development of Taoism and Confucianism merely as local phenomena. Attending more to the temporal, dynamic, and self-evolutive process in culture, my criterion is the sequence, order, and inner necessity of the development of consciousness itself. I view the rise of Taoism and Confucianism as the self-bifurcation of the cultural complex which at a very early time was already a loosely unified whole called Sinism. Coming from the same roots Taoism identifies with the spirit of the south and represents the conservative branch, while Confucianism identifies with the northern spirit and is the progressive branch of the Sinitic complex.

Among classical Taoist texts the *Chuang Tzu* is most critical of Confucius and what he represents. Here is a typical example:

> In Lu there was a man named Shu-shan No-Toes who had had his foot cut off. Stumping along, he went to see Confucius. "You weren't careful enough!" said Confucius. "Since you've already broken the law and gotten yourself into trouble like this, what do you expect to gain by coming to me now?" No-Toes said, "I just didn't understand my

duty and was too careless of my body, and so I lost a foot. But I've come now because I still have something that is worth more than a foot and I want to try to hold on to it. There is nothing that heaven doesn't cover, nothing that earth doesn't bear up. I supposed, Master, that you would be like heaven and earth. How did I know you would act like this?" . . .

No-Toes told the story to Lao Tan. "Confucius certainly hasn't reached the stage of a Perfect Man, has he? What does he mean coming around so obsequiously to study with you? He is after the sham illusion of fame and reputation and does not know that the Perfect Man looks on these as so many handcuffs and fetters!" Lao Tan said, "Why don't you just make him see that life and death are the same story, that acceptable and unacceptable are on a single string? Wouldn't it be well to free him from his handcuffs and fetters?" No-Toes said, "When Heaven has punished him, how can you set him free?"

(Watson: 71–72)

This passage illustrates the main difference between Confucianism and Taoism. Confucianism builds upon law and order, on moral distinctions and cultivation; it encourages the pursuit of "fame and reputation" through distinguished service to society. Taoism, transcending the distinction of morality to the unity of all in the ground, sees all these as "so many handcuffs and fetters." It regards not punishment for civil or moral transgressions, but the very distinction between right and wrong, as penalty from heaven.

From the Confucian viewpoint, Taoism is unacceptable exactly because in abiding in the unity of the ground, it neglects the problem of the coming forth of the many from the one. The *Tao Te Ching* harps on the need to return to and become rooted in Tao. Since all beings become identified in the ground, it advocates the equality of all beings. For the Confucians hierarchy and distinction of ranks are necessary measures to obtain order in the realm of the many. In this spirit Hsün Tzu (fl. 298–238 B.C.) criticizes Lao Tzu for deficiency in the art of coming forth *(hsin)*: "Lao Tzu saw the importance of retreat, but not of coming forth *(hsin)*. . . . When there is only retreat but no coming forth *(hsin)*, the distinction between the noble and the lowly cannot be made" (Watson, 1963b: 87). For the same reason Hsün Tzu claims Chuang Tzu was "obsessed by thoughts of heaven *(t'ien)* and did not understand the importance of humans" (cf. *Ibid.*: 125). To the Taoist, heaven *(t'ien)* stands for the transpersonal, creative, and wonderfully transformative power governing all beings in the universe, a power from which humans may declare independence only at their own peril. The *Tao Te Ching* says: "The world *(t'ien hsia)* is a spirit vessel" (ch. 29: 1). The *Chuang Tzu* says: "Thus it is said that one must not allow the mind to contribute to Tao, nor allow humans to assist heaven" (Watson: 78). While for the Taoists heaven is a holy order embracing both nature and humans, for Hsün Tzu heaven or nature is simply the given prior to the contribution of human intelligence and labor. What is holy is the reasoning power in humans enabling them to ascend to the moral plane, thus establishing civil society: "Heaven has its seasons, earth has its wealth, humans have their government" (Watson, 1963b: 80).

The Grand Historian's concluding statement in the biography faithfully sums up the *Tao Te Ching's* central teaching. No-action (*wu-wei*, chs. 2.3, 3.3, 37.1, 48.1, 57.3), self-transformation (*tzu-hua*, chs. 37.1, 57.3), tranquillity (*ch'ing-ching*, chs. 15.3, 45.2), and self-equilibrium (*tzu-cheng*, ch. 57.3) are the expressions of this wonderfully self-balanced world. If humans aspire to live in peace with themselves and with nature, they would do well to adopt the same rhythm nature so successfully demonstrates.

Conclusion

T'ang Chün-i thinks that it is entirely fitting that Ssu-ma Ch'ien should leave us with only a vague portrait of Lao Tzu; the vagueness of the person of Lao Tzu faithfully reflects his philosophy (154). While the Confucian aims at establishing his fame and thereby his immortality in the memory of the living, the Taoist goal is to retreat to the source, to lose his identity until he becomes one with the creative principle.

Kuo Mo-jo observes that the problem of the authenticity and date of the *Tao Te Ching* arose only after the Ch'in dynasty (255–206 B.C.), beginning with Ssu-ma Ch'ien's need to write Lao Tzu's biography (1962: 26ff). By Ssu-ma Ch'ien's time Lao Tzu had become a legendary figure and different versions of his life appeared, but before Ch'in, said Kuo, there was no problem about who Lao Tzu was. We have seen that in the *Chuang tzu*, the *Lü-shih ch'un-ch'iu*, the *Han Fei Tzu*, and the *Hsün Tzu*, the dates and authenticity of which are determined, there was no question about who Lao Tan was or what he said. Lao Tan was venerated by pre-Ch'in thinkers as a wise man who fully grasped the spirit of the ancient Tao and taught the virtues of softness and yielding, a philosophy embodied in the *Tao Te Ching*.

Hu Shih maintains that each argument against the text as a work of 600 B.C. can be separately refuted, and thus none of the new theories on its date and authorship present enough evidence to warrant adoption (1937). From the references in classical texts, we consider untenable the view that the text was first composed ca. 300 B.C. In fact, shortly after and even before 300 B.C., various schools of thought widely quoted the *Tao Te Ching* not so much to criticize or attack it, but rather to use it as a time-honored tradition lending support to their arguments.

Pre-Ch'in texts quote the *Tao Te Ching* more often than any other work, sometimes attributing statements to it not found in today's versions, albeit compatible and complementary to its thought (Ma Hsü-lun: 201). The *Chuang Tzu*, the *Han Fei Tzu*, and the *Chan-kuo Ts'e* do directly quote the *Tao Te Ching* and attribute the quotes to Lao Tan, but in the majority of cases these same texts quote it without explicit attribution. The *Lü-shih ch'un ch'iu* mentions Lao Tan five times (1/10a; 2/10a; 13/7a; 17/18a; 18/6a), informing us of Lao Tan's philosophy and also that Confucius studied under Lao Tan (2/10a). It quotes the *Tao Te Ching* many times, sometimes almost verbatim, other times paraphrasing it; not once, however, explicitly attributing these quotes to it. The fact that these classical texts drew from the *Tao Te Ching* so readily without crediting it shows that in the minds of these authors the work was so familiar to the Chinese mind that the references would be immediately recognized.

Sometimes classical texts attribute statements in the *Tao Te Ching* to other texts such as the *Book of Chou* and the *Book of Yellow Emperor*, both long lost[1] This shows that the teaching of the *Tao Te Ching* does not stand alone but is part of the ancient tradition. Lao Tan did not create a new system but transmitted the old wisdom. Chapter 42.3 says: "What others teach, I also teach." The *Shuo Yüan*, a repository of ancient sayings by Liu Hsiang, informs us that Lao Tan's teacher was Ch'ang Ts'ung who imparted the teaching of the soft (10/4a–b).

The *Tao Te Ching* does not so much represent the thought of one person as the embodiment of the spirit of a living tradition. Yet, the thought contained in it has such unity that it certainly is not merely a loose collection of ancient sayings culled from pre-Ch'in texts, as those who could not grasp its unique message have contended (Giles, 1958: 57, Maclagan: 70). Karlgren's detailed study of the poetical parts in the *Tao Te Ching* conclusively proves that considering its use of language and imagery, it dates no later than 300 B.C., and also, in terms of its body of thought, is mainly the work of one person (1932). That it was quoted by so many thinkers of ancient China only testifies to its vast influence and early existence.

Han Fei Tzu (d. 233 B.C.) appropriated the *Tao Te Ching* freely so that it agreed with the legalistic concepts he advocated. Nineteen out of the 81 chapters are quoted and commented on in chapters 20 and 21 of the *Han Fei Tzu*. I disagree with Takeuchi Yoshio that these two chapters may not belong to the body of the *Han Fei Tzu* but may have been inserted by mistake (280). In my judgment the thought contained in these two chapters is decisively legalistic and the style of writing agrees well with the rest of the work. Further, if the *Tao Te*

---

1. Ma Hsü-lun: 17, Kao Heng, 1956: 18–19. Recently, the *Huang Ti ssu ching* unearthed at Ma-wang-tui in 1973 has been determined to belong to the *Book of Yellow Emperor*. See Lung Hui and T'ang Lan.

Ching was intended to be a refutation of legalistic thought, it is extremely unlikely that a member of the legalist school would want to comment on nineteen chapters of the *Tao Te Ching* to support the legalist position and to include the commentaries in the body of the *Han Fei Tzu.* The freedom with which the *Han Fei Tzu* commentary interpreted the *Tao Te Ching* indicates that before 233 B.C., the text was already a long-established classic and a work of great antiquity, its truth accepted universally, although its meaning could be interpreted freely to lend support to one's own arguments and convictions. Unless the *Tao Te Ching* had already existed for a long time and was familiar to the educated class in general at about 233 B.C., it could not have been quoted and treated in such a manner.

We have seen that among Confucian texts, the *Li chi* records the meeting of Lao Tan and Confucius. The *Analects* makes no direct reference to Lao Tzu or his teaching. In one statement by Confucius, however, we encounter the term "Lao P'eng": "To transmit without creating, to be faithful to and loving the ancient way, I dare compare myself to Lao P'eng" (7: 1). This term has been interpreted to mean Lao Tzu, the Old Master, and P'eng Chu, the Chinese Methuselah who lived to be 800 years old. Two important teachings of the *Tao Te Ching* are also discussed in the *Analects* without reference to it: the idea of governing by non-action and the idea of repaying injury with virtue. Confucius accepts the former (15: 4) but rejects the latter (14: 36) because it does not satisfy retributive justice.

If the *Tao Te Ching* appears to be a polemic against the Confucian emphasis on rites and learning, Confucius himself and later Mencius (371–289 B.C.?) were not opposed to its teaching. The *Analects* shows us a Confucius also looking back to the golden age when sage kings ruled and nature was perfect. The aim of education, as well as the mission with which Confucius felt himself entrusted, was to restore this perfect state of nature through education and correct conduct. Taoism and Confucianism were closely allied in their veneration for nature. Mencius attacked Yang Chu, the hedonist individualist Taoist thinker, but his own thinking was faithful to the spirit of the *Tao Te Ching:* Human nature, as nature in general, is good in its pure state which needs only to be restored and preserved. Not until Hsün Tzu was Confucianism aware of itself as developing toward a position declaring humankind's independence of nature.

Hu Shih believed that at least in their formative stages, Confucianism and Taoism were not two distinct schools of thought (1962: 19, 34). Their difference lay between the old and the new. Confucianism represented a new way of thinking evolved from the older tradition represented by Lao Tzu. This would explain why some Confucian texts acknowledged that Confucius apprenticed with Lao Tzu on rites. This old tradition, the bedrock from which the various classical currents of thought flowed, did not represent any particular school of thought. When the new tradition forged by Confucius threatened to take over, the old tradition was forced to assert itself. It called itself Taoism and took its place alongside those schools of thought developed from it. The old tradition, affirming itself after other schools of thought had established independence from it, became itself a new school of thought. Ssu-ma T'an, the Grand Historian's father, claimed that in his own time Taoism incorporated all the strengths of the other schools of thought while avoiding their errors (*Shih chi* 130/1a–30b).

While the original inspiration of the *Tao Te Ching* was no doubt of very ancient origin, it is possible that the text we have today did not reach its final form until ca. 300 B.C. or earlier. Kimura Eiichi surmised that at about 300 B.C. the need for a basic Taoist text was keenly felt (92). Hence, the *Tao Te Ching* was committed to writing, explaining why it contains terms that according to some did not become current until ca. 300 B.C., when China entered the Warring States Period. Yet, it also contains ideas and terms so archaic and incomprehensible by 300 B.C., that any one could interpret them as he saw fit. This perhaps also would explain why in texts antedating the *Chuang Tzu* (ca. 370–290 B.C.) we do not find direct quotes of the *Tao Te Ching* text or unequivocal mention of Lao Tzu's name.[2]

Against Ch'ien Mu and others, the predominant theme contained in the *Tao Te Ching* could not have come about ca. 300 B.C. (the modern theory) nor even ca. 600 B.C. (the traditional account) but reaches back to the primordial consciousness of the Chinese. We may even say that the most distinctive features contained in the text were not the insight of one person but rather the product of a whole race, a sort of accumulation of the whole of Chinese wisdom. From its insemination to its final form—whether we date this ca. 600 or 300 B.C.—it went through a long development. Some modifications and additions naturally occurred, but not to the effect that the work became a mere collection of unrelated sayings. In our view, because it represents a profound living experience through the purifying process of time, it came to be crystallized into a coherent body of thought, preserving even today its original vitality and marking itself out sharply from forms of thought developed later in China.

Of all the ancient classics still extant, the *Tao Te Ching* alone draws its inspiration from the female principle. To argue that the feminine emphasis was a protest against masculine power and thus could not arise until the consolidation of male domination in Confucianism is to read today's issues into the past. The *Tao Te Ching* does not pit the feminine form against the masculine; it appeals to all forms and beings to remember their root in the womb of non-being.

Whatever the actual date of its composition, it must have appeared much earlier than, and gained wide circulation long before, 300 B.C. Hence, chapter 33

2. There is no mention of Lao Tan in today's *Mo Tzu* text, though in the *T'ai-p'ing yü-lan* (Imperial Collection of the T'ai-P'ing Period, no. 513), we find the *Mo Tzu* quoting chapter 4 of the *Tao Te Ching*.

of the *Chuang Tzu* could praise Lao Tan as one who caught fully the ancient spirit of Tao, Hsün Tzu could criticize the author as knowing only how to retreat to the ground, and by 233 B.C. one aspect in its thought helped shape the legalistic philosophy of Han Fei Tzu who studied under Hsün Tzu. The ancients could have misquoted the *Tao Te Ching* or mistaken a statement in it to be from elsewhere and vice versa, but belonging to diverse schools in different times they could not have conspired to fabricate a grand hoax, invent a nonexistent person called Lao Tan, attribute a book to him, and then quote, paraphrase, criticize, develop, or twist the thoughts contained therein.

2

The *Tao Te Ching* as a Religious Treatise

From the western religious perspective, the *Tao Te Ching* does not appear to be a religious text. With most of its chapters concerning how to be a sage ruler, it seems more a political treatise than a religious tract. Yet, it must be treated as a religious tract. Its conceptions of politics and of the reintegration of humans with nature, their fellow beings, and Tao are all influenced by the notion of salvation. Duyvendak has translated the term *sheng jen*, the sage ruler, which appears thirty times in twenty-six of the eighty-one chapters, as "saint," "because it gives more emphasis to the magical power, which is proper to a saint" (1954: 24). To associate *sheng jen* with magical power, if it means the human will to overcome the forces of nature, is inappropriate. But the term "saint" aptly lends a religious aura to the political figure. Rather than distinguishing between the kingdom of heaven and the human kingdom, the *Tao Te Ching* distinguishes between the way Tao governs and the way humans govern, both of which are in this world. It proposes that human government attune itself with the government of Tao; indeed, it proposes that human government fade away so that the government of Tao pervades over all. The reversion of human society to the society of Tao is an important part of the *Tao Te Ching's* total salvation vision; without it religion becomes a matter of mere private concern.

There are many senses of being religious. What from one perspective is religious may be seen as not religious from another. In his *Outline of the History of Chinese Philosophy* Hu Shih praises the *Tao Te Ching* author as a revolutionary who produced the first work in China able to liberate itself from an anthropomorphic or religious conception of heaven to propound a pure naturalism opening the way for the development of the ideas of universal law and science in ancient China. This naturalism, he adds, must again play its role for China to develop a scientific spirit to catch up with the West (1938: 53–59). In his work on the *Huai-nan Tzu* he also congratulates the *Tao Te Ching* for liberating Chinese philosophy from the yoke of religion and blames later Taoists for returning it to religion (1962: 161). In taking this position Hu Shih grouped the *Tao Te Ching* with the general Chinese mind, which he took to be not very religious.

> They had a very simple religion consisting chiefly in a worship of their own ancestors, a belief in the spirits and the powers of the natural forces, a worship of a supreme God or heaven (which was probably evolved out of the worship of natural objects), and a belief in divination. To these they added a belief in the idea of a retribution of good and evil. There was neither Hell nor Paradise; no life after death, only a firm belief in the importance of the perpetuation of the family line, probably primarily for economic reasons. This was the original religion of the Chinese.
>
> (1934: 80–81)

We shall not comment on Hu Shih's simplistic views about religion here. Earlier in the same work on the *Huai-nan Tzu* he also wrote: "The world view and political philosophy in the *Tao Te Ching* are crystalizations of hundreds and thousands of years of human experience, containing a maximum degree of religious faith" (1962: 32). Thus, in the same work he gives two different, conflicting assessments of whether or not the *Tao Te Ching* is religious in orientation.

This inconsistency, we suggest, arises from two different conceptions of religion. When Hu Shih speaks of the Chinese as not very religious, he sees religion as otherworldly, the worship of a Supreme Being separate from and transcending the temporal process. In this sense the Chinese people in general may be considered not very religious. When he speaks of the *Tao Te Ching* as containing a maximum degree of religious faith in its world view and political thought, he takes religious faith to mean an awareness of the holy in all aspects of life. In this sense the Chinese people may be said to be most religious. These two conceptions of religion, one viewing the holy as distinct from and transcending the world, the other taking life and earth to be the very seat of the holy, are incompatible. The Chinese may be judged to be religious or not religious depending on which meaning of religion takes precedence. The *Tao Te Ching,* not religious in the commonly accepted meaning of religion as human transcendence of the world, as a work of fundamental ontology calling humans back to the remembrance of the ground for the peace and harmony of all beings, furnishes us with a most profound religious vision.

The *Tao Te Ching* as a religious text preaches peace between humans and the natural world and thereby peace among humans. To bring out this religious message and to contrast this teaching with the teaching of many other religions, I shall present a history of religions from the perspective of the dialectic between humans and the natural world. Our treatment of the history of religions is admittedly narrow, perhaps even naive, missing the deepest function of religion as the spiritual transformation of the human race. However, this is exactly the question I wish to raise concerning religion's true function. Religion as the ultimate concern has in its own way produced ultimate problems for its practitioners. We shall view religion, from its very inception, as aiding humans in their struggle against the natural world, which yet often entails struggle against their fellow beings. As such, religion in the conventional sense has been more an instrument of war than of peace.

The Function and Role of Early Religions

Various theories on the origin of religion have given us some universal characteristics concerning religion's role and function. Religion grows out of the necessities of life as an aid to human struggle against the difficulties of the world. From its very inception religion's main function has been the maintenance and propagation of life, not so much of the individual but of the tribe or species. If we take this definition of religion, then religion is part and parcel of human struggle for survival. Its method may be different, but its goal is the same as that of science and philosophy which developed later. E. O. James says:

> Everywhere and at all times food and children are the two chief concerns of a primitive community. . . . Thus, the primitive religious impulse seems to be directed primarily to one end, viz. the conservation and promotion of life so that the good is food and fertility, and evil is hunger and barrenness.
>
> (43)

Edward B. Tylor gives a minimum definition of religion as "the belief in spiritual beings" (8). This is the theory of animism. From the animating principle in humans, the soul or life, all natural phenomena, the sun, moon, and stars, trees and rivers, wind and thunder, were considered to possess souls or spirits that could bring blessing or harm to humankind. The natural world was populated and controlled by these souls, spirits, or demons, which became the gods of the early peoples. According to Tylor nature cults, ancestor worship, polytheism, and eventually monotheism all developed from animism.

For James George Frazer the age of religion was preceded by an age of magic that he analyzes as two kinds, both to be comprehended under the general name of sympathetic magic. The first kind, homeopathic magic, is based on the association of ideas by similarity: The sorcerer or shaman believes that by drawing the outline of a person and shooting the drawing, he can injure the person represented. The second kind, contagious magic, is based on the association of ideas by contiguity: The magician believes that by doing something to the hair or nail clippings of a person, he is acting directly on the person. Magic teaches us not only what to do, but what to avoid. These negative precepts are taboos.

It is clear that magic was also a way of facilitating life's necessities. It was used not only to control nature, but also to dominate other human beings who posed a threat to one's life. Frazer points out that since magic's purpose is control or manipulation for specific human purposes, it is like science and unlike religion. Religion "assumes that the course of nature is to some extent elastic or variable, and that we can persuade or induce the mighty beings who control it to deflect, for our benefit, the current of events from the channel in which they would otherwise flow." Magic and science, on the other hand, "assume that the processes of nature are rigid and invariable in their operation, and that they can as little be turned from their course by persuasion and entreaty as by threats and intimidation" (I: 224).

If magic and religion adopt different approaches to solving the difficulties of the world, their goal—to facilitate human survival and make life here and hereafter easier for the believer—is the same. Humans have always felt themselves inadequate and unprotected against the forces of the world and have always needed the protection of powers greater than themselves. Whether by magic or religion, spells or incantations, propitiations or briberies, humans hope to bend or appease those unseen powers. Both magic and religion are ways of forging alliances with those natural forces that can be channeled to assist in our survival or contribute to our prosperity.

This is also the case with ancestor worship, which, according to Herbert Spencer, is the root of all religions (I: 411). Faced with the terrifying forces of nature, humans sought allies among the unseen spirits or souls. By invoking the names of illustrious ancestors among the ranks of the spirits, the ancients hoped to become fortified. Ancestor worship recognizes that the dead ancestors can be enlisted to assist living descendants in their struggle for survival. On the other hand, the dead had become a part of the forces of nature and could be a source of fear as well as protection. If not properly propitiated, they could inflict harm on their living descendants, providing another reason for ancestor worship.

In totemism a group or tribe believing itself descended from an animal or from other natural objects celebrates this relation in a sacramental meal in which the animal, normally taboo, is ritually eaten. The totem animal was once the main staple of food for the clan but since has been consecrated as one's ancestor, so that its consumption is forbidden except as religious communion. Connecting the clan to the totem animal or vegetable spirit establishes one's link with the food source. This is another sign of religion's basic concern with life-sustaining food.

According to Tylor, totemism is only one case in the cult of animals. The ancestor's soul was believed to have entered the body of an animal or plant through reincarnation. According to Emile Durkheim, however, religion originated in the worship of the clan, tribe, or society. The totemic principle was none other than the clan itself. Thus, totemism is not actually animal worship; it acknowledges a bond or kinship between humans and their totemic animal so that humans can "regard the animals of the totemic species as kindly associates upon whose aid they think they can rely" (139).

Andrew Lang also rejected Tylor's view that the origin of religion is in animism (201f). Tylor had maintained that the idea of God developed from the belief in nature spirits and the cult of ancestor worship. Lang found that among some aboriginal peoples like the Australians and Andamaneses there is no ancestor worship or nature cult but a belief in high God. The belief in high God among aborigines was also maintained by Wilhelm Schmidt who explained polytheism, the worship of many gods or spirits, as a corruption of primordial monotheism (Eliade, 1964).

According to Durkheim, the procurement of food is not viewed as a painful task in totemism. Rather, the bond between oneself and the source of one's food (the totemic animal) is celebrated joyously. It seems, therefore, that at the foundation of totemic religion we do not find struggle between humans and other creatures, but rather their unity and common ancestry. Perhaps the totemic age can be considered a pre-religious golden age when the difficulties of the world were not yet felt and humans were seamlessly united with nature. This would correspond to the age of perfect *te* discussed in the *Tao Te Ching* and the *Chuang Tzu,* an age prior to the birth of religion and morality.

This view was shattered by Freud's psychoanalytic discoveries. Freud traced the origin of totem and taboo to parricide. He borrowed from Darwin the idea of the primal horde headed by a "violent jealous father who keeps all the females for himself and drives away the growing sons" (235). The sons, envious of their father's power and resenting the prohibition of their sexual relations with the females, united to murder and eat the father, giving rise to the religion of totem and taboo. After this murder the sons, overcome by guilt and remorse, reinstated the ban on incest and murder, thus establishing morality. Their love for their father also returned. The ritual eating of the father or the totem animal became the symbolic way to commune with the father, who has since become the deity. Freud shows that religion was not only part and parcel of the human struggle for survival. In this case the breeding instinct is given priority over the need for food, but this struggle is nakedly exposed as humans' struggle against their fellow beings, indeed, as a struggle within the family. Freud's theory brings to the fore the cruelty and violence at the very root of religion and morality, perhaps explaining why even to this day religion and morality carry conflict and struggle as their trademarks. In Chinese mythology the founding of society, thereby religion and morality, was also frought with violence. Thus, it seems that religion was born out of humankind's awareness of alienation from the sacred, and the religious act, performed ostensibly to reunite humans with the sacred, serves rather to maintain their separation (Legge, 1971: 230). From the *Tao Te Ching* viewpoint, religion as conscious project perpetuates the state of alienation and conflict.

The above short survey shows that for the early humans life—its mysteries and maintenance—was the supreme concern. Religion's basic aim was the preservation of life. As archaic religions gave way to high religions, the original function of religion did not change. The perception of survival, however, did change.

Religions of the Axial Period

During what Karl Jaspers calls the "Axial period" (1962)—the age of great individuals like Zoroaster, Buddha, Lao Tzu, Confucius, Thales, Solon, Aeschylus, and Socrates—the tribal and nature gods were replaced by more universal and spiritual conceptions of deity. God, now identified with Heaven, became a transcendent principle no longer confined to a locality. We may call this the birth of high religions, which, in general, are world negating. The opposition between heaven and earth, soul and body, eternity and time, and culture and nature, distinguish high religions from religions of an earlier age.

In archaic religions humans feel powerless against the natural world, needing to ally themselves with the controlling powers in nature. High religions abandon this initial naïveté. Humans give up their attempt to control the world. Instead, as their God, Heaven, or Nirvana transcends the earth, they find security and happiness away from earth. The religions of Heaven offer hope and escape from earth's bondage.

The God of high religions is the product of what J. N. Findlay calls the logic of perfection that impels the worshipper of many gods to arrive at the belief in one God. As the being than which none greater can be thought, God can only be one, infinite, all powerful, and all knowing. Such a God can no longer be identified with any worldly beings but must transcend the world to be its source and creator. In high religions, therefore, the natural world is no longer fit to be the abode of the holy. To the westerner reared in Christianity, the natural world is so completely devoid of spiritual value that Louis Dupre mistakes this basically Christian bias to be a universal attitude: "For man, as a rule, does not directly experience the divine in nature at all. His view of nature is mainly functional and pragmatic, rarely contemplative and almost never religious" (583).

As the earth is emptied of gods, the natural world loses its reality. It is now the realm of *maya* (Hinduism), *samsara* (Buddhism), opinion (Parmenides), shadow (Plato), or the vale of tears (Christianity). Human struggle against the difficulties of the world loses its urgency. Fear of the natural world turns into dissatisfaction, impatience, weariness, and disdain for the world. A Greek saying has it that it is better not to be born, but once one is born the best thing is to die young. The Pythagoreans believed that on earth the soul is in exile, thus the world and the body are the prison and tomb of the exiled soul. For Socrates, philosophy is the practice of death, a process of withdrawal from the body and this world (*Phaedo,* 67). The *Katha Upanishad* distinguishes between the way of pleasure, which leads from death to death on earth, and the way of joy, which leads to true wisdom and liberation through denial of earthly pleasures (Macnicol: 195–206).

Since in high religions humans set their goal in heaven with earth only a temporary abode or testing ground, religion's main function is not in assisting humans to satisfy their biological needs. The needs of the body, which belong to this world, are now spurned as obstacles to salvation. The war to win a foothold in nature in archaic religions becomes the war against nature and the body. In one way or another high religions prescribe asceticism as the way to salvation. Formerly religion was an ally assisting believers in life, rendering their land and bodies fertile; now religion liberates believers from life altogether. In Buddhism, *Nirvana* as true liberation from suffering, thus true peace, is compared to a mountain on which nothing ever grows (Conze: 92–102). Religion as a spiritual discipline marks its spirituality through nihilism and world renunciation, so much so that earth- and life-affirming religions, like Confucianism and Taoism, have difficulty being classified as religions. We have seen that because Chinese religions never turned against life on earth, even Hu Shih conceded that the Chinese were not very religious.

Of course this repudiation of earthly life is not a repudiation of life clear and simple: it is the repudiation of a life tainted with finitude for a life that is endless. In archaic religions even gods were born and died; the eternal was the cyclical process tied to the earth's own life cycles. The deity in high religions is eternal by transcending the world of change. The worshipper also aspires to eternal life free of the changes of the world; only eternal happiness can be the true human *desideratum,* says Thomas Aquinas, since no amount of success in the finite world can satisfy the infinite desires of humans (*SCG,* Bk. III, ch. 48). High religions are religions of sublimation. The Heavens of Plato and Christianity are transfigurations of all that is good and precious on earth rendered perfect and imperishable. Instead of praying for a long and fruitful life on earth, the faithful in high religions trade the corruptible life of the body for the incorruptible life of the soul. Moreover, the herd instinct of the archaic person gives way in high religions to the idea of the individual self, meaning that survival is no longer equated with the perpetuation of the tribe. Aristotle was confident of the immortality of the species, but Thomas Aquinas argued for the immortality of the individual soul (*The Soul,* a. 14).

This disenchantment with earth was a sign that the most elementary forms of life have been conquered and that culture has come to replace nature, at least as far as the aristocracy was concerned. While the poor prayed for their daily bread the ruling elite could no longer be contented with a good but terminable life. In preparation for the hereafter they spent their entire earthly lives building sumptuous tombs and pyramids. Culture in this sense is a struggle against the transitoriness of nature, as in Keats's celebrated line: "A thing of beauty is a joy forever."

We owe to high religions the splendor of classical and medieval cultures and the birth of high ethical ideals. The idea that deity or heaven is universal, belonging to all peoples, gave rise to the idea of the universal brotherhood of all humanity, though conceived negatively as the universal misery of humankind. The Jewish and Christian religions teach that we are all sinners in need of redemption. In Buddhism and Hinduism the highest virtue is *ahimsa,* non-killing, born of compassion for the sufferings of all sentient beings. Only in Chinese religions was the universal kinship of humankind not uttered as a protest against earthly life. When Confucius said that "within the four seas all men are brothers" (*Analects* 12: 5), he said it with genuine gratitude to heaven and earth as the universal parents of all humanity.

Perhaps world negation is a necessary phase in the religious development of humankind, and in this high religions have not abandoned the deepest secret of religion, which is to assist humans in their struggle for survival. Only now religion's main task is not survival on earth but to show the way to heaven. The battlefield has moved within. The struggle between humans and nature in archaic religions is replaced by the struggle between the body and soul, or nature and supernature, within the believer.

Freud saw in the rise of magic a belief in "the omnipotence of thought"; the development of high religions owes no less to this. While a person's powers are limited, a person's ambitions are boundless. Neitzsche shows that behind asceticism is the thirst for conquest or the will to power. A human being's secret desire is to be like God who has power over everything, hence the *Upanishad* declares: "That thou art," or "Atman is Brahman." The fierce determination on the face of the Buddhist arhat is a model of defiance against the powers of the world. Even while renouncing the world the believer's secret desire is world conquest, though at this stage it is expressed only as self-conquest.

The progress of science was slow during this otherworldly phase of religion, with human struggle against the physical world temporarily in abeyance. Believers were engaged in the combat within the self. Science itself was considered an otherworldly project with a transcendent origin and destiny. Aimed at the speculative knowledge of the world or the eternal forms of things, science's goal was not to assist humans in changing and improving conditions on earth but to help them contemplate the eternal wisdom of their transcendent God.

World negation, however, is only one phase in the development of religion. A pure world-negating religion, such as original Buddhism, would be pure escapism. Even though as escapism it harbors a secret desire to conquer the world, as escapism it is ineffective, in reality amounting to a surrender to the forces of the world. In the case of the Christian West, this world-negating phase in retrospect prepared for real conquest of the natural world. Christianity's desacralization of the natural world was an intermediary stage assisting humans in their passage from magic to science, continuing in this way the dialectic between humans and nature.

Arthur O. Lovejoy speaks of the Western religious consciousness under the influence of Plato as containing two conflicting strains of thinking regarding God and the world. On the one hand, God as the *ens perfectissimum* is self-sufficient, never in need of any other being (42). The existence of the world adds nothing to God's perfection. The religious mystic turns away from the world to God as the ultimate and only completely satisfying object of contemplation. This is the source of the otherworldly strain in Christianity. On the other hand, for Plato the maker of the world is good, devoid of envy, and desirous that everything should be so far as possible like Himself. The Good as self-diffusive is a self-transcending fecundity necessitating the creation of the world to complete its own goodness and perfection (49). This is the source of world affirmation in Christianity. Though in medieval Christendom the world-negating strain predominates, the world-affirming strain, never completely absent, gained ascendency in the modern period.

In the modern period human struggles against nature enter a third phase. As science becomes more and more successful in its domestication of the natural world, facilitating the world-affirming strain in religion, we witness the modern believer altering his course, again giving attention to the earth.

Humans Become Gods on Earth

We learn that even in high antiquity, the high God of some religions gradually retired and became remote from the world, a *deus otiosus* who left the world to lesser gods and humans. Lucretius informs us in his long poem that the Olympian gods also withdrew, leaving the affairs of the world to humans (1969: 249, Bk. V, l.146). We have seen that this departure of God from the world in high religions inspired their believers to abandon the world. The absence of God from the natural world produced yet another effect: It freed humans from inhibitions to explore the world.

Modern Western science is the achievement of a mentality fostered by Western religion. The early Christians who refused to worship the nature deities were accused by their contemporaries of being atheists. From the viewpoint of archaic religions, which hold nature to be the abode of the gods, the Christian view of nature is, in the words of Harvey Cox, "atheistic propaganda" (23). The Christian God is not a nature deity; as the cause of nature His power is in nature but He Himself transcends the natural world. Everywhere Christianity triumphs the Christian God, banishing the nature gods from their niches, effects a desacralization of the universe. This desacralization has been generally recognized as necessary before science can conquer (Whitehead, 1925: 19; Dawson, ch. 8). In archaic religions, the natural world was the seat of sacred and mysterious forces and not open to human experimentation. Later, the crosses of Jesus on mountaintops cleared away the demons and nature deities in pagan lands and opened these lands to scientific exploration. Humans were now headed toward the secular city, "a field," says Cox, "of human exploration and endeavor from which the gods have fled" (1).

At the beginning scientific interest in the world was motivated by religious need. According to Thomas Aquinas we can have no direct knowledge of God in our present life, yet, through knowledge of the world we may acquire an indirect knowledge of God. Although the world as an order of reality does not contain God and is outside the order of the divine, as God's handiwork it reveals His wisdom. If Christians as mystics turn their backs to the world because it is not God, as philosophers and scientists they gather vestiges of God in the world.

To the extent that modern science has produced modern atheism, Thomas Aquinas, who under the influence of Aristotle fostered a positive attitude toward science, has been said to have opened the way to contemporary atheism. John Courtney Murray says: "Scholasticism in the Thomist style did indeed authorize a mode of rational inquiry, philosophical or scientific, that was methodologically atheist. It did not start with God but only with experience" (89). We might say that Thomas Aquinas adopted this so-called "methodological atheism" because he was convinced that every effort to provide a scientific explanation of human experience eventually led to God, as his famous five ways try to show. Modern science, from the eighteenth century on, no longer held this view. Science does not require the hypothesis of God, Laplace confidently asserted. Just as archaic religions by the logic of perfection surrendered to high religions, these in turn by preparing the ground for science's success have led to today's atheism.

Science is now a more effective way to combat nature. The introduction of the modern scientific mentality, the explanation of natural events by natural causes, frees humans from their reliance on God for their daily bread. Indeed, with every advancement in science and technology humans assume the roles of the former gods in controlling world events. As the world yields to our probing, humans become more and more absorbed in the world's problems. The result is secularization, humankind's turning away from the world beyond toward this world.

We have seen that in the first phase religion arose as a human response to the difficulties of the world and the human need to seek alliances in the world. In the second phase humans turned away from the world following their God's retreat from the world. The third phase of religion is the arrival of the secular city. Its function fulfilled, religion becomes outmoded. Secularization and various forms of contemporary atheism declare humans gods of the earth. Whereas in the first phase humans were supplicants to nature, in the third phase nature is passive while humans are active and powerful. Nature has become, in Dewey's words, "a plastic material of human desires and purposes" (350).

Secularization is humankind's return from the religion of world renunciation to the religion of world conquest. Those Christian theologians who saw the inherent danger of this world-building without God have been comforted by others who interpret secularization as the fulfillment of the biblical message. If we interpret the Old Testament as Harvey Cox does, there is real continuity between the Christian religion and today's secularization. In the pristine condition humans under God were given the right to dominate all other creatures. Through sin they lost this right and became subservient to nature. Through redemption, however, they regained this right, made manifest in the secular city. Science is the means by which humans recapture their birthright to dominate the world (Miltmann: 128). Secularization, the control and domination of the desacralized universe by humans, is celebrated by both

Friedrich Gogarten (Shiner) and Dietrich Bonhoffer as "man's coming of age" (Cox: 2). The secular city testifies to the triumphal return of humans to the position of domination on earth. Human creativity is expressed through our efficient control and command of both the natural and social worlds. Thus, the secret of the biblical religion, and perhaps of all religions, is human struggle against nature. The culmination of Western religious consciousness is in the secular city; human triumph and domination over nature is the fulfillment of God's design.

In the secular city humans turn their interest to earth. Yet, since the world is devoid of the holy, thanks to the desacralization effected by Christianity, we cannot be really devoted to the earth. Religion becomes the passionate commitment to science, reason, humanity, and progress, all centered on humanity. This interest in the self began with the Enlightenment when Pope declared that "the proper study of mankind is man." Auguste Comte (1798–1857) speaks of three periods in the development of religion: a magical period in which humans interpret nature through numinous forces, a cosmological period in which they rationalize nature, and a positive period in which they themselves assume absolute power (Bk. 6, Ch. 6). True to the spirit of the time Comte tried to found a church of humanity in which humanity replaced the traditional God as the Great Being, and names of scientists and scholars replaced saints. Finally, Ludwig Feuerbach (1804–1872) reveals that the secret of religion consists of human beings worshipping the projection of their own species being.

The omnipotence of thought, through the experimental method in science, is finally vindicated. If archaic magic was unsuccessful, science, the modern magic, is largely efficacious. The vast improvements science and technology have brought to human life cannot be denied. In unfolding the dialectic between humans and nature, clearly the religion of humanity heralds the successful conquest of nature by humans. Nature has become Descartes's extended substance, a passive ground for humans to vent their destructive as well as creative energies. Without a deep-seated reverence for the integrity of nature and her creatures, the process of secularization turns out to be both the homecoming of humans and the destruction of their habitat. In Western religious consciousness the world is still regarded as an enemy; thus humans return with a vengeance. The ecological crisis today follows at the heels of the technological revolution. Even in its world affirmation, the world-negating strain in Western religious consciousness is at work.

We have seen that to the extent that Confucianism and Taoism never renounced the earth, they did not join the mainstream of world-negating religions in the axial period. Since the process of desacralization of the earth did not occur in China, science and technology as the uninhibited human exploration of nature did not develop. The Chinese regard the natural world or the earth as a sacred vessel not to be lightly tampered with. This is not to say that in China science and technology did not develop; the work of Needham and Sivin shows that Chinese science was in advance of the West up until the dawn of the modern period. This is quite understandable since only in the modern period did Western religious consciousness pass its world-negating phase. In China, however, science and technology did not develop as human torture of nature. The aim of science in China is not to conquer the natural world but rather to accommodate and facilitate nature's own processes. Taoism has been hailed as the main influence on the development of science in China. If this is true, then the tribute goes to religious, not philosophical Taoism. In the Baconian dictum that nature is to be conquered by obedience philosophical Taoism supplies only the second ingredient, that nature is to be obeyed. Only in religious Taoism is the first ingredient, the conquest of nature, also present. There is really no intention to conquer nature in religious Taoism; there is only the intention to conquer—or at least to delay—death, and that is to be done by stealing from nature its own secrets.

We must now turn our attention to the equally important question of whether humans can refrain from dominating other human beings when we dominate nature. Struggle among humans has existed from the beginning of history; in the past it has been overshadowed by the more pressing struggle between humans and nature, but now it takes on new proportions. Today human survival is threatened not so much by the forces of nature as by the conflicting claims of different ideologies that are contemporary forms of religion.

Two Pseudo-Religions of the Twentieth Century

Capitalism and communism are the two most powerful pseudo-religions of the twentieth century. Both continue the *hubris* of the Western mind in regarding all salvation as centered on humans. Both are based on the idea of struggle, and in both humans hold the same stance toward the natural world—our right to exploit and dominate it.

Capitalism, following upon scientific and technological triumphs, is the new secular religion replacing Christianity. It is Christianity turned worldly. As an otherworldly religion Christianity condemns the rich to bless the poor, who are promised the inheritance of Heaven (Matt. 5: 3). In capitalism the situation is reversed. The capitalist measures hopes for salvation by a person's success in his worldly endeavors (Weber, 1958; Novak, 1981). Material wealth gives the capitalist certainty that he is among God's elect, as opposed to the lazy masses.

It has been argued that the master-slave relationship was a necessary condition when the natural world was inadequate to provide for the well-being of all. Under capitalism, however, the scientific and technological conquests of nature and the advent of machines—new slaves increasing productivity and wealth, and rendering human slavery unnecessary—have not liberated all humanity. Rather, if we follow Herbert Spencer, laissez-faire capitalism constitutes the application of the Darwinian idea of survival of the fittest. Founded on greed and aggressiveness, capitalism at its inception did not bring about justice and peace among humans. As in Christianity there are those who are saved and others who are damned, in capitalism there are winners and losers. Industrialization devastates not only the natural environment, creating pollution and vast ecological imbalances with its by-products, it also devastates the less fortunate of humanity, creating a new class of poor. Where capitalism spreads, slums surround the cities.

Under capitalism Christianity acquiesced to the condition of earth, marking the capitalists with the sign of salvation (Novak). Communism declares that the poor shall inherit the earth. The proletariat is certain that history is on its side, that by overthrowing the capitalist oppressors it shall be the instrument of salvation for all. According to Marx the scientific and technological revolutions by themselves will not bring about the salvation of all humanity. On the contrary, human triumph over nature under capitalism has turned into the triumph of some humans over others, or rich over poor, resulting in the mass dehumanization of humanity and the need for a communist revolution. Only in the communist state, with the positive abolition of private property and all forms of alienation, can the earth's wealth be enjoyed by all (K. Marx, 1977: 77–95). The solution to history's riddle lies in communist revolution. Communism alone deserves to be heir to all previous human achievement. Communism represents the revolt of the disinherited mass to seize the wealth of the earth. Human struggles against nature having arrived at a decisive outcome, humans now must struggle against humans: the classless society is to be established by class struggle.

The struggle between capitalism and communism is not merely political or economic, it is unmistakably religious. On both sides there is the certainty of the elect, and the certainty that those outside are excluded from salvation. Both are atheistic, glorifying in humanity's salvation by itself on earth. Marx considers atheism as the beginning of communism which builds heaven on earth. Today the theology most representative of capitalism is called Christian Atheism or the Death of God Theology (Altizer).

The two pseudo-religions of capitalism and communism, represented by two superpowers, may differ in their understanding of the relationship among humans. Both, however, are premised on the same relationship between humans and nature, i.e., humanity's right to dominate and exploit nature in the name of its own liberation. The secular city created by capitalism has been hailed as the fulfillment of the biblical teaching on humanity's right to dominate all other creatures on earth. While Marx speaks of communism as the naturalization of man and the humanization of nature (Rouner), the relationship between humans and nature is also a one-sided conquest of nature by humans. Indeed, according to Marx, the very emancipation of the worker hinges on the successful conquest of nature.

Machines, which have helped to settle the conflict between humans and nature, are now instrumental in ushering in a new stage in the dialectic of conflict. Since humans have become gods on earth we are now faced with the specter of the wars of the gods, which promise to destroy not only the existence of these gods but also all life on earth. The certainty of "mutual assured destruction" guarantees that if ever a major conflict erupts, the peace that ensues will be what Hegel calls the peace of death.

Our present condition is the consequence of a long development in human religious consciousness. Ideas do not remain on the ideal plane; they spread and transform the earth's landscape as they are constantly being translated into concrete situations. Human behavior, including acts of war, expresses deep religious convictions. Certain mental states justify and sharpen conflict while others are more conducive to peace. The problem seems inherent in the very development of consciousness—a phenomenology of mind that has developed toward the opposition between humans and nature inevitably unfolds in like manner concerning the opposition among humans. With the threat of nuclear holocaust posed by the two superpowers, we must reexamine the meaning of religion.

Religion For or Against Life

A single thread weaves through the various stages of the unfolding of religion. Religion, together with philosophy and science, has always been a means to overcome the limits posed by the natural world as the non-ego, whether by magic and ritual in archaic religions, by worshipping a transcendent deity in high religions, or by outright conquest of the natural world in the modern period. At the same time, humanity's relationship with nature has always been mediated by our relationships among ourselves, which means that human struggles against nature have always been translated into struggles against our fellow beings. When nature is scanty, personal or communal survival sometimes requires that other tribes perish.

Early religions modeled their deities on the warrior whose mode of existence was struggle or conquest. Auguste Comte points out the affinity between the theological and military regime (537ff). Religious language is suffused with the language of conquest, whether in archaic religions, high religions, or today's secular religions. Wars were undertaken not only for a people's own survival but for the survival of their ancestors and gods as well. The *Tso chuan* (Tso's

Commentary on the *Spring and Autumn Annals*) says: "The major events of the state consist in sacrifices to ancestors and the carrying out of warfare" (The Duke of Ch'eng, thirteenth year). The former, in sustaining the afterlife of the dead, secures their protection and blessing, while the latter, by enlarging the territories of the living members at the expense of other tribes, further enhances the glory of the dead. In this way religion and aggression went hand in hand to ensure the survival of the tribe. In ancient China a conquered state had to cease all sacrifices to ancestors and tribal gods, hence, in defeat not only the living perished but their gods and ancestors as well. Paul Tillich for this reason calls the pagan gods gods of space. When the locality or tribe is destroyed, the gods are destroyed along with it (35–36).

High religions in general do not shed the warrior syndrome. Religious wars, past and present, prove that in high religions, as in archaic religions, the concern is with survival. Although the deity is now universal transcending tribal and local divisions, each religion claims to be the exclusive vehicle of salvation and, in the face of other religions, wages unending warfare. The Hebrew God in the Old Testament was a warrior God. As long as the Hebrews remained loyal to Him, Yahweh would assist them in their wars against their enemies: "For the Lord your God is He that goeth with you, to fight for you against your enemies, to save you" (Deut. 20: 4). The very concept of the chosen people gave the Hebrews the certainty that they, alone of all peoples, would win in the struggle for survival. The claim of being God's chosen has been made also by Christians and Moslems. The militarism of Islam is well known: "And slay them wherever you catch them, and turn them out from where they have turned you out; for tumult and oppression are worse than slaughter" (Quran 2: 191). Catholics were once told that outside the church there is no salvation. Religion teaches its faithful to love their neighbors, but most of all it teaches them to love those of the same faith or of the same sect. Every religion excludes outsiders from salvation, which is the religious language for survival.

Tillich defines religion as ultimate concern (42). To extend Tillich, we may say that in the archaic period human ultimate concern was survival on earth; in high religions human ultimate concern is still survival, but at the transcendent plane of Heaven or Nirvana; in modern times it is embodied in the slogan "science, progress, and humanity." We have now entered a darker phase of religious consciousness. Our ultimate concern is not how humans may survive on earth, but how both nature and culture may survive the awesome destructive capabilities of humans themselves.

Advancements in science and technology have helped us turn the tables on nature. Yet, the conquest of nature has not brought about peace among peoples, but has only intensified our struggles against one another. The aggressive instinct that Konrad Lorenz describes as the innate species-specific behavior patterns forged in the long process of evolution as a safeguard for human survival has now become outmoded and detrimental to our very survival today. Lorenz observes that a male fish with no enemies against whom to vent its aggressive instincts soon kills its mate. In the same way the modern person who does not struggle against the saber-toothed tiger turns his aggressive instincts directly toward his fellow human beings. The dialectic seems unavoidable. "Hell," says Jean-Paul Sartre, "is—other people" (1955: 47).

As long as the warrior stakes his life for the sake of preserving the lives of his fellow citizens, religions that encourage the faithful to dominate others may be said to be on the side of life. Today, however, this is no longer possible. How do I maintain my domination over an enemy with whose fate I am inextricably tied, an enemy whose destruction involves my own destruction? Since in a nuclear holocaust there are likely to be no survivors, any religion today willing to go to war to prove its validity declares its intention to abandon all lives, including those of its own faithful. Hence, both capitalism and communism as religious ideologies are untenable. Josiah Royce once said:

> Whatever may hereafter be the fortunes of Christian institutions, or of Christian traditions, the religion of loyalty, the doctrine of the salvation of the otherwise hopelessly lost individual through devotion to the life of the genuinely real and Universal Community, must survive, and must direct the future both of religion and of mankind, if man is to be saved at all.
>
> (xix)

The phrase "genuinely real and Universal Community" cannot be limited to the human community alone. Perhaps this is at the very root of our problem, that most religions have taught us to be loyal only to the human race. Religion as the expression of human self-importance, as upholding human solidarity against the world, sets the stage for the wanton destruction and abandonment of the world. More than loyalty to the human community we must say with Whitehead that "religion is world-loyalty" (1926: 60). Humans must be loyal to the earth if they are to be truly loyal to themselves.

Can we work out a vision of the future, a vision of peace and harmony among peoples and nations, based upon the traditional religious attitude of conflict between humans and nature? If religion is to be on the side of life today, it must shed its former ideology of domination and conquest to adopt the language of harmony, a harmony not only among all humans, but among all creatures. It is time we rejected the religion of hierarchy in which those in higher positions have the right to subjugate those beneath them for a religion of diversity that cele-brates the worth and dignity not only of each and every human being, but of each and every species on earth. A religious vision that glories in the human conquest of nature must be replaced by one of harmony and symbiosis between humans and nature, for only when there is fellowship between humans and nature can we speak meaningfully of fellowship among peoples. Such a theology, vital for saving the spiritual heritage of humankind as well as the precious non-human life forms that have evolved on earth, is the urgent task today. Jurgen Moltmann says:

> Investigations into the ecology of survival on the subhuman level have shown that in "the struggle for existence" symbioses between competing organisms have a far greater chance of survival than conflicts of competing organisms. The subject-object relationship of man to nature, and the pattern of domination and exploitation do not lead to any symbiosis between human and nonhuman systems that would be capable of survival; they lead to the silencing of nature and to the ecological death of both nature and man
>
> (129)

There is little theological writing in the West to serve as the foundation for this new theological vision. Christianity so far admittedly lacks a theology of nature, notwithstanding the example of St. Francis of Assisi, the patron saint of ecology. From Augustine to Luther Christianity ignores the role of nature in the scheme of human salvation. When Augustine declares that he desires only to know God and the soul (*Soliloquies,* I.ii.7.), he implies that Christians want nothing to do with the earth. Furthermore, Christianity is noted for its arrogance toward nature, an arrogance which, according to Lynn White, Jr., is at the root of our ecological crisis.

Christian arrogance toward nonhuman creatures, a remnant of *Genesis* thinking, does not reflect the essence of Christianity. What is the essence of Christianity if not the birth of the child Jesus, the death of this God on the cross upon reaching maturity, and his resurrection and ascension into heaven followed by the descent of the Holy Spirit? The incarnation has been interpreted too long as the exclusive love affair between God and humans; it is time that it is also recognized as a love affair between heaven and earth. The Christian God loves not only humans, for whose sake the Son comes into the world, but also the earth. Christianity does not preach human alienation and domination of the earth, but the grand unification of heaven, earth, and humanity. We must recognize that in Christianity this God's reconciliation with humanity is also humanity's reconciliation with earth. The Christian soul, truly imitating God, must love the earth.

There is a new spiritual consciousness today, that all forms of life on earth make up one spiritual world. This new spirituality, more in evidence in the conservation efforts of ecologists and field scientists, is gradually spreading among theologians. A theology of nature is building in the West. James Buchanan expresses this new sentiment well when he says: "As *homo religiosus* the demand of creation is the experience of ourselves as creatures among creatures, as full participants within a cosmos whose desacralization can mean only self-desacralization" (42).

The Vision of Peace in the *Tao Te Ching*

Claude Levi-Strauss speaks of Western societies as hot or mobile societies that are progressive, acquisitive, and inventive, and traditional societies as cold socie-ties that maintain their equilibrium and are longer lasting, though seemingly more static (233–236). Today the hot societies, with their accelerating momen-tum, are approaching the point of explosion unless they slow down and turn colder, so as to last longer. The problem is how to change a dynamic, self-destructing civilization, one built on Nietzsche's motto "transcend and perish," to one that is cyclical, continuous, and unending. Most religions pursue eternity through the destruction of time. Taoism offers an alternative vision of the ever-lasting life as a non-transcending, cyclical, perpetually self-regenerating temporal process that would be the despair of Sartre (1949).

Comparing Western to Chinese civilization Bertrand Russell says:

> The distinctive merit of our civilization, I should say, is the scientific method; the distinctive merit of the Chinese a just conception of the ends of life. It is these two that one must hope to see gradually uniting. Lao-Tzu describes the operation of Tao as "production without posses-sion, action without self-assertion, development without domination." I think one could derive from these words a conception of the ends of life as reflective Chinese see them, and it must be admitted that they are very different from the ends which most white men set before themselves. Possession, self-assertion, domination, are eagerly sought, both nationally and individually (205).

Wei Yüan (1794–1856) calls the *Tao Te Ching* a book of salvation (2). In what sense may we call this text that even 2,000 years ago was called "The Old Master" *(Lao Tzu),* a book of salvation today? The *Tao Te Ching* does not fit into any of the categories of religion we have discussed so far. Notwithstanding Waley's tendency to interpret its sage as practicing magic, as a text it definitely does not belong to a stage of religious consciousness we call magical. It is critical of religions that resort to divination or prognostication (ch. 38.6). Unlike other mystical religions its ultimate reality, Tao, is not posited as transcending the physical world. Its most vehement attacks are, however, reserved for religions of culture, such as Confucianism, which take humans to be superior to other crea-tures by virtue of their reasoning power. For Taoists, possession of this so-called "divine" gift is exactly what alienates humans from Tao. Confucius traveled to various states trying to enlighten rulers on the nature of the good, hoping thereby to bring about peace in the world. The *Tao Te Ching* regards the cultural and moral values treasured in Confucian humanism as so many useless appendages. It is exactly this dedication to such moral ideals supposedly lifting humans above the rest of nature that leads to wars. Confucianism is a humanism or a religion of secularization in which humans eventually replace God or gods.[1] Taoism protests not so much against gods who transcend the world as against humans masquerading as gods. It would also be critical of atheists like Feuerbach and Marx who, in calling humans back from the religion of heaven, end up with a religion that regards humans as gods on earth. The *Tao Te Ching* is truly revolutionary in that it insists on carrying out the return process, not only from heaven to earth or God to humans, but also from humanity's preoccupation with its own power back to its roots in nature, prior to the separation and alienation from nature.

It has been observed that Chinese civilization, which values gentleness and yielding, is a plant civilization, as opposed to Western civilization, which is modeled on animal life and characterized by struggle, conquest, and the survival of the fittest. This observation is fitting if we take the *Tao Te Ching* to be the fundamental expression of Chinese civilization; its secret is its idea of Tao, modeled on the life of a plant.

Just as a living plant is tender and yielding (ch. 76.1), so is Tao weak and yielding (ch. 40.1). With plants the hidden roots support the visible leaves and flowers, which return to the roots upon perishing (ch. 16.2). Likewise, Tao is the hidden root (ch. 6.2), the non-being from which all beings spring (ch. 40.2) and to which all beings return (ch. 34.3). The life of a plant is conditioned by seasonal rotation. So is the movement of Tao in four stages: great (summer), disappearing (fall), far away (winter), and return (spring) (ch. 25.2). In the same way does the Taoist model spiritual life after a plant. A living plant is tender and pliant, while a dead plant is stiff and hard (ch. 76.1); one who is with Tao is also tender and pliant, while one who departs from Tao is stiff and hard. The plant kingdom is a quiet kingdom (ch. 16.2) that sleeps in beauty; Taoist quietude is the spiritual condition for regeneration. A plant grows at its own pace. One must not, like the farmer in the *Mencius* (2A: 2), help the growth of the corn stalks by pulling them up. In the same way the Taoist allows events to unfold according to their inner rhythms; he acts by non-action *(wu-wei)*, which is acting with, not against, the inner rhythms of things. A plant is always renewing itself; the Taoist celebrates perpetual childhood (ch. 55.1).

Working from within the Christian tradition George S. Hendry gives a rough definition of a theology of nature as the knowledge of nature in the light

---

1. Indeed, through a reverse process of euhemerism the former gods became in Confucianism great human rulers or heroes (Bodde).

of God, while natural theology is the knowledge of God in the light of nature (14). According to the *Tao Te Ching* nature is the most direct and faithful revelation of Tao. Its theology of nature is grounded in natural theology, i.e., our knowledge of Tao comes through the observation of nature. Nature is the realm of grace. Everything spiritual we learn from the natural world; its beauty and perpetual youth require only that we open our eyes and look. Water flows downward; this is the highest form of goodness (ch. 8.1). Water is yielding but overcomes the strong (ch. 78.1). Such is the power of Tao that it conquers by weakness. Nature is a self-corrective process: "Hence a squall lasts not a whole morning, a rainstorm continues not a whole day" (ch. 23.1). This is also the justice of heaven and earth: the sweet rain falls on all (ch. 32.2). Nature bears no rancor (ch. 63.1); if we are to hit upon the perfection that is Tao, we must forgive and forget. With assistance from Prigogine Taoism would claim that the law of entropy does not apply to the natural world, but exists only in the cultural world created by humans.

Other religions command humans to transcend the earth; the *Tao Te Ching* teaches them to transcend this very urge. With all their transcending humans remain earthbound creatures. Religion ought to be basically a reverence for the inherent dignity in all beings. Every being, with or without life, has its inherent character, deserving our respect and gratitude. Furthermore, respect for people presupposes respect for things. The current human rights stand that people should be respected since they are not objects but subjects is ineffective from the standpoint of Taoism: The way we treat things will inevitably reflect on our treatment of people. In renouncing our right to dominate things once and for all, we remove the intellectual ground for the antagonism between people and nations.

The religion of the *Tao Te Ching* is a reversal of the whole religious process of humankind. From the very first chapter onward it may be said to be the divinization of the Receptacle (Chaos or Nothing) which has been repudiated by religions and philosophies of the axial period. The *Tao Te Ching* is a religious text of homecoming to the world, born of the love for Tao as the mother and cradle of all beings. In one set of symbols or another, humans must make peace with the world in which their lot is cast. We need to invert Plato's allegory of the cave and descend from the stratosphere of the unchanging Absolute, through the realms of science and culture, to touch finally upon the earth where the chemistry is perfectly suited to support life in its biological, cultural, and spiritual expressions. There is need to make the world sacred again. The divine is not away from the world, but is the very life pulse of the world. Time is not the moving image of eternity, but its very unfolding. Finite beings are not separate from the infinite ground, but its very fulfillment.

Peace between humans and nature, and among nations and states, comes from the realization that we all have the same origin, live in one common environment, and share the same destiny. Such a religious consciousness must play an important role in shaping the religion of the future, a future which in Brian Swimme's story of the universe is called the Age of the Earth (23). To usher in the Age of the Earth we need to justify our love of earth. As the voice of the primordial ground that has given rise to all, the *Tao Te Ching* shall serve as the credo of this new religion of earth.

3

Use and Translation of the Text

The Title

Traditionally, the *Tao Te Ching* is called the *Lao Tzu* (The Old Master). The book did not have the status of *ching* (a sacred text) until Emperor Ching (reigned 156–141 B.C.) of the Han Dynasty. This emperor was so deeply impressed by the *Lao Tzu* text transmitted by Huang Tzu that he decreed that henceforth it was to be designated a *ching* (Ma Hsü-lun: 7; Chiang Hsi-ch'ang: 471). Thus, the *Tao Te Ching* was officially elevated from being a philosophical work (*tzu*, a work by a master) to a religious or sacred text. This act, however, could be merely an official confirmation of what had already taken place. The bibliographical section of the *Han shu (History of the Former Han Dynasty)* recorded the existence of three editions or schools that transmitted the *Lao Tzu* text, each with the character *ching* in its title (30/20 a–b), showing that at least within the school the *Lao Tzu* was revered as a sacred text before the official elevation.

In his biography of Lao Tzu the Grand Historian informs us that "Lao Tzu wrote a book in two parts, expounding the meaning of Tao and *te* in more than five thousand words." Officially the *Lao Tzu* was not called the *Tao Te ching* until 741 A.D. The emperor Hsüan Tsung (reigned 713–756 A.D.) of the T'ang dynasty, having commented on both the Tao and *te* parts of the *Lao Tzu*, first named the text the *Tao Te Ching* (Chiao, Chuan 7: 21a; Couling: 545).

The Oldest *Tao Te Ching* Texts

The oldest extant text of the *Tao Te Ching* is found in the *Han Fei Tzu* commentary. It is as fragmented as the commentary is incomplete. Prior to the discovery of the Ma-wang Tui texts in 1974, the oldest complete extant text was the *Chiao-ting ku-pen Lao Tzu (Ancient Text of the Lao Tzu Collated)* edited by Fu I (555–639 A.D.) of the T'ang dynasty. Fu I's edition was based partly on the text discovered in 487 A.D. in the tomb of the mistress of Hsiang Yu (233–202 B.C.) (Yen Ling-feng, 1957: 25–26). This text, now lost, predated the Ma-wang Tui texts by about twenty or thirty years. It could have been the origin of the Wang Pi text which is close to the Fu I text, and which in turn has been the source of other scholarly editions.

Another ancient text is in the *Lao Tzu chih-kuei (Essential Principles of the Lao Tzu)* by Yen Tsun (fl. 53–24 B.C.) of the Han dynasty. From early on it was very fragmented (Chiang Hsi-ch'ang: 8–10). Yen's text is said to have been the origin of the Ho-shang Kung text which developed into two versions. The northern version, containing 4,999 words, is said to be closer to the ancient *Lao Tzu.* The southern version has 5,302 words (Chu Ch'ien-chih: preface).

The Ma-wang Tui texts unearthed in 1974 (Jan Yun-hua, 1978) are now the oldest complete texts, version A being determined to date prior to 206 B.C. and version B to be from 206–195 B.C. Prior to the discovery of the Ma-wang Tui texts, the most popular texts belonged to the two most important commentaries, those by Wang Pi and by Ho-shang Kung. The Wang Pi text circulated among scholars and intellectuals. As a result emendations and refinements have been added to the text. Some characters that had become obscure were dropped and rhyming schemes were altered after pronunciations changed. On the other hand, because the Ho-shang Kung text circulated mainly among the illiterate mass, it has been better preserved with fewer deliberate changes. For this reason some scholars consider the Ho-shang Kung text superior to the Wang Pi text.

The opinion that the Ma-wang Tui texts will become the definitive versions of the *Tao Te Ching* is unwarranted. There is no reason to believe that their order of arrangement is the earliest. Beginning with chapter 38 most likely their order represents a late arrangement to accommodate the special needs of the Legalist school, the last of the classical schools. When Wang Pi (226–249 A.D.) wrote his commentary (he commented on all but chapters 31 and 66), he well could have been using a text version older than the Ma-wang Tui texts.

After a preliminary study of the Ma-wang Tui texts, Hsü Fu-kuan concluded that they do not change our overall understanding of the text. The different number of words in the various text versions consists mainly of the use of auxiliary modes of speech and different local pronunciations. These differences do not alter the central insights, nor do they affect the overall meaning and intention of the text. No doubt the Ma-wang Tui texts can help to clarify some textual problems. In this translation I have used mostly the Wang Pi and Ho-shang Kung texts, but where there are textual uncertainties, or discrepancies between the Wang Pi and Ho-shang Kung texts, I have used the Ma-wang Tui texts to arbitrate.

Division into Parts and Chapters

The division into two parts probably dates back to the very beginning of the text. The Grand Historian stated: "Lao Tzu wrote a book in two parts." The division into chapters, according to tradition, began with the Ho-shang Kung commentary. In both the Wang Pi and Ho-shang Kung texts the *Tao Te Ching* is a work in two parts divided into eighty-one chapters. The first part (chs. 1–37), with chapter 1 opening with "Tao" and supposedly treating mainly metaphysics and cosmology, is called the *Tao ching (The Canon of Tao)*. The second part (chs. 38–81), with chapter 38 beginning with *"shang te"* supposedly treating mainly ethics and politics, is called the *Te ching (The Canon of Te)*. Strictly speaking, this division into two parts cannot be said to be according to subject. In the metaphysical first part *(Tao ching)* there are ethical and political statements, and metaphysical and cosmological statements appear in the second. Moreover, in the *Tao Te Ching te* in its primary meaning does not stand for ethics or politics. It means nature, the manifestation of Tao in the world, as well as the condition when humans are at one with nature. The second part therefore gets its name because *te,* as the peace and harmony between humans and the natural world, is the central idea in almost every chapter.[1] In general we may say that the Tao part concerns fundamental ontology while the *te* part concerns cosmology, which in the *Tao Te Ching* includes the social and political orders since humans are a part of the natural world.

The reason why the text traditionally is divided into eighty-one chapters is given in numerology. Nine, a sacred number, is the square root of eighty-one. Some explain that the first part refers to heaven, whose number is odd (thirty-seven chapters), while the second part follows earth, whose number is even (forty-four chapters). The Yen Tsun text, however, is divided into seventy-two chapters, with forty chapters in part one and thirty-two chapters in part two. Here seventy-two is explained as the product of eight, which represents *yin* (feminine) and nine, representing *yang* (masculine). Wei Yüan divided the text into sixty-eight chapters by grouping chapters with similar contents.

1. In the Tao part, only four chapters contain the character *te* (10, 21, 23, 28), but in the *te* part, twelve chapters contain the character *te* (38, 41, 49, 51, 54, 55, 59, 60, 63, 65, 68, 79). Even when *te* does not appear, it is the central idea in many chapters.

It appears that when the need arose to divide the text into chapters, it had already reached a relatively stable form not to be tampered with at random. Although there are no chapter divisions in the Ma-wang Tui texts, there are many places that have dots corresponding to today's chapter divisions (Henricks). The Ma-wang Tui texts have the *te* portion of the text preceding the Tao portion. Yet, with only three exceptions each chapter's integrity and sequence remain the same.[2]

Various Arrangements of the Text

The arrangement of the Ma-wang Tui texts, which open with chapter 38, the first chapter of the *Te* treatise, solves the long-standing historical puzzle why the *Han Fei Tzu* commentary, the earliest extant commentary on the *Tao Te Ching* begins not with chapter 1 but with chapter 38. Obviously, this was the practice in the Huang Lao school of Taoism, to which both the Ma-wang Tui texts and the *Han Fei Tzu* commentary belong. Apart from starting with chapter 38 the *Han Fei Tzu* commentary does not follow the order of the Ma-wang Tui texts and so we cannot be certain that the Ma-wang Tui text version was actually used by Han Fei when he wrote the commentary.[3]

Despite the different arrangements of the *Tao Te Ching* text already in existence, I object to today's commentators and translators transposing or eliminating sections of the text as they see fit. If every commentator or translator takes this liberty, the *Tao Te Ching* will soon cease to be a viable text, being completely at the mercy of whoever happens to be working on it. The arrangement of the text as found in the Wang Pi and Ho-shang Kung texts is not haphazard. In most cases the transition from one chapter to the next is easy and natural, either presenting a connected chain of reasoning or naturally leading to a related topic. Rarely are there such abrupt changes of topic that connections between chapters become difficult or impossible to make. This means that the chapter divisions and their sequence are not the result of chance, but were thoughtfully arranged. I have indicated in the commentary the connections or similarities in thought patterns or sentence structure between the various parts of the text when they occur.

In matters of textual studies I have relied mostly on the works of previous

2. In the Ma-wang Tui texts chapter 40 follows chapter 41, chapters 80 and 81 precede chapter 67, and chapter 24 is placed before chapter 22.

3. Indeed, it does not follow any particular order. Chapter 20 of the *Han Fei Tzu* comments on twelve chapters of the *Tao Te Ching* in this order: 38, 58, 59, 60, 46, 14, 39, 1, 50, 67, 53, 54, and chapter 21 comments on thirteen chapters of the *Tao Te Ching* in this order: 46, 54, 26, 36, 63, 64, 52, 71, 64, 47, 41, 33, 27.

scholars. Occasional departures from traditional readings are either supported by established scholarship or are obvious upon examination. This means that while my interpretation of the *Tao Te Ching* may be highly unconventional, my reading of the text is rather conventional. The difference lies in that now that a new key has been found, the entire work can be seen in a new light.

The Need for a New Translation

In writing the commentary, I found it necessary to render a new translation of the text. Every translation is an interpretation, representing the translator's understanding. The key ideas and their mutual relationship form the architecture of the Taoist universe. This same architecture must be reflected in the translation. For the sake of clarity and consistency, I have tried to render the same terms or ideas in the original text into the same terms in English. If there is need for a different rendering, the reason is given and the relationship between its first rendering and its new meaning pointed out. Since no previous translations needed to be so highly sensitive to the demand for consistency in the rendering of key terms, a new translation displaying the key ideas and their mutual relationships prominently became necessary.

The same need for clarity and consistency in the *Tao Te Ching* translation of the text calls for retranslation of many passages I have quoted from other classical sources. My purpose in citing these texts is to support discussions of particular points in question and to illustrate that my interpretation of these terms applies not only to the *Tao Te Ching* but is also supported by other ancient texts. It is foolhardy to expect such consistency among different works translated by different individuals under different circumstances. Unless I mention the translator's name, all quotes from other classical sources, whether or not they have been previously translated, are my own. As a rule I have consulted and benefited from previous renderings. References are usually given for well-known translations.

On the Transliteration of the Chinese

The transliteration of the Chinese follows the Wade-Giles system of Romanization. Since most works already published in the field of religious thought and metaphysics use the Wade-Giles system, our use of the pinyin system, now standard in the People's Republic of China and in many ways superior to the Wade-Giles system, would create great confusion for students of traditional Chinese thought. One of the glaring examples of such a confusion is shown in the title of a paper presented at the thirty-second annual meeting of the Association for Asian Studies in 1980: "Metaphysics of Taoism and the Meaning of Dao." To retain the word Taoism, but to spell Tao as Dao, is an offense against consistency and good sense. For the convenience of readers, however, the pinyin spelling, when different from the Wade-Giles system, is given in parentheses in the Chinese glossary.

The *Tao Te Ching*
A New Translation
and Commentary

1

---

1. Tao that can be spoken of,
Is not the Everlasting *(ch'ang)* Tao.
Name that can be named,
Is not the Everlasting *(ch'ang)* name.

2a. Nameless *(wu-ming)*, the origin *(shih)* of heaven and earth;
Named *(yu-ming)*, the mother *(mu)* of ten thousand things.
Alternate,
2b. Non-being *(wu)*, to name *(ming)* the origin *(shih)*
of heaven and earth;
Being *(yu)*, to name *(ming)* the mother of ten thousand things.

3a. Therefore, always *(ch'ang)* without desire *(wu-yü)*,
In order to observe *(kuan)* the hidden mystery *(miao)*;
Always *(ch'ang)* with desire *(yu-yü)*,
In order to observe the manifestations *(chiao)*.
Alternate,
3b. Therefore, by the Everlasting *(ch'ang)* Non-Being *(wu)*,
We desire *(yü)* to observe *(kuan)* its hidden mystery *(miao)*;
By the Everlasting *(ch'ang)* Being *(yu)*,
We desire *(yü)* to observe the manifestations *(chiao)*.

4. These two issue from the same origin,
Though named differently.
Both are called the dark *(hsüan)*.
Dark and even darker,
The door to all hidden mysteries *(miao)*.

General Comment

This chapter sets forth in a nutshell the entire project of the text: (1) and (2) on the nature of Tao, (2) and (3) on how Tao evolves and becomes the world, and (3) and (4) on how we may return to Tao. Ho-shang Kung gives it a fitting title: "On the Substance of Tao" (T'i Tao).

Detailed Comment

1. In its opening statements the *Tao Te Ching* points out the limitations of language, spoken or recorded, in conveying to us the nature of ultimate reality. Language, as Bergson points out, is invented to express and deal with the determinate and immobile (1929: 275). The everlasting, transcending all determinations, cannot be spoken or named.

All religious traditions speak of the Absolute as beyond speech and name. The *Tao Te Ching*, however, is unique in the reason why Tao is beyond speech and name. The everlasting transcends the finite not because it is "a being than which no greater can be conceived" (Anselm), but because it is a cyclical movement or becoming. The everlasting *(ch'ang)* Tao is thus a verb, not a noun. When forced to give it a name, the sage calls it Tao, the Way or Path (ch. 25.2). We shall see that Tao is the everlasting rhythm of life, the unity of the polarity of non-being and being.

2. These lines and those in (3) can be read in two different ways. The traditional reading (2a, 3a), found in the Ho-shang Kung, Wang Pi, and Ma-wang Tui texts, holds that *wu* (non-being, nothing) and *yu* (being, having) are adjectives modifying the characters following them. The Ho-shang Kung commentary understands Tao from two aspects. As formless, Tao is nameless; as heaven and earth giving rise to all beings, it is the named. The named is not Tao as such, but heaven and earth that give rise to all beings: "The nameless is Tao. Tao being formless cannot be named. The named refers to heaven and earth, which having forms, positioning *yin* and *yang,* and containing the yielding and the firm, have names." The modern reading (2b, 3b) treats *wu* and *yu* as nouns standing by themselves. Modern commentators like Ma Hsü-lun, Kao Heng, Yen Ling-feng, and Duyvendak believe that the traditional reading is wrong. According to them these lines say that Tao, which strictly speaking cannot be named, can be given two names, non-being *(wu)* and being *(yu),* depending on how we look at it. If we regard Tao in itself, prior to heaven and earth, Tao is named non-being. If we look at Tao in its relationship to the world, as giving birth to all beings, Tao is named being.

The traditional reading, taking Tao to be both nameless *(wu-ming)* and named *(yu-ming),* is well supported in the text. Tao is said to be not only nameless *(wu-ming,* chs. 32.1, 37.2, 41.2), but impossible to name *(pu-k'o ming,* ch. 14.2), and having no name *(pu ming-yu,* ch. 34.2), though at the same time Tao is also the name that never goes away (ch. 21.3). Also, Tao is characterized by the negative, *wu,* in all sorts of manners. It is not only nameless *(wu-ming),* but desireless *(wu-yü,* chs. 34.3 and 37.2), without action *(wu wei,* ch. 37.1), without partiality *(wu-ch'in,* ch. 79.3), without limit *(wu chi,* ch. 28.2), etc.

The same cannot be said of the modern reading. Non-being *(wu)* and being *(yu)* as independent concepts appear only in one instance in the text (ch. 40.2). In chapter 2.2 we read: "Being *(yu)* and non-being *(wu)* give rise to each other." Here being and non-being are parallel to the difficult and easy, long and short, etc., i.e., complementary opposites in the realm of finite beings. They are not names of Tao as the *arche* and mother of all beings.

The modern reading, however, is superior in conceptual clarity. Yen Ling-feng points out that it brings out more sharply the aspect of pure negation in Tao, while the traditional reading gives only particular aspects of Tao's negative nature, e.g., its namelessness or desirelessness (1959: 14–15). Whichever reading we adopt there is a progression of thought from (1) to (2). The everlasting Tao or Name as the process of becoming is seen in its dipolar aspects as non-being and being, or the nameless and named. As *arche* Tao is non-being or nameless. As giving rise to the world of ten thousand things and mothering them Tao is being or named. We move from fundamental ontology to cosmology.

3. Here we move to religious psychology. There are two postures a person may take in relation to Tao and the world. He may either view the world in its hidden aspect in Tao, or he may view Tao in its visible aspect as the world.

Depending on whether you follow the traditional or modern reading in (2), you will take the traditional or modern reading in (3). In the traditional reading, *wu* (to have not) and *yu* (to have) not only modify the noun following them, they are also preceded by the character *ch'ang*, in this context meaning not "the everlasting," as in (1), but "always," hence "always without desire" and "always with desire." This is the reading in Wang Pi, and Ho-shang Kung, as well as in both versions of the Ma-wang Tui silk manuscripts.

The hidden Tao is desireless (ch. 34.3), while the world is the realm of desire. From the small *(miao)* and hidden, things grow to become the manifest and great *(chiao)*. To desire is to desire being; it is to belong to the world of being and having. On the other hand, to be desireless, empty of any content in either mind or possession, is not to dwell in the realm of being and having. When one enters the desireless state, one observes the hiddenness of things; when one is in the state of desire, one observes their manifestation. The traditional reading, equating the hidden with the desireless and the coming out of ten thousand things with desire, may point to some esoteric spiritual practice: by conditioning oneself psychologically in the desireless or desiring state, the Taoist can attain a vision of things either in their hiddenness in Tao, or in the fullness of their coming out process.

In the modern reading (*wu* and *yu* as independent concepts standing for Tao) the ontological significance of the character *ch'ang* as "the Everlasting" is fully preserved. The Everlasting Tao or Everlasting Name in (1) is divided into the duality of Everlasting Non-Being *(ch'ang-wu)* and Everlasting Being *(ch'ang-yu)*. The psychological condition of the Taoist, his desire or lack of it, does not occupy center stage. The issue is how to grasp Tao as the Everlasting *(ch'ang)*. As the Everlasting Non-Being *(ch'ang-wu)* Tao is hidden, as the Everlasting Being *(ch'ang-yu)* Tao's creativity overflows and becomes the world. By projecting ourselves to Tao as the Everlasting Non-Being, we transport ourselves to a stage before creation when all beings are still hidden in Tao. By projecting ourselves to Tao as the Everlasting Being, we witness Tao coming forth to become the manifest world.

Kuan, translated as "to observe," is also the title of one of the *Four Texts of the Yellow Emperor* unearthed at Ma-wang Tui. Joseph Needham interprets *kuan,* composed of the radicals "bird" and "to see," as a method of divination: One predicts omens by observing the flight of birds (II: 56). This interpretation may not be accurate. From its etymology *kuan* may well mean to see the world as the birds do, i.e., from on high. A Taoist temple is called *kuan.* The identity of *kuan* with Taoist temples began relatively late in Chinese history (Yang Lien-sheng: 58; Sun K'o-k'uan: 127). Originally *kuan* meant an imperial building or palace with a tower on it (ch. 26.2). In the *Tao Te Ching kuan* connotes transcendence or rising high to attain vision into the truth of things (ch. 16.1).

4. This concluding stanza leads us back to the first. Names in the coming out process belong to the conscious. They do not lead to Tao. In the return process they serve as portals to the dark, mysterious, unconscious Mother, the root of heaven and earth (ch. 6.2). While the Everlasting *(ch'ang)* Tao cannot be said or named, the duality that issues from it can. Non-Being and Being are the primal pair of opposites issuing from the Everlasting Ground. Through them we are again led back to the hidden secrets of Tao.

Hsüan, usually understood as the dark color of water, originally meant the dark color of the sky *(hsüan t'ien)*. The dark color of water is a reflection of the sky or heaven, since water comes from the sky. When the *Tao Te Ching* says *"hsüan chih yu hsüan,"* it refers to heavenly hydraulics, as De Santillana says of the water of Thales. *Hsuan* as the darkness of heaven is the depth of heaven from which all things come. As the color of heaven it is contrasted to *huang* (yellow), which is the color of the earth. In the *I-ching* we read: "Black *(hsüan)* and yellow *(huang)* are heaven and earth in confusion. Heaven is black and earth yellow" (R. Wilhelm: 395). The Chinese call themselves the children of *hsüan* and *huang,* meaning the children of heaven and earth, and their first ruler was called Huang Ti, The Yellow Emperor (literally, the ruler of the earth).

In other texts of the *Tao Te Ching hsuan* also appears as *yüan,* a cognate. *Yüan* means the original or primal principle. It has a more positive connotation than *hsüan.* As the first metaphysical principle *yüan* is equivalent to the Greek *arche.* The line *"hsüan chih yu hsüan"* (the "dark and even darker"), if read as *"yüan chih yu yüan,"* would mean "the primal of the primals," "the origin of origins," or "the *arche* of *archai.*" Though both readings are acceptable, we consider *hsüan,* the negative and mystic way, the older and superior version. Both versions of the Ma-wang Tui texts, the Ho-shang Kung Text, and most other texts have *hsüan* in chapters 1, 6, 10, 15, 51, 56, and 65. The Wang Pi text in different editions, has both *hsüan* and *yüan.*

Hsüan connotes the dark and mysterious, a descriptive term for something which is strictly speaking indescribable and ineffable (ch. 10.3). The vision of the dark is obviously the language of the mystics. Moving backward to the dark and darker or the origin of origins we enter the door to all hidden secrets.

2

1. When all under heaven know beauty *(mei)* as beauty,
There is then ugliness *(o);*
When all know the good *(shan)* good,
There is then the not good *(pu shan).*

2. Therefore being and non-being give rise to each other,
The difficult and easy complement each other,
The long and short shape each other,
The high and low lean on each other,
Voices and instruments harmonize with one another,
The front and rear follow upon each other.

3. Therefore the sage manages affairs without action,
Carries out *(hsing)* teaching without speech *(yen).*
Ten thousand things arise and he does not initiate them,
They come to be and he claims no possession *(yu)* of them,
He works *(wei)* without holding on,
Accomplishes *(ch'eng)* without claiming merit.
Because he does not claim merit,
His merit does not go away.

General Comment

This chapter stamps the *Tao Te Ching* as pro-nature and anti-culture. Value distinctions cause the very ills they are supposed to cure, but natural opposites complement and enhance each other. If the sage in governing human society imitates nature's way, converting moral opposites into natural opposites, peace and prosperity will reign in human society as it reigns in nature.

Detailed Comment

1. *Mei*, the beautiful, is the desirable or attractive, and *o*, the ugly, is the repulsive or abhorent (ch. 31) to our senses and sentiments. Wang Pi says that the beautiful or the ugly pertain to the human heart *(hsin)* and its emotions and feelings—what arouses pleasure or pain in us so that we move toward or flee from it. In the same way the good and not good are what we judge to be right or wrong, fitting or not fitting. They pertain to our conscience and our sense of justice. Both the beautiful and ugly, the good and not good, have a psychological origin, being products of human consciousness and valuation, but the very consciousness and pursuit of beauty and goodness as values are accompanied by the consciousness and presence also of the ugly and not good as disvalues. Opposites, including moral and value opposites, issue from the same ground and always accompany each other. According to the *Tao Te Ching* human awakening to moral and value consciousness, which marks the so-called advancement into culture, is in truth a declension from the harmony and oneness in nature. Consciousness of the beautiful and the ugly, the good and not good, splits the world into two without hope of reuniting them.

2. If value opposites war against each other, natural opposites are inseparable. They arise together, depend on each other while they exist, and perish together, as illustrated by the six pairs of natural opposites mentioned here.

The first pair, being *(yu)* and non-being *(wu)*, are not to be equated with the *wu* and *yu* in chapters 1 and 40. There *wu* and *yu* represent the duality within the unity of the Primal Principle, with *wu* preceding and giving rise to *yu*. In this chapter *yu* and *wu*, ranking with the easy and difficult, long and short, high and low, etc., do not stand for the dual principles in Tao, but describe a duality in the realm of finite beings.

Since *yu* commonly means to have, and *wu* means to have not, Marxist philosophers in China have interpreted them to mean the propertied and propertiless classes (Hou Wai-lu, 1946). The same line would then read "the haves and have-nots live by one another." This interpretation is refreshing and quite acceptable within the chapter's context. Just as the long and short, high and low, and voices and sounds (from musical instruments) support each other, the rich and poor or strong and weak also sustain each other. Did not Aristotle maintain that slavery was in the interests of both master and slave (*Politics*, Bk. I, ch. 6, 1255b12)? The *Tao Te Ching* was also written at a time when the mutual dependence of masters and slaves was taken for granted.

The *Tao Te Ching's* position, of course, is decidedly not Marxist. For the *Tao Te Ching* all opposites depend on each other, including the haves and have-nots, and the good and not good. Though it complains of the injustices of human laws (ch. 77.2) it proposes no revolutionary ideology to eliminate the rich, for that would also mean the elimination of the poor. Instead, it proposes we treat the unnatural opposition between rich and poor like natural opposites: If human laws do not help the rich become richer, the imbalance between rich and poor will be naturally taken care of by the way of heaven, which takes from the rich to give to the poor. Marxism preaches the necessity of class struggle to abolish the opposition between rich and poor, and thus operates within an intense value system quite alien to the spirit of the *Tao Te Ching*.

The last line, "The front and rear follow upon each other," is given a Confucian twist by Ho-shang Kung to mean that inferior persons follow superior persons, conjuring the image of a court procession. In this line the front and rear are purely natural opposites with no value distinctions as to which is superior.

3. The first line, managing without action, parallels the second line, teaching without speech[1]. The basic ideas from line 3 on are repeated in chapters 10.7, 34.2, and 51.4. They describe the presence of Tao in the world as an absence of power and coercion. The sage, imitating Tao, also practices non-action. Shedding the values and moral consciousness of humans, the sage personifies the creativity of nature that allows all to come to be and fulfill themselves.

The modern version of the third line reads: "Ten thousand things arise and he does not decline them *(pu tz'u)*." Our translation follows the ancient version *pu wei shih* (he does not initiate them, Chu Ch'ien-chih: 6–7), which brings out the spontaneous character in all beings. The point here is not that the sage cares for all beings (he does not decline them), but that all beings arise by themselves without his planning or design. In the same way the sage does not claim any credit, since all things happen on their own accord. This reading, which is confirmed in the B version of the Ma-wang Tui texts, would also justify Kuo Hsiang's interpretation in his *Commentary on the Chuang Tzu:* "Then by whom are things produced? They spontaneously produce themselves, that is all." (Chan, 1963a: 328)

---

1. Duyvendak, following Ma Hsü-lun, moves the first two lines in (3) to chapter 43, and the rest of (3) to chapter 51. This is unwarranted. Without (3), which sums up and unifies (1) and (2), the chapter is incomplete and aimless.

3

1. Do not honor *(shang)* the worthy *(hsien)*,
So that the people will not contend *(cheng)* with one another.
Do not value *(kuei)* hard-to-get goods,
So that the people will not turn robbers.
Do not show objects of desire *(k'o yü)*,
So that the people's minds *(hsin)* are not disturbed.

2. Therefore, when the sage rules:
He empties the minds *(hsin)* of his people,
Fills their bellies,
Weakens their wills *(chih)*,
And strengthens their bones.
Always he keeps his people in no-knowledge *(wu-chih)* and no-desire
   (wu-yü),
Such that he who knows dares not act.

3. Act by no-action *(wu-wei)*,
Then, nothing is not in order.

General Comment

This chapter applies the insights of chapter 2 to society. The role of the ruler
is again to revert value opposites, which separate and cause strifes among the
people, to natural opposites, thereby restoring them to the ease of instinctual
living.

Detailed Comment

1. *Hsien,* which appears also in chapter 77, means the able, wise, and prudent. According to Hou Wai-lu, the appearance of the worthy person *(hsien jen)*
from the ranks of common people in ancient China was a relatively late event
(1979: 282–314). Honoring the worthy *(shang hsien)* was an important teaching in the Confucian school as well as in the Mohist canon (Watson, 1963a:
18–33).
   Wang Pi, with his Confucian background, found it hard to accept literally
what is said here. He therefore softens its tone by saying that the Taoist sage

uses and gets the services of the worthy but does not lavish praises upon them, lest the people become jealous, and that the sage uses rare goods but does not publicly show his fondness for them, lest the people want to steal them, etc. To Wang Pi, the Taoist ruler makes distinctions but does not openly profess them. This makes the Taoist ruler a hypocrite. According to the *Tao Te Ching*, however, the struggle for superiority or worthiness is not conducive to peace and unity among humans. Intellectual and moral achievement foster pride in those who possess them, encourage hypocrisy in those who don't (ch. 18.2), and, in general, intensify competition among individuals. When the government elevates the worthy among its citizens, it encourages its people to contend *(cheng)* with one another for advancement, thus to become petty-minded and selfish.

In the same way when the government sets high values on rare objects, it is tempting the people to become robbers and criminals. Given the severity of the ancient penal code, in the end their lives are mutilated or lost. The multiplication of sensual desire does not lead to peace and contentment but only disturbs the hearts and minds of the people (ch. 12.2). Out of compassion for these errant individuals, the *Tao Te Ching* speaks out against those leaders who, by valuing hard-to-get goods while promulgating harsh laws, create the conditions for crime and punishment (ch. 57.2).

2. These lines, smacking of devious tactics employed by dictators to control the people, have made many commentators uneasy. Some take these statements as representing the legalistic position (Creel, 1970: 37–47). Duyvendak, on the other hand, grasps the spirit of these lines when he says: "in its political application Taoism may be said to be anti-cultural." These radical statements must be understood in the light of the *Tao Te Ching's* primitivism in which the highest value is life, not thought. The mind is the knowing and discriminating faculty as opposed to the belly, the seat of instinct. To the extent that thought negates life, the *Tao Te Ching* is against mind *(hsin)* and its executive power, the will *(chih)*. The belly and bones represent the body with its instinctual life while mind and will are perceived as forces detrimental to the smooth functioning of life (ch. 55.3). The mind controlling the vital force is the will, a will to struggle, to contend, and above all, to power. The Taoist does not have a strong will; his is a will to live and let live. The sage therefore empties the minds and weakens the wills of his people, while he fills their bellies and strengthens their bones. Kao Heng is right when he says: "By weakening the will (of the people) is meant that the people do not contend, do not rob, do not create disorder, that they act by no-action."

For Anaximander (frag. 1) all beings commit transgressions against one another by the very fact that they come to be. According to the *Tao Te Ching* nature without the evaluating mind knows no transgressions. It is mind with its value distinctions and desire that leads people to acts of transgression. Desire *(yü)* here does not mean the natural desires of the body represented by the belly. It refers to the unnatural desires that arise with the awareness of the self and the development of value consciousness. Mind stirring up selfish desires prompts the will to dominate and conquer. To ensure peace in society the ruler empties the minds of his people. In the *Chuang Tzu* chapter 4, this emptying of the mind and weakening of the will is fine tuned to become the mystic's discipline called "fasting the mind" *(hsin tsai)* (Watson: 57–58).

3. With no-knowledge *(wu-chih)*, no-desire *(wu-yü)* and no-action *(wu-wei)*, we have a complete program of the Taoist art of government. Knowledge leads to desire, which leads to action, which disturbs the peace of society. When peoples' minds are empty, their desires are few. Under such a condition even if some few have ideas that lead them to agitate society, they would not dare do so, for then, as chapter 74.1 points out, they would be easy to arrest and execute. When the people are so rooted in nature and so lethargic in their minds, those with knowledge cannot lead them astray. By not leading the people onto the paths of knowledge *(chih)*, desire *(yü)*, and action *(wei)*, and by keeping them in the simplicity of nature, the Taoist ruler allows the peace of nature to pervade society.

4

---

1. Tao is a whirling emptiness *(ch'ung)*,
Yet *(erh)* in use *(yung)* is inexhaustible *(ying)*.
Fathomless *(yuan)*,
It seems to be the ancestor *(tsung)* of ten thousand beings.

2. It blunts the sharp,
Unties the entangled,
Harmonizes the bright,
Mixes the dust.
Dark *(chan)*,
It seems perhaps to exist *(ts'un)*.

3. I do not know whose child it is,
It is an image *(hsiang)* of what precedes God *(Ti)*.

General Comment

In chapter 1 we witness the bifurcation of the everlasting Tao and name into the duality of non-being *(wu)* and being *(yu)*. In chapters 2 and 3 we are given the distinction between natural opposites that arise together and complement each other and value or moral opposites that break up the unity of nature and vitiate human life. In this chapter we see how opposites, which issue from Tao, become again identified when they return to Tao. Tao is the dark womb that pours out (1) and receives back (2) all beings. Its unceasing fecundity is due to its unceasing activity, blending and preparing all that have returned to it for their reemergence into the light of existence. As this unceasing creativity Tao hardly seems to exist, yet it is prior to God or the Lord on High.

Detailed Comment

1. Depending on how we interpret *ch'ung* (the empty), *yung* (to use), and *ying* (the full), the first two lines can be read in a number of ways. *Ch'ung*, according to Fu I (555–639), is written *chung*, which means an empty vessel. As the empty, *ch'ung* is the opposite of *ying*, the full (chs. 22.1, 39.1, 2). Thus interpreted, Tao is compared to a magic jug which, though empty, pours out (ch. 34.1) to fill everything. The first two lines would read: "Tao is like an empty vessel *(ch'ung)*, yet when used *(yung)* there is nothing it does not fill *(ying)*."

It is not clear whether the character *yung* (to use) means to pour out from the empty vessel, or to pour into the empty vessel. Always seeing the return of all beings to Tao, Wang Pi adopts the latter meaning. Also, he interprets *pu ying*, not filled to the full, to mean *pu i*, not to brim over. Ordinary vessels can be made to brim over. Tao absorbs the sharp, entangled, bright, and dusty; indeed, it absorbs all the world's beings and still does not brim over. For Wang Pi this shows the impassivity and ineffability of Tao. Wang Pi interprets both *ch'ung*, the empty, and *yung*, to use, in the passive sense so that Tao is the empty receptacle or bottomless pit that can never be filled. Following Wang Pi's interpretation, the first two lines would read: "Tao is like an empty vessel *(ch'ung)*, yet when used *(yung)* it is not filled *(ying)*."

Kao Heng argues that if we are to follow Wang Pi, taking *pu ying* to mean not full or still empty we have a mere repetition of *ch'ung*, the empty vessel. But the grammatical structure of the line with the character *erh* at the beginning indicates a change of mode or meaning. According to Kao Heng, these lines say that although Tao is empty, its use in pouring out to become all beings is inexhaustible for it is the origin of all beings. If this is the case, *ying* should be read *ch'eng* or *ch'ing*, meaning "to be exhausted" or "depleted." Thus *pu ying* would mean "not exhausted."

Kao Heng's reading that Tao is an empty vessel that when poured is inexhaustible is confirmed and supported in many chapters (chs. 5.2, 6.3, 35.3, 45.1). Chapter 45.1 almost repeats the first two lines: "Great fullness *(ying)* appears empty *(ch'ung)*, its use *(yung)* is inexhaustible."

Kao Heng also quotes the *Shuo Wen* on *ch'ung* as meaning to shake or agitate. This dynamic interpretation of *ch'ung* (the empty) indicates an even more dynamic reading of these two lines. In chapter 42.1 *ch'ung* is used in the line: *ch'ung ch'i i wei ho* (Activating the airs to reach harmony), as a verb meaning the activation, confrontation, resolution, and harmonization of the dual airs *yin* and *yang*, resulting in the coming to be of all things. Thus, it seems clear that *ch'ung* does not describe Tao passively as an empty vessel receiving back all things, as Wang Pi interprets it. This chapter describes Tao throughout as the dynamic self-diffusive creativity (1) as pouring out all beings and (2) as receiving back all beings. Tao as a dynamic emptiness is not a thing determined (ch. 1.1): It is the whirling vortex whose motion is ceaseless. This same dynamic character of Tao as ever pouring out is also portrayed in the next two chapters, 5.2 and 6.3. Our translation of the first two lines adopts Kao Heng's emendation of *ch'ung* and *ying*.

The Sung scholar Wang An-shih (1021–1086) said that *ch'ung* indeed means the *ch'ung-ch'i*, the empty whirling vortex revolving between heaven and earth. A dynamic whirling vortex, however, could no longer be the ultimate principle of the world to a Neo-Confucian who elevates immobility above change. Typical of the Neo-Confucian exaltation of the unchanging, Wang An-shih thought that movement has to issue from the unmoved. In his commentary, this Ch'ung-ch'i (the Agitating Air) becomes subordinated to Yüan-ch'i (the Primal Air), which is immobile and gives rise to the Ch'ung-chi. In the *Tao Te Ching* there is no Yuan-ch'i beyond the Ch'ung-ch'i. Tao is *ch'ung* and the Ch'ung-chi is the original dynamism of the world.

The last two lines of chapter 4.1: "Fathomless *(yüan)*, it seems to be the ancestor *(tsung)* of ten thousand things," parallel the last two lines of 4.2 "Dark *(chan)*, it seems perhaps to exist." *Ch'ung*, the agitating, *yüan*, the fathomless, and *chan*, the dark, all have the water radical: *ch'ung* is the sound of rushing water, and *yüan* means abysmal water, while *chan* is the dark color of deep water.

2. These lines describe the functions of Tao as the receptacle of all beings. In its bosom sharp things are blunted, entangled parties are untied, glaring differences are softened, and all that come from the dust return to the mixing bowl to become one again.

These first four lines of 4.2 are repeated in 56.2 as describing the psychological state of the Taoist. By withdrawing into himself he receives and harmonizes all things into his own unified ground *(yüan t'ung)*. The oppositions and conflicts of the many are resolved as they melt in the ground.

If we take Tao's dark emptiness as a whirling vortex, then the return to the ground is not what Whitehead calls a return to sleep. This blunting, disentangling, harmonizing, and mixing activity is the activity of what the next chapter calls a bellows or blasting furnace preparing for new beings emerging into light. The moving away *(shih)* process is a preparation for reappearance (ch. 25). Things return to the bottomless pit not to sleep or disappear forever, but to provide ingredients for future becoming. The old renews itself by resolving conflicts into harmony. Tao as pure becoming provides the ground for this process of renewal.

The last two lines of 4.2 in the Ho-shang Kung text reads *chan hsi, ssu jo ts'un* which has the same meaning as *mien mien jo ts'un* in chapter 6.3. Most commentators interpret this to mean that Tao is the everlastingly existing. According to the *Shuo Wen*, however, *chan* means to be hidden or submerged under water. Also, Wang Pi has *chan hsi, ssu huo ts'un* and he interprets the line to mean, "dark, it seems perhaps to exist," i.e., Tao's existence is questionable. Wang Pi's interpretation here is more consistent with the overall position of the *Tao Te Ching*. Tao as the ground, dark *(chan)*, empty *(hsü* or *ch'ung)*, and non-being *(wu)*, gives rise to beings that emerge into the light of existence with determinate features. When these cease to exist they are reabsorbed into the dark ground that, as the ground of what exists, only seems to exist. The Wang Pi text is happily confirmed by the Ma-wang Tui silk manuscripts.

3. Christian sinologists were perplexed with the idea that Tao is even before Ti or God (Carus, 1909: 13; Maclagan: 77). The character Ti meaning God or Lord of Heaven appears in the oracle bones and in the *Shou Wen* as the picture of a flower. Its homonym *ti* means the fruit or the bud. Ti, or God, thus is either the flower, the beginning state of the flower, or the fruit that results from the flower, all symbols of life and fertility. Tao is beyond Ti, being the hidden root giving rise to the flower that bears the fruit. Ti originally meant the first ancestor in the Shang dynasty, the first progenitor of the ruling house who as ancestor is now the Lord on High (Kuo Mo-jo: 13–16, 23). Wang Pi comments on Ti as the Lord of Heaven. Ho-shang Kung says: "Tao is prior to the Lord of Heaven. This means that Tao exists prior to heaven and earth." As the first ancestor and Lord, Ti marks the beginning of life and being *(yu)*, but Tao is the non-being *(wu)* that gives rise to being (ch. 40.2).

The dark, hidden *Urgrund*, the mother of all, itself is motherless and fatherless. Indeed it is nameless. The name Tao is only an image *(hsiang)* of the unnameable *Urgrund*. Wang Huai says that Tao is not verifiable by experience but is posited by the mind as prior to all being (23). Han Fei explains the connection between *hsiang* meaning image, and *hsiang* meaning elephant when commenting on chapter 14 of the *Tao Te Ching:*

> Men rarely see living elephants *(hsiang)*. As they come by the skeleton of a dead elephant, they imagine its living according to its features. Therefore it comes to pass that whatever people use for imagining the real is called "image" *(hsiang)*. Though Tao cannot be heard and seen, the saintly man imagines its real features in the light of its present effects. Hence the saying: "It is the form of the formless, the image of the imageless."
>
> (Liao: I: 193–194)

The choice of the character *hsiang* (image) points to the concreteness with which the ancients grasped Tao. Tao is not the Kantian ideal of reason nor an empty concept. It is the fruit of an act of imagination in an effort to capture this prior as the dynamic creativity whose effects are all the beings that ever come to be.

God (Ti), the greatest and most powerful being, is not the source of all. God is rooted in Tao whose existence is in question.

5

---

1. Heaven and earth are not humane *(jen)*,
They treat the ten thousand beings as straw dogs *(ch'u kou)*.
The sage is not humane *(jen)*,
He treats the hundred families as straw dogs *(ch'u kou)*.

2. Between heaven and earth,
How like a bellows *(t'o yo)* it is!
Empty and yet inexhaustible,
Moving and yet it pours out ever more.

3. By many words one's reckoning *(shu)* is exhausted.
It is better to abide by the center *(shou chung)*.

General Comment

The central theme running through chapters 4, 5, and 6 is not the providence of heaven and earth, but their unceasing creative activity. In chapter 4 all beings returning to Tao return to the melting pot that prepares them for reemergence. In chapter 6 we shall see Tao as the mystical female pouring out ever more. In chapter 5.2 heaven and earth are compared to a world bellows or blasting furnace that absorbs all beings back to itself when their life functions are over. From the creature's perspective the return to the blasting furnace means the tragedy of perishing.

Detailed Comment

1. To detractors of the *Tao Te Ching* these lines are the most damaging evidence against it as a deeply spiritual tract. In openly declaring that heaven and earth are not humane *(jen)*, that is, they are unkind, these lines have puzzled its ethically-minded Confucian admirers. Recently they have also provided grounds for attack by Christian critics (Lo Kuang: 72–74). Wei Yüan's (1794–1856) comment on these lines is typical of the Confucian effort to divest the *Tao Te Ching* of this offensive trait and color it with Confucian sentiments:

> Lao Tzu saw that in a time of chaos the lives of the people were precarious. Thus touched at heart he said: "Ah! How unkind are heaven and earth at times, treating the ten thousand things like the grass underfoot, letting them live or die by themselves! When the sage is unkind, he treats his people like the trampled grass with no sympathy at all!"
>
> (4)

Wang Pi, however, was able to defend these lines without apology:

> Heaven and earth follow the natural way of things, they neither act nor make. The ten thousand things govern themselves. Therefore heaven and earth are not humane *(jen)*. The humane one makes and transforms, dispenses favors and acts. But when things are made and transformed, they lose their genuineness; when favors are dispensed and actions are taken, not all things may flourish. If not all things may flourish, the earth would not be a place bearing forth all things. But the earth has not produced the grass for the beasts and yet the beasts feed on the grass; it has not produced the dogs for humans and yet humans feed on the dogs. Doing nothing to the ten thousand things, yet the ten thousand things all find their right use. . . . The sage's virtue

(te) corresponds to that of heaven and earth. He treats the hundred families as grass and dogs.

Wang Pi's comment brings out the unintentional character of the universe. The non-humane way of heaven and earth means the absence of design. To act humanely is to choose this and reject that, to apply something like Leibniz's principle of sufficient reason allowing certain possibilities to be actualized and others to be suppressed. The humane way is one of conscious selection and planning; Tao's way is pure sponteneity. Because heaven and earth are not humane, having no value distinctions or any principle of selectivity, everything is allowed to come forth, to find its place and use. This inhumanity on the part of heaven and earth, Su Ch'e (1039–1112) points out, is indeed the greatest kindness. The non-providential character of heaven and earth turns out to be real providence to the ten thousand things.

Wang Pi interprets *ch'u kou* as grass *(ch'u)* and dog *(kou)*. In the *Chuang Tzu* chapter 14, *ch'u kou* stands as one term meaning the straw dogs used for sacrifice.

> Before the straw dogs *(ch'u kou)* are presented at the sacrifice, they are stored in bamboo boxes and covered over with patterned embroidery, while the impersonator of the dead and the priest fast and practice austerities in preparation for fetching them. But after they have once been presented, then all that remains for them is to be trampled on, head and back, by passers-by; to be swept up by the grass-cutters and burned.
>
> (Watson: 158–159)

Once a thing has served its purpose, it is speedily destroyed. Heaven, earth, and the sage treat all beings and all people as unfeelingly as straw dogs, mere means in the universal process of becoming. To Hegel, all individuals, even great heroes, are subject to the cunning of reason that victimizes them for the appearance of the higher universal in the world historical process. Existence is a procession in which each individual has an appointed time and place. Once that role is played out, room must be made for others.

> Once their objective is attained, they fall off like empty hulls from the kernel. They die early like Alexander, they are murdered like Caesar, transported to Saint Helena like Napoleon. This awful fact, that historical men were not what is called happy—for only private life in its manifold external circumstances can be "happy"—may serve as a consolation for those people who need it, the envious ones who cannot tolerate greatness and eminence.
>
> (1953: 41)

The *Tao Te Ching* does not regard history as the progressive unfolding of the higher universal in the realization of the absolute idea. It is also typically against the worship of heroes (ch. 19.1). There are no great world historical figures in Taoism.

Though its benevolence is not to be measured against the standard of human kindness *(jen),* Tao is a benevolent power (chs. 34, 62, 77, 81). Tao is the great image that brings the blessings of peace and tranquillity to all who come to it (ch. 35.1). Chapter 41.3 says that Tao alone helps and fulfills all. Chapter 79.3 says: "The Tao of heaven has no partiality, it is always with the good people."

Yet, in this chapter heaven and earth, functioning as the bellows of the universe, undeniably form the devouring mouth in which all beings must perish. The return of all beings to the womb of Tao is necessary to the continuous pouring out of new beings in the world. Erich Neumann presents the rationale of ancient fertility cults:

The womb of the earth clamors for fertilization, and blood sacrifices and corpses are the food she likes best. . . . Slaughter and sacrifice, dismemberment and offerings of blood, are magical guarantees of earthly fertility. We misunderstand these rites if we call them cruel. For the early cultures, and even for the victims themselves, this sequence of events was necessary and self-evident.

(1954: 54)

Both the *Tao Te Ching* and the *Chuang Tzu* (Watson: 84–95) hold the conviction that the harmony and creativity of the whole is more important than the demands of the individual. Heaven and earth pay no heed to an individual's private needs. The dynamic outpourings of creativity are emphasized, not the right of the individual to stay around and state his or her claims. If the death of the individual is necessary for the unending life of the whole, so be it. In chapter 6 we shall see that only the whole is an inexhaustible and deathless life force.

2. The characters that stand for bellows are *t'o yo*. *T'o* is the external cover of the bellows, and *yo* is the bar that produces the air flow with back and forth movement. Heaven and earth form the furnace that absorbs and remolds all beings. The art of metallurgy was highly developed in ancient China. The beauty of Shang bronzeware has not been matched elsewhere in the world, but the lore of the ancient smiths has not been fully explored. Marcel Granet speaks of Taoism as going back to the days of the guilds of the smiths, custodians of the most wondrous of the magical arts (1926, II: 161). Mircea Eliade says: "The first smith, the first shaman, and the first potter were blood broth-

ers" (1971: 81). It is generally accepted that Taoism, both religious and philosophical, descended from ancient shamanism. There is also a reference to the potter in chapter 11.

T'o yo also symbolizes the reproductive activity of the male and female. According to Kao Heng, *yo* also means *mou*, the male animal, key, or the hill. The activity of the bellows symbolizes the interaction of the male and the female, here understood as heaven and earth. The emptiness between heaven and earth makes for continuous motion explaining the world's inexhaustibility.

On yet another plane *t'o yo* stands for a musical instrument. *Yo* also means a flute that produces music because of its hollowness. This is how Wang Pi interprets *yo*. The secret of Tao's inexhaustible creativity thus lies in its emptiness. In the *Chuang Tzu*, chapter 2, the music of earth is said to be produced by the spontaneity of the wind (Watson: 36–37). The music of heaven is the music of silence, the message in the next verse.

3. The *Tao Te Ching* generally takes a negative attitude toward speech *(yen)*: Heaven does not speak (ch. 73.2), nature speaks little (ch. 23.1), and the sage teaches wordlessly (chs. 2.3, 43.2). Speech and discourse as the externalization of thought means the loss or falsification of the real. They belong to the coming out process, thus leading us away from Tao. It is by keeping to the silence of the center that one holds on to the root.

Shu literally means number or counting. In the *Chuang Tzu*, chapter 2, there is a passage that states that the counting or numbering from one to two to three pertains to the coming out process that will never lead us back to Tao (Watson: 43). Language and numbers lead to the many, not to the source of all beings. Wang Pi takes *shu*, number, to mean the reasoning principle *(li)* in things. In this sense the first line would read: "By many words the principles are exhausted." According to Ma Hsü-lun, *shu*, number, stands for a homophone, meaning speed or quickness. Language *(yen)* as the objectification of thought speedily disperses one's life energies so that one becomes quickly depleted. To preserve one's life energies it is better to keep silent.

Duyvendak translates *chung* as the "middle course," giving the impression that these lines refer to the Confucian mean governing speech and action. Such an interpretation is unwarranted. *Chung* as the opposite of speech means the center that does not come out, hence, does not distinguish or falsify. As chapter 56.1 says: "He who knows does not speak, he who speaks does not know," the Taoist mystic who has the vision of the unceasing creativity of Tao does not argue about the merits or demerits of humanity *(jen)* and righteousness *(i)*. Was it the same insight that prompted Wittgenstein to say: "Whereof one cannot speak, thereof one must be silent"?

6

1. The Valley Spirit *(ku shen)* is deathless,
It is called the Dark Mare *(hsüan p'in)*.

2. The door of the Dark Mare,
Is called the root of heaven and earth.

3. Continuous *(mien mien)*, it seems to exist *(ts'un)*,
Yet in use *(yung)* it is inexhaustible.

General Comment

This chapter continues the theme of the two preceding chapters on Tao as
the dynamic vortex from which all beings come and to which all beings return. In this chapter Tao acquires two new names: the valley spirit and the
dark mare *(hsuan p'in)*, both symbols of fertility. In the *Lieh Tzu* (ch. 1)
this chapter is quoted as from the *Book of the Yellow Emperor* (*Huang Ti
shu*), showing that the *Lieh Tzu* author considered it part of the Huang Lao
tradition.

There are three ways to interpret this chapter. One is a literal interpretation.
Valley spirit, dark mare, empty, root, inexhaustible, all indicate that Tao is the
feminine creative power. This is my approach.

A second way is that of sublimation. When the references to female reproductive power were no longer comprehensible in a male-dominant society, they
were transformed into the ideas of vacuity, emptiness, nothing *(wu)*, or receptacle, which characterize the mind or spiritual state of the practitioner. Now that
the male principle had come to dominate, the feminine power, deprived of its
concrete political arena, turned inward and retreated to what is called the spiritual
or metaphysical realm; compared to the original active and dynamic valley it is
but a pale reflection. This was the way of philosophical Taoism represented by
Wang Pi, whose interpretation became the standard. As a philosophy of retreat
philosophical Taoism was the *yin*, the passive hidden spiritual reserve at times
rebellious and heterodox, complementing the *yang*, the active, politically dominant orthodoxy of Confucianism. Philosophical Taoism has forgotten its roots,
though everywhere the original meaning reveals itself. The emphasis on vacuity
as the quality of mind and spirit in the East shows the lingering influence of the
feminine. We suspect that the same happened in the West—when Aristotle

speaks of the mind as a receptacle of forms, he betrays the influence of the feminine of a prior age.

A third interpretation represented by religious Taoism results from the adaptation of the ancient fertility cult to the different needs of the religious individual in a later age, only in this case it is not the question of ultimate reality but the salvation of the individual that takes center stage. The deathlessness of the valley spirit is to be appropriated by the Taoist adept through the proper cultivation of the breathing technique. This is the interpretation in the Ho-shang Kung commentary. The valley, the earth as womb, that produces and nourishes all beings, is equated with the power in the human body that nourishes the spirits of the five viscera: the spiritual soul *(hun)* in the liver, the animal soul *(p'o)* in the lungs, the spirit *(shen)* in the heart, the semen *(ching)* in the kidneys, and the will *(chih)* in the stomach. "If one is able to nourish the spirits, one does not die." "If all of the five viscera are hurt, then the five spirits flee." The Ho-shang Kung commentary also inverts the female and male roles. In the *Tao Te Ching* the female is prior to the male (chs. 6.2, 10.5, 28.1). In emphasizing the male spirit (the spiritual soul) and in regarding the female soul as impure, the Ho-shang Kung mentality belongs to the Confucian period. Religious Taoism has also forgotten its ancient roots. Its interest in personal immortality and revolt against perishing is quite alien to the spirit of the *Tao Te Ching*, which accepts the necessity of perishing and has no teaching on personal immortality (E. M. Chen, 1973). In the next chapter we shall see that only one who transcends the self can be immortal.

Detailed Comment

1. The valley is where the waters gather to become clarified so that life may stir again (ch. 15.3). As the receptacle that receives and renews all, we may look upon the valley as the Taoist equivalent of storehouse consciousness *(Alaya-Vijnana)* in Buddhism, although it is neither conscious nor, being empty, a storehouse. Ho-shang Kung takes *ku*, valley, to be a verb meaning "to nourish" so that the first line reads: "By nourishing the spirit one dies not." The Neo-Confucian master Chu Hsi (1130–1200 A.D.), whose bias against the *Tao Te Ching* generated much negative criticism among his followers, nevertheless singled out this chapter as the best in the text (Ch'ien Mu, 1971, III: 612; Chan, 1963b: 110). To him the valley symbolizes the creative life-giving power of the universe. He even traced the idea of *sheng sheng* (production and reproduction) in the *I Ching*, a major teaching of his teacher Ch'eng I, to the idea of the valley here (Chan, 1975).

Hsüan, the dark, is the color of deep water (ch. 1.4). *P'in* literally means mare. Duyvendak enumerates four meanings of *p'in*. As stillness, passivity, female, and weakness, *p'in* is associated with K'un, the second hexagram and the symbol of earth in the *I-ching*. As gully or valley, *p'in* is the antonym of *mu*, the male, elevation, or hill (ch. 61.1). As keyhole, *p'in* is the image of the gate leading us back to the womb (Duyvendak, 1954: 30–31).

The valley spirit and the dark mare, identifying Tao with the feminine principle, probably point to some primitive religious belief. The valley is the seat of fertility, giving birth to and nourishing all beings. The dark mare is the invisible mystical womb from which all beings are born. The *Shan Hai Ching (Book of Mountains and Seas)*, chapter 9, mentions a valley spirit of the rising sun, a water god. The valley spirit may also point to the moon, which is deathless through its transformations. A Sung collection of lost texts mentions a lost edition of the *I-ching* called the *Kuei Tsang (To Return and Become Hidden)* in which hexagram 60, Chieh, has a text reading *"ch'ang mu jo ku"* (the everlasting mother is like the valley). Later texts give the version *"ch'ang mu ku yueh"* (the everlasting mother is the valley in the moon; Ma, Kuo-han, I: 21 and 23). We have seen that in chapter 1.1 Tao is *ch'ang*, the everlasting, and in many chapters (1.2, 20.6, 25.1, 52.1, 59.7) Tao is *mu*, the mother of all beings. Legend has it that a great archer's wife named Ch'ang O, having partaken of the vial of immortality given to her husband by the Queen Mother of the West, escaped to the moon to become the immortal spirit of the moon (Yüan K'e: 195–201).

2. In the *I-ching* we read: "In the I there is the Great Ultimate (T'ai-chi), which is divided into the Two Poles." The two poles are understood to be heaven and earth. The door of the dark mare where heaven and earth unite is the door to the Great Ultimate or the archetypal feminine into whose secrets chapter 1 promises to initiate us: "Dark and even darker, the door to all hidden mysteries."

According to the Ho-shang Kung commentary, the dark mare does not stand for the one that gives rise to the two of heaven and earth or male and female. It itself is two, with dark standing for heaven and mare standing for earth. These two lines are then integrated with chapter 10.5: "In opening and closing the gate of heaven, can you be the female?" Both, according to Ho-shang Kung, refer to the breathing technique through the nose and the mouth.

3. Most commentators and translators read *jo ts'un* (seems to exist) to mean *chiu ts'un*, (long existing or everlasting). I prefer to translate it literally as "seems to exist." There is no question that Tao is everlasting (*ch'ang*, ch. 1.1). The reason why it is everlasting, however, is because it only seems to exist (ch. 4.2). Chapter 11 tells us that the functioning, activity, or use *(yung)* of a being is through its non-being. This valley spirit or dark mare, which is the inexhaustible creative function *(yung)* that produces without end, is the root of heaven and earth, a being that verges on non-being, thus only seeming to exist. Chapter 35.3 also speaks of Tao as the invisible and inaudible, something of questionable existence, yet "when used *(yung)*, however, it is inexhaustible."

7

---

1. Heaven and earth are long lasting *(chiu)*.
The reason why heaven and earth are long lasting:
Because they do not live for self *(pu tzu sheng)*.
Therefore they last long.

2. Thus the sage puts his body *(shen)* behind,
Yet his body is in front.
He regards his body as external,
Yet his body remains in existence *(ts'un)*.
Is it not because he is selfless *(wu szu)*,
That he can fulfill himself *(ch'eng ch'i szu)*.

General Comment

This chapter serves as a transition from the discussion of cosmology and the universal creativity of Tao in chapters 4, 5, and 6 to the subject of ethics in the next two chapters. In particular, the chapter tells us how to live a long life resulting from regarding the self the right way. It begins with heaven and earth which, as the first pair born of Tao, most closely resemble Tao, and ends with the nature of the self and how it can be fulfilled.

The thought pattern in this chapter (heaven and earth, being selfless, are long lasting; the sage, like heaven and earth, does not live for self and so also lasts long) parallels that in chapter 5.1 (Heaven and earth are not humane *[jen]*; the sage, like heaven and earth, is not humane). Both chapters illustrate the *Tao Te Ching's* basic reasoning process which, as delineated in chapters 16.3 and 25.4, is also the process of liberation. When the particular follows the universal, or when humans follow earth and heaven, which in turn follow Tao, they are as long lasting as Tao.

In moving from the universal (heaven and earth) to the particular (the self) this chapter gives us three notions of the self. *Tzu* in stanza 1, line 3, is a self-reference; etymologically it pictures a finger pointing to the nose, implying the awareness of the self as distinct from others. *Shen* in the first four lines of stanza 2 means the body, the locus of the self as a person as well as a physical entity; my body, which attests to my existence, allows me to share my existence with others and participate in the realm of existing beings. *Szu* in the last two lines of stanza 2 means the private self and implies selfishness.

Detailed Comment

1. Heaven-earth *(t'ien ti)* as a term has already appeared in chapters 1.2, 5.1, and 6.2. Heaven and earth are long lasting because as universal powers they are not aware of self. The long-lasting quality of a being is proportionate to its approximation to non-being, i.e., its universality and lack of selfhood. Particular beings, determined and limited, are perishable. Tao is everlasting because it has neither being, existence, nor selfhood. The *Chuang Tzu* informs us that awareness of self brings death into the world (Watson: 97).

Wang Pi comments on *"pu tzu sheng"* this way: "To live for self, a thing has to contend against others; in not living for self, a thing will be that to which all things return." The former, the mode of being of particulars, leads to conflicts, while the latter, the mode of being of universals, is conducive to peace. Whatever lives for self necessarily comes into conflict with others. The problem of how to live in harmony with others, while maintaining the concept of self, is solved in Confucianism by a clear definition of each individual's rights and duties according to his or her station in life. In so drawing and consolidating the lines separating the individuals, order and peace are maintained in society. Among those well-bred (the *chün tzu* or gentlemen) there is the added virtue of humility or politeness, inculcated through an education in ritual (*li,* propriety) and righteousness *(i)*. These virtues draw the individuals farther in from their boundary lines and create a wider interpersonal space to facilitate interpersonal transactions.

Taoism solves the problem of the many through a different route. Harmony among the many is attained by dismantling the boundaries separating individuals and by forgetting the self in Tao. Taoism believes that peace resulting from clear territorial demarcations does not lead to long life. The very maintenance of such boundaries and the struggle against violators demand an expenditure of energy which hurries individuals to their death (*Chuang Tzu,* Watson: 37–38). For long life it is better to forget the self. By imitating the selflessness of heaven and earth, the Taoist has no territories to maintain and thus does not conflict with others.

2. My body *(shen)* is what identifies me as a being among other existing beings. In some forms of religious mysticism, the destruction of the body is a way to return to the universal. In the *Tao Te Ching,* however, there is no hatred for the body nor any hint of asceticism. Existence by virtue of having a body is a good, though having a body also subjects me to evils and misfortunes (ch. 13). The belief is that by letting go of anxiety about one's body, one enjoys a longer life span. The wise and successful ruler puts his body behind (ch. 66). One of the three Taoist treasures is "dare not be at the front of the world" (ch. 67).

What exactly is meant by the last two lines—that fulfillment of the self *(ch'eng ch'i szu)* is through selflessness *(wu szu)?* If being selfless is but a means of preserving the self, the sage after all lives for the self. The question is, does the sage practice true self-renunciation, or does he renounce it only to reclaim it? We encounter the same problem when we read sermons of Christian saints. While repudiating material goods, the most selfless saints often pursue spiritual goods and preach selflessness with the same gusto a capitalist preaches the benefits of delayed self-gratification. St. Francis of Assisi once gave a sermon on voluntary suffering:

We have promised great things,
And still greater have been promised to us.
Let us keep the promises we have made;
Let us long for the fulfillment of those made to us.
Pleasure is fleeting, but its punishment eternal;
Suffering is light, but the glory to come is infinite.

(Englebert: 156)

8

1. A person with superior goodness *(shan)* is like water,
Water is good in benefiting *(li)* all beings,
Without contending *(cheng)* with any.
Situated in places shunned *(o)* by many others,
Thereby it is near *(chi)* Tao.

2. (Such a person's) dwelling is the good earth,
(His/her) mind *(hsin)* is the good deep water *(yuan)*,
(His/her) associates are good kind people *(jen)*[1],
(His/her) speech shows good trust *(hsin)*,
(His/her) governing is the good order,
(His/her) projects *(shih)* are carried out by good talents *(neng)*,
(His/her) activities *(tung)* are good in timing.

3. Because he does not contend *(pu cheng)* with any,
He commits no wrong.

1. The last character in the Wang Pi text has *jen* 仁, benevolence or humanity. Earlier text versions had *jen* 亻, a human being. (Ma Hsu-lun, 1964:44)

General Comment

The character *shan* (the good) appears nine times in this chapter, showing it to be the key idea in the chapter. The main characteristic of the good, according to this chapter, is its self-abnegation and non-contention *(pu cheng)*.

Detailed Comment

1. The question we asked in the preceding chapter: "How does the sage fulfill the self by forgetting the self?" is answered in this chapter. The true fulfillment of the self is through fulfilling others. One who forgets the self is like water flowing downward to benefit all, collecting itself only at the lowest point shunned by others.

Wang Pi comments on the character *chi* (near) this way: "Tao is non-being *(wu)*, but water is being *(yu)*, therefore it is near *(chi)* Tao." Like heaven and earth, water is being, but even as being, it reflects the non-being of Tao by its self-abnegation, just as heaven and earth reflect the non-being of Tao by not existing for self.

To Confucius water was the symbol of intelligent activity: The wise rejoice in water, while the virtuous rejoice in the mountain (*Analects*, 6: 21). The *Tao Te Ching* speaks of water as nearest to Tao for a different reason: by dwelling at the lowest places, water receives all the rejects of the world into itself. To dwell in lowly places shunned by the many is not a Confucian's choice. Tzu-kung, a disciple of Confucius, said: "A gentleman hates to 'dwell on low ground.' He knows that all filth under Heaven tends to accumulate there" (*Analects*, 19: 20). The role of the Taoist sage, on the other hand, is exactly to play the low ground, to receive all the filth under heaven (ch. 78.2). What is called superior goodness here, then, is the religious notion of goodness that transcends the ethical distinction between good and evil. It does not seek self-aggrandizement but self-donation.

2. These lines, containing no subject terms, appear at first reading difficult to decipher. Wang Pi has not commented on them. In their effort to make some sense out of these lines, most commentators and translators have interpreted the character *shan* (the good), which appears in every line, as the object of human love, choice, or valuation. In defining the good as the conscious choice of humans they cut off this part from the rest of the chapter. We keep in mind that the overall theme of the chapter is the nature of perfect goodness. It is also reasonable to assume that what is said here in (2) confirms and sheds light on the notion of the good presented in (1) and continued in (3).

We find the key to unlocking these lines in chapters 27 and 49.2. Perfect goodness is not only good in whatever it does, it also transforms whatever it touches into something good. Thus, the first line *chü shan ti* does not mean that the good person selects a good site to make his dwelling, but that wherever he dwells is good ground. The second line *hsin shan yüan* does not mean that the good person trains his mind to draw only from the good source *(yüan)*, the Confucian way, but that whatever issues forth from his mind issues from a good source (ch. 4.1 speaks of Tao as *yüan*). The third line *yu shan jen* does not mean that the good person associates only with good human beings, but that he considers all his associates good human beings (chs. 49.2 and 62.2). Line 4 *yen shan hsin* does not mean that the good person intends his speech to be trustworthy *(hsin,* ch. 21.2), but that he trusts all he addresses (ch. 49.2). Line 5 *cheng shan chih* does not mean that the good person in governing produces good order, but that under his rule the original good order of nature prevails in civil society. Line 6 *shih shan neng* does not mean that the good person selects able persons to accomplish projects *(shih),* but that by practicing *wu wei* he lets the people ably accomplish their projects by themselves (ch. 17.3). The last line *tung shan shih* does not mean that the good person schedules activities at the right time, which is important, but that since all activities take place of their own accord they take place spontaneously at their own good time. In sum, perfect goodness neither calculates nor discriminates, it just happens, and when it happens, it is good (ch. 27.1).

3. This sums up the chapter's key message. Perfect goodness is humble, it does not contend, therefore it does not commit any wrong. We shall find chapter 66.4 ends with the same message.

9

1. To hold and fill (a vessel) to the full *(ying),* [1]
It had better not be done.
To temper and sharpen a sword,
Its edge could not be kept *(pao)* long.

1. Wang Pi's interpretation of the first line to mean holding and filling *te* (nature) is rejected by all other commentators. Wing-tsit Chan concurs with Waley that this line can be interpreted to mean stretching a bow to its breaking point. My translation follows the Ho-shang Kung commentary. The character *ying* (chs. 4, 9, 15, 22, 39, 45) refers to filling a vessel or hollow space, not to stretching a bow.

To fill the hall with gold and jade,
There is no way to guard *(shou)* them.
To be rich, exalted, and proud,
This is to invite blame *(chiu)* upon oneself.

2. When work is done *(sui)*, the person *(sheng)* retires,
Such is the Tao of heaven.

General Comment

Chapters 7, 8, and 9 are on the same theme. Chapter 7 tells us that selflessness ensures long life. Chapter 8 shows that self-abnegation and non-contention disarm everything and transform everything they touch into a good. This chapter tells how selfishness invites the destructive forces of the world, thus again illustrating the theme that, through the retreat of the self, the self is fulfilled (ch. 44.3).

Detailed Comment

1. In the Ho-shang Kung text, this chapter is called "Yün I," the movement of change, or as translated by E. Erkes, "How to Let Ease Circulate" (25). "I" (pronounced as the "e" in easy) means both the easy and change; what changes naturally is easy (ch. 70.1). The principle of change operates in all things. When one extreme is reached its opposite takes over. Humans, however, try to hold on to one extreme only. Since this cannot be done, they find the world difficult, and their efforts are foredoomed.

2. The Ho-shang Kung commentary interprets these lines this way:

He who does not retreat from his previous position shall meet with harm. For this is the constant Tao of heaven, as for example the sun begins to sink when in the zenith, the moon begins to wane when full, plants begin to fade when in full bloom, music becomes moanful when in full swing.

Wang Pi comments: "The four seasons rotate, each, when its work is done, moves on." The dynamism of the universe requires that the old yield to the new. To refuse to withdraw after accomplishing one's functions is an act against the way of heaven. These concluding lines introduce the next chapter on the need to retreat to the one, mother, and source, which, having given birth to all, does not hold on to them.

10

1. In bringing your spiritual *(ying)* and bodily *(p'o)* souls to embrace the
One,
Can *(neng)* you never depart *(li)* from it?

2. In concentrating your breath to attain softness,
Can you be like an infant *(ying erh)?*

3. In cleansing your mirror *(lan)* of the dark *(hsüan)*,
Can you make it spotless?

4. In opening and closing heaven's gate *(t'ien men)*,
Can you be the female *(tz'u)?*[1]

5. In being enlightened *(ming)* and comprehending all,
Can you do it without knowledge?

6. In loving the people and governing the state,
Can you practice non-action?

7. To give birth, to nurture.
To give birth yet not to claim possession *(yu)*,
To act *(wei)* yet not to hold on to,
To grow *(chang)* yet not to lord over *(tsai)*,[2]
This is called the dark virtue *(yüan te)*.

General Comment

The last chapter speaks of the futility and danger in holding on to worldly
possessions. In this chapter we are called back to the safety of the womb. The
Chuang Tzu, chapter 23, quotes this chapter as offering "the basic rule of life

1. This line in the Ma-wang Tui text, version B, has *neng wei tz'u* (can you be the female).
The Wang Pi and Ho-shang Kung texts read *neng wu tz'u* (can you be without the female).
Both commentaries, however, interpret this line to mean *neng wei tz'u* (can you be the female).

2. *Chang erh pu tsai* can also be translated "to govern without killing." *Chang* as a verb
means to make something grow; as a noun it means an elder who is qualified to govern. *Tsai*
means to lord over or to kill, since he who lords over has the power to give or deprive life.

preservation" *(wei sheng chih ching,* Watson: 253). The Ho-shang Kung commentary treats stanzas 2 to 4 as describing the breath control technique for the prolongation of life. Max Kaltenmark speaks of this chapter as containing "positive directives concerning the methods for achieving long life." (1969: 63) Duyvendak says: "This chapter deals with the art of nourishing the vital force." Waley treats this whole chapter as referring to a yoga practice like the Dhyana in Buddhism and as presenting a technique by which the Taoist rules the world in a trance state. The main thrust of this chapter, in our view, is the establishment of a long-lasting society through the mystical vision of the Taoist ruler; the six stanzas prior to the conclusion instruct how to *(neng)* reach the vision.

Since the individual is a microcosm mirroring the universe as the macrocosm, we can read every line with at least two levels of meaning: as pertaining to the psychology of the mystic, and as referring to a cosmogonic event. Thus, every psychological reference is overlaid with cosmological significance, while ever reference to cosmology has its psychological application. In this light, prolonging one's life by nourishing the vital force in oneself is but a happy consequence of the individual's reconnection with the vital force that nourishes all beings. This union of the Taoist ruler with the cosmic force has its main event in the transformation of the Taoist ruler into the image of the divine creative force that sustains and permeates the universe.

In content this chapter should be read together with chapters 51 and 52. Chapter 51 portrays the mystical *te* as the great mother; chapter 52 speaks of the need to become united with the great mother; this chapter maps the way to reach Tao as the great mother.

Detailed Comment

1. Traditionally, the Chinese believe that each individual has three spiritual and seven bodily souls. A human being begins with his bodily souls *(p'o)* at conception, then acquires his spiritual souls *(ying* or *hun)* at birth or later *(Ko, Hung,* Ch. 4; de Groot, IV, Bk. II).

Wang Pi and Kao Heng take the "one" in the psychological sense to mean a person's unity (Kao Heng, 1956: 23), i.e., when the bodily and spiritual souls adhere to the same person, not dispersing into the atmosphere, which results in death. From the cosmogonic perspective the "one" is the original Chaos or Hun-tun (ch. 25.1) born directly from Tao as non-being (ch. 42.1), the formless vortex at the world's beginning (ch. 14.1) from which all things receive their determination so that they are what they are (ch. 39.1). In the *Ch'u Tz'u (Elegies of Ch'u)* by Ch'u Yüan (343–277 B.C.) the line "Carrying my spiritual and physical souls I rise up into the rainbow sky" has been understood as a direct reference to these lines (Hawkes: 84, line 46; Fung, 1959: 100ff). If this is so, the *Ch'u Tz'u* equates the one to heaven or the rainbow sky. "To embrace the One" refers to a spiritual journey back to the source.

2. The vortex of heaven, the stuff of air, is to be approached by the breathing technique. The infant, not knowing the union of male and female (ch. 55.5), holds on to the "One," which is the womb of the universe. Breathing softly and possessing the power of life in the fullest degree, the infant is harmed by nothing (ch. 55.1). To breathe softly like the infant is called womb-breathing (*Chuang Tzu*, Watson: 253). If Freud shows life from infancy on to be one of struggle, conflict, and neuroses, the Taoist retreat to infancy and the womb is a way back to the peace and bliss in the universal ocean of life (Smith: Appendix).

3. Three interrelated meanings of *lan* can be given: as contemplation, as mirror, and as heaven plate. The most obvious meaning of *lan* is meditation or contemplative vision.[3]

Now *lan* 覽 in the Ma-wang Tui texts, version A, is *(lan)* 藍. In version B, it is *chien* 監, the archaic form of *chien* 鑒, bronze mirror. Composed of eye, 臣 a human being 人, and a vessel containing water 皿, 監 depicts the act of a person looking into a vessel of water to see his or her own reflection. In the earliest times water was the instrument for reflection, later replaced by bronze and glass mirrors. *Lan,* meaning contemplative vision, is derived from *chien* as mirror (Kao Heng, 1956: 24, 1974: 6). The mirror is a familiar word of the mystics. According to the *Tao Te Ching* the mind reflects the hidden mysteries of Tao by an inner light called *ming* (chs. 27.2, 36.1, 52.3). We are all familiar with the celebrated story of Hui Neng (638–713), who won his robe to become the Sixth Patriarch in Ch'an Buddhism by presenting a more spotless mind's mirror than that of the head monk Shen Hsiu (605?–706, W. T. Chan, 1963c: 35–41).

There is a third and more esoteric meaning of *lan* as heaven plate. In Taoist lore a Taoist mirror has the magical quality of protecting its owner from demonic forces. E. H. Schafer describes a recently excavated T'ang Taoist mirror representing various Taoist deities, as well as the Big Dipper and the lunar mansions exactly as they are found on the heaven plate of Han cosmic board *(shih)*. Donald J. Harper concludes that the heaven plate served as the prototype for the mirror, and that the magical potency of the mirror derives in large part from its association with the Big Dipper (Harper: 1–10, J. Needham, IV: 261–273, 314–334). Now Ho-shang Kung actually identifies "heaven's gate" *(t'ien men)* in (4) with the Big Dipper. Also, in chapters 22.2 and 28.2 the sage is literally called the *shih,* heaven plate or model of the world, because he models himself upon heaven, which is the "One." The Taoist mystic keeps his interior vision (mirror) clear so that he reflects faithfully the dark way of heaven.

---

3. Part II of the *Lü-shih Ch'un-ch'iu (Spring and Autumn of Lu),* a syncretic work compiled in 239 B.C., is divided into eight Lans or meditations, each of which consists of eight parts, thus consisting of sixty-four parts, reminding us of the sixty-four hexagrams of the *I-ching.*

4. Heaven's gate has also been interpreted psychologically to mean the five senses that open us to the external world. Hsün Tzu says: "Ears, eyes, nose, mouth, and body all have that which they perceive, but they cannot substitute for one another. They are called the heavenly faculties" (Watson, 1963b: 80–81). In opening heaven's gate the Taoist abides in the bright realm of the many; in closing heaven's gate he withdraws into the unity of the dark ground, thus becoming free from toil (ch. 52.2). According to the *Tao Te Ching* one does not have to step out the door to know Tao (ch. 47.1).

Ho-shang Kung interprets heaven's gate both macrocosmically as astronomical phenomenon and microcosmically as breathing activity. In the former sense heaven's gate points to the Pole Star or Big Dipper, the pivot of the universe. The latter means the nostrils—the opening and closing of heaven's gate means the proper inhaling and exhaling techniques, that ensure long life. In religious Taoism these lines also hint at the practice of sexual hygiene.

Cosmogonically the opening and closing of heaven's gate is the creation of the world. The *I-ching* says: "Therefore they called the closing of the gate the Receptive (K'un), and the opening of the gate the Creative (Ch'ien). The alternation between closing and opening they called change" (R. Wilhelm: 318).

Here the goal is reached. The journey begins with the ascent (or descent) from the many to the one with the process of rolling back psychological time whereby he becomes again an infant, wiping out the concept of the self that obstructs the vision of the dark and finally leading to the door of the mystical female, the root of heaven and earth (ch. 6.2). Entering the Uroboros (Neumann, 1955), the Taoist now becomes one with the archetypal feminine at the foundation of the universe.

5 and 6. Interpolation on the art of statecraft amidst instructions on mysticism is quite usual—proof enough that Taoist yoga, as far as the *Tao Te Ching* is concerned, does not involve any renunciation of the world. The fruit of the mystical vision is the formation of the ideal ruler to bring peace to all. The philosopher king ideal is as alive here as it is in Plato. In Plato's Allegory of the Cave (*The Republic*, Bk. VII, 514a–519c) the philosopher who has ascended to the real world must return to the cave to enlighten the prisoners therein. The Taoist ruler after his vision must also come back to the world, in his case to undo the work of consciousness. Having returned to ignorance himself (ch. 20.4) he protects his people from the dangerous paths of knowledge (ch. 65.1). His motto is "do not act" *(wu-wei)*.

7. These concluding lines, found also in chapter 51.4, show that the aim of the mystical vision is to make a ruler in the image of heaven as a mystical female. To claim possession, to hold on to, to lord over, are works of an alienated consciousness. It is heaven's way to retreat when work is done (ch. 9). The dark vision *(hsüan lan)* produces dark virtue *(yüan te)*. The Taoist ruler nurtures and accomplishes all things without dominating any of them.

11

---

1. Thirty spokes share one hub to make a wheel.
Through its non-being *(wu),*
There is *(yu)* the use *(yung)* of the carriage.

Mold clay into a vessel *(ch'i).*
Through its non-being *(wu),*
There is *(yu)* the use *(yung)* of the vessel.

Cut out doors and windows to make a house.
Through its non-being *(wu),*
There is *(yu)* the use *(yung)* of the house.

2. Therefore in the being *(yu-chih)* of a thing,
There lies the benefit *(li).*
In the non-being *(wu-chih)* of a thing,
there lies its use *(yun).*

General Comment

This chapter gives an excellent illustration of the relationship between being *(yu)* and non-being *(wu)* in the everyday workings of things. Non-being, the self-effacing, empty, or receptive, is the way of Tao; being, that which exists, affirms itself, or has a specific essence, is the way of things. Yet, non-being lodges within the very heart of being. It is through the presence of non-being that beings fulfill the reason of their being.

Detailed Comment

1. Wheels, vessels, and houses are beings, but their usefulness *(yung)* is through the emptiness contained in them. The emptiness in the hub allows the spokes to unite and form a wheel so that the the carriage can be used; the emptiness in the vessel allows it to be a container; and the openings and emptiness in the house allow it to serve as habitation. Thus, the use (form or function) of a being is derived from its non-being.

2. The process of *yu-chih* is the process of coming to be. *Li* has been translated "advantage" by Waley, Duyvendak, and Chan. More accurately, *li* means "to benefit," as opposed to "to harm" (ch. 81.3). It is good that all things come to be. Tao, in giving birth to all beings, benefits *(li)* them all, just as in *Genesis*, having made the world God pronounces it good.

Yung, "to use," refers to the power of being to act, work, and serve. This power to function comes from the non-being contained in being. If being refers to the concrete particular physical existence of something, non-being is the universal dynamism contained within every particular being. Tao is this universal dynamism present as the non-being in all beings. While to be is to be served and provided for, to be useful one must serve and provide. This is done when one makes room to accommodate others. Realization of this truth, that the usefulness of a being is measured by how much non-being is contained within it, tames the aggressive instincts in humans.

In the process of serving its purpose, a thing dispenses and uses itself up; being, in the process of its functioning, eventually exhausts itself and returns to non-being (the hub is worn out, the vessel is broken, the house collapses). This is the process of *wu-chih*, a process of nihilation and return to non-being, through which a thing fulfills its destiny (ch. 5). If to benefit *(li)* pertains to the order of being and having, to function *(yung)* pertains to the order of becoming and perishing. Through its nothingness (emptiness) while existing, a thing is useful; through perishing and returning to nothingness, a thing attains its purpose. Being stands for name and form; it is the process of coming to be. Non-being stands for activity and becoming through which a thing returns to formlessness. Being is the concretization *(li)* of non-being, while non-being is the activity *(yung)* of being.

The process of *yu-chih*, coming to be, and the process of *wu-chih*, ceasing to be, are the two phases in the reversive movement of all things. In the forward movement we witness the birth of ten thousand things; in the return movement we witness their reabsorption into the root (ch. 16.2). The two movements of coming out and return, of appearance and disappearance, of making being and making nothing, complete the circle of Tao. *Yu-chih*, the movement toward being, is one of creation and making resulting in a world good and beneficial *(li)* to have. *Wu-chih*, the movement back to non-being, is one of retreat and fulfillment. Through this process of self-abnegation, the abolition of the particularity in individual beings, individuals attain their usefulness and destiny *(yung)*. The *telos* of a being is not fulfilled as long as it tarries in being. It is in returning to non-being that being fulfills its destiny. In being's return to non-being lies the full value of having-been. This is the secret relationship between being and non-being; being in giving out its power and light returns to its dim root in non-being (ch. 52.3).

12

---

1. The five colors blind a person's eyes;
The five musical notes deafen a person's ears;
The five flavors ruin a person's taste buds.

2. Horse-racing, hunting and chasing,
Drive a person's mind *(hsin)* to madness.

3. Hard-to-get goods,
Hinder a person's actions.

4. Therefore the sage is for the belly, not for the eyes.
Therefore he leaves this and chooses that.

General Comment

This chapter, on the danger of going beyond the limits of nature, reflects back to chapter 9. Consciousness comes to ruin when it madly pursues the objects of desire.

Detailed Comment

1. This is a persistent primitivistic theme in the text—that humans should be contented with the simple pleasures of life (ch. 80) and that the overstimulation of the senses renders them incapable of functioning smoothly. The *Tao Te Ching* does not counsel withdrawal from sensual pleasure out of arrogance toward the world. It advocates living out the wholesomeness of one's natural endowment, not seeking external stimulants that disrupt the life rhythm within.

2. Horse racing, hunting, and chasing, favorite royal sports, not only needlessly cause animal suffering and death, they also harm the mental equilibrium of the participants.

3. Humans are value-creating creatures trapped by their own inventions. Theft of highly valued things is among the diseases of civilization. Just as hard-to-get goods are superfluous to nature, crimes are superfluous to good living. The *Tao Te Ching* believes that by removing one superfluity (hard-to-get goods) the other superfluity (acts of theft) will remove itself.

4. Wang Pi comments: " 'For the belly' means to allow things to nurture the self; 'for the eyes' means to allow things to enslave the self." According to Wang Pi the issue is between preservation or dissipation of the self. The sage makes things serve him; he does not enslave himself to things. Food, which is for the belly, serves to sustain the body, but the eyes lead us to outside distractions and dissipate the body's energies.

We suggest that the symbols of the belly and the eyes go deeper. The belly, representing instinct, the unconscious, and the unopened self, is the seat of life and unity (Gebser: 145). The eyes, opening us to the external world, represent consciousness, sight being the most refined and intellectual of the senses. The opposition between the belly and the eyes is the opposition between body and mind, or instinct and intelligence. That "the sage is for the belly, not for the eyes" means that his choice is the body, not the mind (ch. 3.2).

In chapter 9 of the *Shuo Kua (Discussion of the Trigrams)* of the *I-ching* we find the root meaning of why the sage is for the belly but not for the eyes:

> The Creative (*ch'ien*, male) manifests itself in the head, the Receptive (*k'un*, the female) in the belly, the Arousing in the foot, the Gentle in the thighs, the Abysmal in the ear, the Separation (*li*, brightness)[1] in the eyes, Keeping Still in the hand, the Joyous in the Mouth.

> (Cf. R. Wilhelm: 274)

The belly is the symbol of the womb or the valley spirit (ch. 6.1) containing all beings. Chapter 4 of the *Shuo Kua* says: "K'un is for storing." (Cf. R. Wilhelm: 267). The eye is the symbol of the coming out or standing apart of things. It represents the trigram Li (Separation) when things become fully illuminated. Chapter 5 of the *Shuo Kua* says: "Separation *(li)*, it is the state of light *(ming)*. The ten thousand things all perceive each other. It is the trigram of the south. That the sage faces south to attend to (*t'ing*, listen) all under heaven, that he governs by facing the light *(ming)*, is derived from this trigram" (*Ibid.:* 269).

While the Confucian sage governs by the trigram Li (Separation), the Taoist sage avoids this trigram. Instead he abides by *shou* (chs. 28.1, 52.1), the dark womb which contains and nurtures all beings. When things stand apart to perceive one another there is alienation and strife. The state when all beings are still in the womb of the mother remains the most peaceful and blissful state for the Taoist.

---

1. Wilhelm translates *li* as clinging, which is just the opposite of its exact meaning. *Li* means separation or standing apart under the condition of full illumination. It is a clinging to the sensual world, not to the source.

13

---

1. Accept honors and disgraces as surprises,
Treasure great misfortunes as the body.

2. Why say: "Accept honors and disgraces as surprises"?
Honors elevate *(shang)*, [1]
Disgraces depress *(hsia)*.
One receives them surprised,
Loses them surprised.
Thus: "Accept honors and disgraces as surprises."

3. Why say: "Treasure great misfortunes as the body"?
I have great misfortunes,
Because I have a body.
If I don't have a body,
What misfortunes do I have?

4. Therefore treasure the body as the world,
As if the body can be entrusted to the world.
Love the body as the world,
As if the body can be entrusted to the world.

General Comment

There are many turnings in this chapter. The premise is that the Taoist loves his body. Yet, if he loves his body he must also accept the possible misfortunes his body is subject to. Love of the body and hatred of its possible misfortunes is the cause of our primordial anxiety; love of the body and acceptance of its possible misfortunes gives us primordial trust. Do I hate my body because it is subject to misfortunes? The Taoist answers: "No, I love those misfortunes my body is subject to for the love of my body."

This chapter is meant primarily for rulers and ministers whose political lives

1. *Shang* literally means "high" or "to elevate," and *hsia* literally means "low" or "to depress." The Wang Pi text does not contain the line "Disgraces depress," while the Ho-shang Kung text does not contain the line "Honors elevate." Other texts have both. See Chiang Hsi-ch'ang: 68–69.

are always on trial. Here the *Tao Te Ching*'s advice produces peace and tranquillity in a world of uncertainty. If I can transcend the limits of my individual self
and identify my own body with the body of the universe so that the whole world
becomes my own body, I can be freed from the anxieties of independent existence.

Detailed Comment

1. The opening statements seem hard to accept. Since honors and disgraces affect
our very being, making us happy or miserable, it would be hard to take them as
mere surprises, external and accidental to our central concern. Misfortunes ruin
our careers, health, and lives. Yet we are told to treasure them, even as we treasure
our own body. Hence the queries at the opening of (2) and (3).

2. In the *Nicomachean Ethics* (I.5, 1095b22) Aristotle mentions that honor
is one of the ends chosen by people. The trouble is that honor depends on those
who confer it rather than on those who receive it. The same is true of humiliation.
Thus, although we cannot help but feel elated when honored and depressed when
humiliated, the *Tao Te Ching* advises that the proper attitude is to receive them
as surprises and lose them as surprises. Like the Stoic, the Taoist keeps his inner
calm in the face of honors and humiliations (ch. 56.3).

3. The body is the seat of the self (ch. 7.2). It is good to have a body; it is
evil to have misfortunes befalling the body. However, since opposites accompany
and generate each other (ch. 2.2), having a body (a good) also makes one vulnerable to misfortunes (evil). It is senseless to hate misfortunes while loving the body;
they must be accepted or rejected together. Since the body is a good that we
treasure, let us also accept and treasure the misfortunes that having a body entails.

Religious Taoists dream of a condition when the self can be without a body
subject to misfortune. Ho-shang Kung comments: "If I could be without a body,
I would effortlessly *(tzu-jan)* attain Tao. I shall lightly soar to the clouds, wander
in and out where there is no crevice, and penetrate the mysteries with Tao. What
misfortunes could I have."[2]

4. Most translators, following the Ho-shang Kung version of the text, have
rendered these lines in the following manner,

> Therefore he who values the world as himself,
> May be entrusted with the empire.
> He who loves the world as himself,
> May be entrusted with the empire.

2. Cf. Erkes: 32. This is the need for deliverance from the body in religious Taoism. See
Robinet, 1979.

Chapter 12 of the *Huai-nan Tzu* gives us a quite different reading:

Therefore he who treasures his body in serving the world,
How can he be entrusted with the world?
He who loves his body in serving the world,
How can he be entrusted with the world?

To determine the meaning of these lines we ask: What is the central theme of this chapter? Is it how to deal with the issues of glory and disgrace and the fortunes and misfortunes the body is subject to, or is it about who is best qualified to govern the world? The central and predominant theme unifying the whole chapter is the former, not the latter. The translation of these last lines is made in this spirit. The best cure for the anxiety of losing one's fame or life is to identify one's own body with the body of the world, which cannot be lost (ch. 16.3). Here the *Chuang Tzu*, chapter 6, illustrates the message of these last lines well:

You hide your boat in the ravine and your fish net in the swamp and tell yourself that they will be safe. But in the middle of the night a strong man shoulders them and carries them off, and in your stupidity you don't know why it happened. You think you do right to hide little things in big ones, and yet they get away from you. But if you were to hide the world in the world, so that nothing could get away, this would be the final reality of the constancy of things.

(Watson: 80–81)

14

---

1. What is looked at but not *(pu)* seen,
Is named the extremely dim *(yi)*.
What is listened to but not heard,
Is named the extremely faint *(hsi)*.
What is grabbed but not caught,
Is named the extremely small *(wei)*.
These three cannot be comprehended,
Thus they blend into one.

2. As to the one, its coming up is not light,
Its going down is not darkness.
Unceasing, unnameable,
Again it reverts to nothing.
Therefore it is called the formless form,
The image *(hsiang)* of nothing.
Therefore it is said to be illusive and evasive *(hu-huang)*.

3. Come toward it one does not see its head,
Follow behind it one does not see its rear.
Holding on to the Tao of old *(ku chih tao)*,
So as to steer in the world of now *(chin chih yu)*.
To be able to know the beginning of old,
It is to know the thread of Tao.

General Comment

This chapter is on fundamental ontology. It captures the dynamism of Tao at the transitional point between being and non-being. What we have here is the *via negativa*, the language of the mystics. The character *pu*, the not, appears nine times in the chapter. Walter Stace writes: "What mystics say is that a genuine mystical experience is nonsensuous. It is formless, shapeless, colorless, odorless, soundless" (12).

Detailed Comment

1. As the extremely small, Tao is invisible, inaudible, and intangible. It is also the extremely small and extremely great (ch. 41.3). Either way it is beyond our sensual experience. The existence of Tao cannot be verified. Here we move from the phenomenal world of the many to the hidden Tao as one.

2. Our translation of the first line follows the Ma-wang Tui texts. The beginnings of both versions A and B contain two additional characters, *i che* (as to the one), not found in other editions. This addition makes for better continuity between (1) and (2). In these lines Tao as the one further recedes and reveals itself to be nothing or chaos *(hu-huang)*. On the non-being aspect of Tao the *Chuang Tzu* (ch. 22) muses:

Bright Dazzlement asked Nonexistence, "Sir, do you exist or do you not exist?" Unable to obtain any answer, Bright Dazzlement stared intently at the other's face and form—all was vacuity and blankness. He stared all day but could see nothing, listened but could hear no sound, stretched out his hand but grasped nothing. "Perfect!" exclaimed

Bright Dazzlement. "Who can reach such perfection? I can conceive of the existence of nonexistence, but not of the nonexistence of nonexistence. Yet this man has reached the stage of the nonexistence of nonexistence. How could I ever reach such perfection!"

(Watson: 244.)

3. The "Tao of old" *(ku chih tao)* in line 3 pairs with "the world of now" *(chin chih yu)* in line 4. From his philological study Kao Heng determined that *yü* (being) in the *Tao Te Ching* has the same meaning as *yü* (space). Whatever has being occupies space. Thus, *chin chih yu*, the realm of being at the present moment, is "the world *(yu)* of now." If "the world of now" as being means space, "the Tao of old" as non-being *(wu)* is time. The priority of non-being over being (ch. 40) means the priority of time over space, of dynamism over form. This "Tao of old," which is the formless form, the image of nothing, giving rise to beings *(yu)* that have form and occupy space *(yü)*, is none other than the flux of time. This "Tao of old" that informs "the world of now" is what Jean Gebser calls the "Ever-Present Origin" (6, 173–175). Tao is the presence of the absent, an absence that is ever present. Time is this thread of Tao that connects the primordial beginning with the world of now. Thus, the verification of Tao as non-being is exactly through the existence of the world of beings today.

15

1. Those in the past who were good at practicing Tao,
Were subtle, mysterious, dark, penetrating *(wei miao yüan t'ung)*,
Deep and unrecognizable.
Because they were unrecognizable,
I am forced to describe their appearance *(yung)*.

2. Careful, like crossing a river in winter,
Hesitating, like fearing neighbors on four sides,
Reverent, like being guests,
Dissolving, like ice beginning to melt,
Thick, like uncarved wood,

Open, like a valley,
Chaotic *(hun)*, like murky *(cho)* water.

3. What can stop the murkiness?
Quieting *(ching)* down, gradually it clarifies *(ch'ing)*.
What can keep still for long?
Moving, gradually it stirs into life.

4. Those who keep this Tao,
Do not want to be filled to the full *(ying)*.
Because they are not full,
They can renew *(hsin)* themselves before being worn out *(pi)*.

General Comment

Chapter 14 describes the dynamic life of Tao at the moment of disappearance. In this chapter we have a portrayal of the Taoist who, like the vanishing Tao, is at the moment of transition between life, death, and new life. He is captured at his most self-effacing moment: the turning point between being and non-being, the moment of quiet self-regeneration.

Detailed Comment

1. The opening line in the Wang Pi and Ho-shang Kung texts has *shan wei shih che* (one good at military art), the same as in the first line of chapter 68. This chapter, however, does not discuss the appearance of the captain or warrior, but, as the Ho-shang Kung commentary says: "This refers to rulers who have attained Tao." My translation follows the Tang dynasty text, which has the same opening line as in chapter 65.

In the second line, the four characters *wei miao yüan t'ung* are usually descriptions of Tao. *Wei*, the extremely small or subtle, describes the disappearing Tao in chapter 14.1; *miao*, the mysterious, appears in chapter 1.3 and 1.4; *yüan* or *hsüan*, the dark abyss or origin, appears also in chapters 1, 6.1, 10.3, 51.4, 56.2, 65.3, and 4. Although the last character *t'ung*, penetrating or passing through, appears only here in the *Tao Te Ching*, it is a main characteristic of Change in the *I-ching*. The *Hsi Tzu*, II: 2, shows us how Change is everlasting by virtue of its power to penetrate and achieve breakthroughs in all situations: "When Change reaches the point of exhaustion [due to resistance of obstacles], it transforms itself; with transformation, it penetrates *(t'ung)* [i.e., it passes through the obstacles]; penetrating *(t'ung)* [the obstacles], it endures" (Cf. R. Wilhelm: 331–332).

The last two lines on the unrecognizability of the Taoist and that hence one is forced to describe him will be recalled in 25.2, which says that Tao's name cannot be known, thus one is forced to describe it. In the last line the character *yung*, meaning to describe or to give the features, appears also in the first line of chapter 21 in an effort to describe the features of the vast *te* that follows Tao.

2. Kao Heng (1956) points out that the ancient Chinese, fearful of crossing the water, often consulted divination prior to such a risky venture[1]. Here we speak not only of crossing a river but crossing it in winter, the most dangerous season in the year, when living things are caught in the throes of death. In the *I-ching* this refers to hexagram 29, *K'an*, the abysmal water, also the hexagram of the north where life perishes. Therefore, the dominant expression in this section is fear. We find the same expression in Ode 195 as quoted in the *Analects* 8: 3:

> In fear and trembling, with caution and care,
> As though on the brink of a chasm,
> As though treading thin ice. (Waley, 1938: 133).

The idea of the guest in line 3 is also found in chapter 69.1. The guest depends on the master's goodwill and hospitality. Since the world is a spirit vessel (ch. 29.1) with a sacred life not to be tampered with by humans, the Taoist's attitude is one of reverence and circumspection.

While the fourth line "Dissolving *(huan)*, like ice beginning to melt" continues the winter theme, it indicates the arrival at a turning point. *Huan*, to dissolve, hexagram 59 in the *I-ching*, is composed of the gentle wind (Sun) blowing over water (K'an) below. When the ice begins to melt, can spring be far away?

The uncarved wood, the valley (ch. 6.1), and the murky water in the last three lines are feminine symbols: unformed, yielding, and receptive. These indicate that we are no longer at the death throes of things but have advanced to a new stage of cautiously emerging new life. We are now at the transitional stage between non-being (chaos) and being. The same three symbols of wood, valley, and water are found in Ode 196:

> Gentle and respectful, like gathering in trees,
> Worrisome and careful, like arriving in a valley,
> Fearing and trembling, like treading on thin ice.

The Taoist maintains himself in this psychic state, still anchored in the source which is chaos or non-being, yet emerging into new being by virtue of the power of self-transformation.

These seven lines have been interpreted as seven stages of a progressively

---

1. Kao Heng points out that in the *I-ching* the judgments on some lines in hexagrams 5, 13, 18, 26, 27, 42, 59, 61, and 64 have "It furthers one to cross the great water," while other lines in hexagrams 6 and 27 warn: "It does not further one to cross the great water."

profound mystical experience of union with Tao (C.Y. Wu: 150–151). We agree with Wing-tsit Chan that such an interpretation is unnecessary (1963b: 127, note 4). In the very opening lines of the chapter the Taoist is already at one with Tao, being subtle *(wei)*, mysterious *(miao)*, dark *(yüan)*, and penetrating *(t'ung)*, all characteristics of Tao.

3. Wang Pi interprets these lines as the reversive process in nature: "From what is dark, through the organizing principle *(li)*, things attain light; from what is murky, through the quieting down process, things attain clarity; from what is at rest, through motion, things attain existence. This is the Tao of nature *(tzu-jan)*."

Cho, murkiness or turpidity, marks the state of *yin* or the decease of *yang* (Porkert: 22). According to the *I-wei ch'ien-tso-tu*, murkiness is characteristic of earth while heaven's characteristic is *ch'ing* or clarity (Fung, 1953, II: 97–98; Graham: 19). However, that which is murky, when it quiets down, acquires clarity and thus is prepared again for motion and life. *Yin* is the murkiness that gradually clarifies. *Yang* begins with clarity and moves toward dispersion and murkiness. The murky gradually settles down and self-clarifies, the clarified once again stirs and life appears. In this way *yin* and *yang*, rest and motion, and the murky and the clarified alternate with each other.

Murkiness, being dissolution of form, is the individual's point of death. There is a hint here that the Taoist, imitating Tao or Change, is able to undergo death and survive. One who can encompass both life and death, both heaven and earth, lives the deathless life of the round. In the *Chuang Tzu* chapter 7, we have the story of a Taoist adept at locating his life force at any point on the round. Now he is dying, now he is just born. He so befuddled the most competent fortune-teller that the poor fellow ran from town (Watson: 94–97).

4. The retreat or quieting down from life's activities leads to psychic clarification. The retreat is a self-emptying process that prepares the self for spiritual renewal. Thus empty space, necessary for physical motion, is also necessary for spiritual regeneration (chs. 11.1, 48.1), while a full state leaves no room for change or renewal (ch. 9.1). Chapter 22.1 says: "Worn out, thus renewed." The secret of long life is in continuous self-renewal, such that one is never completely worn out.[2]

We shall see in chapter 65.4 that this retreat and withdrawal not only prepares the Taoist for return to the world of activity, it is also necessary to maintain harmony among beings. Without this retreat or self-emptying there would be more conflicts and wars in the realm of the many. The rhythm of retreat and clarification readjusts the balance and brings about harmony in the world.

2. The last line, according to I Shen-ting, should be read: "They can renew themselves before being worn out" (Kao Heng: 38). Duyvendak's translation of this line "they could wear out without renewal" is exactly the opposite of what the text means.

16

---

1. Reach the pole of emptiness *(hsü-chi)*,
Abide in genuine quietude *(ching)*.
Ten thousand beings flourish together,
I am to contemplate *(kuan)* their return *(fu)*.

2. Now things grow profusely,
Each again returns *(kuei)* to its root.
To return to the root is to attain quietude *(ching)*,
It is called to recover life *(ming)*.
To recover life is to attain the Everlasting *(ch'ang)*,
To know the Everlasting *(ch'ang)* is to be illumined *(ming)*.

3. Not knowing *(chih)* the Everlasting *(ch'ang)*,
One commits evils wantonly.
Knowing the Everlasting one becomes all containing *(yung)*.
To be all containing is to be public *(kung)*.
To be public is to be kingly *(wang)*.
To be kingly is to be like heaven.
To be like heaven is to be like Tao.
To be like Tao is to last long.
This is to lose the body without becoming exhausted *(pu tai)*.

General Comment

Chapters 14, 15, and 16 are organically connected. Chapter 14 gives us Tao as moving away from the world to become the far away. Chapter 15 gives us the Taoist withdrawing from the activity of the world into the dynamic still point in the very act of self-regeneration. In this chapter the life of the natural world is seen to be no other than the life of the round. Possessed of the mystical vision of the round, which encompasses all beings both in their coming out and their going back, the Taoist rises above the one-sidedness of individual consciousness to expand in ever-widening circles. To witness the cyclical movement of the natural world is to be one with the life of Tao, is to become immortal and everlasting *(ch'ang)* as Tao is immortal and everlasting.

Detailed Comment

1. The withdrawal into quietude to prepare for the mystical vision is present in many religious traditions (Butler: 33). The pole of emptiness (Hsü-chi), the dynamic still point into which the Taoist has withdrawn to contemplate (*kuan*, ch. 1.3) the life of the round, is the same as the Supreme Ultimate (T'ai-chi) in the *I-ching*, or the pole of non-being (wu-chi, the Unlimited) in chapter 28.2.

The Ho-shang Kung commentary on this chapter sharply contrasts with the Wang Pi commentary. Wang Pi focuses on the return of all beings to the source, not their coming out. When a thing completes its life process, it returns to the quietude of the root. "All beings arise from the empty; all motions issue from the quiet. Thus the ten thousand beings although they are in motion, in the end they all return to the empty and quiet, which is their ultimate destiny."

Wang Pi's comment here, taking emptiness and quietude to be the ultimate state of all beings, shows a strong Buddhist flavor. The Ho-shang Kung commentary, on the other hand, interprets the return as merely one stage in the unending life of the round. The empty and quiet is not the ultimate destiny of all beings, but that to which all beings return to be reinvigorated for reemergence into life. This is brought out more fully in its commentary on (2).

> "Things grow profusely" means that they are full of foliage. Yet the ten thousand things will all wilt and drop to return to the root *so that they may come back to life again.* The quiet is the root. The root being quiet, tender, humble and lowly, does not die. Thus the quiet is revived and will not die. To recover life means to be deathless. This is the everlasting path of Tao.

2. The cosmic tree and its root are familiar religious symbols. Plotinus also compares the One, in his theology the supreme principle standing aloof from the universe, to the root of the universe.

> Or also it is something like the life of a huge tree which pervades the entire plant, the origin remaining what it was before. It does not dissipate itself all over the tree, being situated as it were in the root. This origin procured the entire life for the plant, but it remained itself absolute unity, without multiplicity.[1]

Everything upon perishing withdraws into its root. The whole world returns to Tao as its root, in which the many become the one. From the viewpoint of the *Tao Te Ching* this withdrawal is not the loss, nor the mere completion, of individual life: it is the individual's recovery of the everlasting universal life. The

1. *Enneads*, III, 8, 10. For the cosmic tree as a religious symbol, see Eliade, 1959: 98.

individual sheds individuality, which has a beginning and an end, to become one with the universal life process. This reabsorption into the universal life is the life or destiny *(ming)* of all beings. One who understands this secret, that the return is a return to the source and thereby a recovery of the immortal life in the creative ground, is illumined (*ming,* last line).

The third and fourth lines suggest that noise hampers life, while quietude is conducive to recovery of life. In the preceding chapter quietude *(ching)* is paired with activity *(tung).* Activity dissipates life's energies and leads to murkiness. But in quieting down, signifying a return to the root and a regathering of energies, the murkiness clarifies and one is again prepared for new activity. Though quietude is a winding down of activity, it is not inactivity. Just as non-being is the source of being, the pivot and pole of activity *(tung)* is quietude *(ching).* In the root all is quiet, but an intense activity goes on all the time. From the absolute quietude of the still point all things issue forth. Issuing forth they grow silently and profusely.

3. In this last part we are shown the process of expansion from the narrow individual self to the universal life of Tao. This movement from the particular to the universal is at the same time the liberation of the particular from the perishable to the imperishable.

In Taoism knowledge of the everlasting has a redemptive effect: To know is at the same time to be. Knowledge of the everlasting draws us close to the everlasting, while lack of this knowledge is the reason we commit wanton deeds. Any form of struggle, including moral warfare, is due to blindness to the complementary nature of opposites in the life of the round. This blindness produces the sharp distinctions between the self and non-self. While knowledge of distinctions leads us to strife, knowledge of the round, which embraces (Wang Pi interprets *yung* as all-embracing) all beings, expands our capacity until we become as inclusive as heaven and Tao.

Once we recover the knowledge of the everlasting the self begins to expand. First it becomes *kung,* meaning public, as opposed to *szu* (chs. 7.2 and 19.4), meaning private. *Kung* as a title in feudal enfeoffment means duke. While the king represents the interests of all the citizens of a state, the duke already represents the interest of a large group (chs. 42.2 and 62.3). The term then means public or, according to Wang Pi, the impartial or fair-minded. From the duke, who represents a large group, to the king, who represents all citizens, we move to heaven, which represents all nature, and finally to Tao, the universal creative power of all. If heaven and earth are long lasting (ch. 7.1), Tao is everlasting. When the individual becomes identified with Tao he too becomes everlasting: The loss of the body marks only the loss of the perishable individual. A person who identifies with Tao is one with the life of Tao. Because Tao moves cyclically without becoming exhausted (*pu tai,* ch. 25.1), the individual who identifies with

Tao also does not become exhausted *(pu tai)*. As in chapter 13.4, we are shown here that by identifying one's body with the body of the universe, we can transcend the limitations of the individual body.

The process of liberation from the self to the duke, to the king, to heaven and Tao shows that in the *Tao Te Ching* politics and theology are inseparable. The secular hierarchy flows seamlessly into the sacred hierarchy of being.

17

1. The best government, the people know it is just there.
The next best, they love and praise it.
The next, they fear it.
The next, they revile against it.

2. When you don't trust *(hsin)* [the people] enough,
Then they are untrustworthy *(pu hsin)*.
Quiet, why value words *(yen)?*

3. Work is accomplished, things are done.
People all say that I am natural *(tzu-jan)*.

General Comment

The topic of this chapter is the best form of government. Just as in the preceding chapter bureaucratic hierarchy is integrated into the hierarchy of being (ontology), in this chapter the best human government blends with the government of nature.

Detailed Comment

1. Here we are given four grades of government. The best government is so inobtrusive its people barely know it exists. Such knowing *(chih)*, according to Kao Heng, is mere awareness without sentiments of love, hatred, gratitude, or resentment. Government blends so well with the natural environment that its

actions are indistinguishable from those of nature. Its doings are accepted without inviting emotive responses from its citizens. This happens when the Taoist ruler returns society to nature, as portrayed in chapter 80.

When the distinction between good and bad governments are made, when people love or praise their governments, we have departed from the best form of government. Nature, being unconscious, works without fail. When the people are aware of their government and approve it they have already arrived at value distinctions; the seeds of discord are already sown. At this stage, however, governmental actions are still benevolent. This is the government of legendary Confucian sage rulers like Yao and Shun.

Worse is an oppressive government feared by the people. Government now becomes an added burden, punishing and terrifying. A government controlled by Legalists who emphasize the rule of law may be efficient and strong but the people suffer.

The worst type of government is corrupt and inefficient, punishing the people without offering protection in return. At this time rebellions and violent revolutions will rock civil society.

2. These lines may mean either that the ruler does not trust the people enough or that the people do not trust the ruler enough. We have opted for the former by connecting the *pu hsin* in line 2 to the *pu hsin* in chapter 49.2. The latter says that the most perfect trust (the trust of nature) trusts both the trustworthy and the untrustworthy. This chapter says that it is only when the ruler does not trust the people enough, threatening them with prohibitions and harsh laws, that they become untrustworthy (ch. 57.2). Provided the ruler trusts his people enough, he can dispense with edicts and moral exhortations.

Wang Pi's comment here (followed by Duyvendak) is clearly a Legalistic interpretation. For the Legalists *hsin,* carrying out the strict letter of the law, is an important governmental policy (Duyvendak, 1963: 90, 176, 260). Wang Pi reads the last line not as a question but as an affirmative statement: "Nothing could change their words. If they speak, their words will certainly be carried out. Therefore it is said: 'They value their words highly.' "

Such cannot be the position of the *Tao Te Ching.* A government feared by the people, the third type of government mentioned in (1), is far from being the model. Moreover, the Taoist ruler prefers silence to speech, he "practices the teaching without words" (ch. 2.3). Chapters 15.3 and 16.2 have shown us how silence or quietude is conducive to life and its activity. Nature in its trustworthy regularity "speaks *(yen)* little" (ch. 23.1). Words *(yen)* as externalizations of the inner flow of things tend to falsify (ch. 81.1). A government that relies too much on edicts breeds distrust. To imitate the government of nature the ruler must dispense with words: "Quiet, why value words?"

3. When the ruler dispenses with words and removes all governmental oppressions it is believed that the spontaneity of nature will take over such that

the people barely know the government exists. In this way human society forms one body with the great body of the universe. There is no telling where one begins and the other ends.

18

1. On the decline of the great Tao,
There are humanity *(jen)* and righteousness *(i)*[1].

2. When intelligence *(hui)* and knowledge *(chih)* appear,
There is great artificiality *(wei)*.

3. When the six relations are not in harmony,
There are filial piety *(hsiao)* and parental love *(tz'u)*.

4. When a nation is in darkness *(hun)* and disorder *(lüan)*,
There are loyal ministers.

General Comment

The overall message of this chapter, just as in preceding and subsequent chapters, is that the unconscious state of nature is superior to the conscious state of virtue. Consciousness marks a lack. We are not aware of and do not pursue something until we have already become separated from it. Nature and virtue issue from the same origin. When virtue is perfect and rooted in Tao it is called nature (Tao and *te*); when nature opens and becomes conscious it is called virtue *(jen* and *i)*. Nature, being unconscious, is effortless and successful; virtue, being conscious,

1. In the Ma-wang Tui texts, both versions, the character *an* (how can there be?) has been added at the beginning of lines 2, 4, 6, and 8 resulting in the removal of the intended irony of these lines and drastically altering their meaning (Therefore when the great Tao declines, how can there be humanity and righteousness? When intelligence and knowledge appear, how can there be great artificiality? etc.), making them incompatible with the rest of the text, especially that which immediately follows in the next chapter. This is obviously the work of a none-too-bright copyist.

struggles and fails. From this viewpoint the so-called progress from nature to virtue marks a movement toward strife, not peace.

Detailed Comment

1. We read in the *Chuang Tzu* that when nature was perfect human beings did not know humanity *(jen)* or righteousness *(i)* (Watson, 1968: 105). Their condition being pre-moral, they were naturally good without knowing good from evil. When moral ideas appeared nature had already suffered a loss. Only when humans had lost their original solidarity with the rest of the natural kingdom did they become conscious of the moral values of humanity *(jen)* and righteousness *(i)*, exalting humans above other creatures. Moral values are thus purchased at a price. The *Chuang Tzu* puts it this way: "From the point of view of Tao, things have no nobility or meanness. From the point of view of things themselves, each regards itself as noble and other things as mean" (Watson, 1968: 179).

2. *Wei*, what is done by humans, means art or artificiality in contrast to the work of nature. The natural world is the work of Tao; art or artificiality is the work of human intelligence. Art not only merely imitates nature but lacks an inner dynamism, as Aristotle also observed:

> Antiphon points out that if you planted a bed and the rotting wood acquired the power of sending up a shoot, it would not be a bed that would come up, but wood—which shows that the arrangement in accordance with the rules of the art is merely an incidental attribute, whereas the real nature is the other, which, further, persists continuously through the process of making.
>
> (*Physics* 193a: 13–18)

According to the *Tao Te Ching* the realm of nature is holy and authentic; culture and civilization, the work of human intelligence, stands apart from nature and is the realm of great deceit. To recover its authenticity the work of human intelligence needs to be reintegrated with the work of nature.

3. In the *Lü-shih ch'un-chiu* (SPTK 3/9b) the six relations radiating from the individual are: father, mother, elder brother, younger brother, wife, and son. Wang Pi combines the six relations into three pairs: father-son, elder brother-younger brother, and husband-wife.

For the *Tao Te Ching* the virtues of filial piety *(hsiao)* and parental love *(tz'u)* are not species specific to humans but are found in other creatures; in them they are practiced unconsciously and therefore perfectly. When these virtues are recognized as such and consciously cultivated, it is a sign that the bond between family members has already deteriorated. It is better if natural love pervades so that there is no need for the conscious practice of these virtues.

4. What is true of the family is also true of the state. When human society was one with the great society of nature there was no need for loyal ministers. Wang Pi comments: "If the six relations are in natural harmony, and the country is in good order by itself, then filial sons, loving parents and loyal ministers are nowhere to be found."

19

1. Eliminate sagacity *(sheng)*, discard knowledge *(chih)*,
People will be profited *(li)* a hundredfold.

2. Elminate humanity *(jen)*, discard righteousness *(i)*,
People will again practice filial piety and parental love.

3. Abolish artistry *(ch'iao)*, discard profit-seeking *(li)*,
Robbers and thieves shall disappear.

4. These three pairs adorn *(wen)* what is deficient *(pu tsu)*.
Therefore, let there be the advice:
Look to the undyed silk, hold on to the uncarved wood *(p'u)*,
Reduce your sense of self *(szu)* and lessen your desires *(yü)*.

General Comment

This chapter prescribes a way to remedy the harmful effects of consciousness, thereby to restore the people to the harmony of nature.

Detailed Comment

1. In the other twenty-six chapters where the character *sheng* appears, it appears as *sheng jen,* the sage or ideal Taoist ruler who rules by following Tao. In this chapter the character *sheng* appears alone and is used pejoratively to refer to a so-called sage ruler who promotes knowledge and teaches people to practice virtue. Such a sage leads the people away from the path of nature to the path of "virtue," thereby also to alienation and lack of virtue.

2. The virtues of humanity and righteousness as conscious love for one's kinsfolk *(jen)* or members of one's own group *(i)* not only foster exclusivity, division, and fanaticism, they indicate the existence of alienation and strife even among one's kinsfolk and within one's group (ch. 18.3). The *Tao Te Ching* believes that if the ruler stops preaching conscious virtues of humanity and righteousness, the natural love of offspring for their parents (filial piety) and parents for their offspring (parental love), witnessed in many living creatures, will reappear in human families.

3. Human art or ingenuity *(ch'iao)*, adding value to natural materials, brings profit to those who engage in it. This so-called enrichment of nature is called culture. However, the added beauty and value also arouses unnatural desire in peoples' hearts, inducing them to thievery. Generally anti-culture and anti-civilization (ch. 12), the *Tao Te Ching* is against embellishments of nature that produce societal disturbances (ch. 57).

4. These three pairs: sagacity and knowledge, humanity and righteousness, ingenuity and profit-seeking, are civilization's achievements. Nature is contented and adequate (chs. 33, 44, 46). Human beings, plagued by desire *(yü)* and self-awareness *(szu)*, always feel inadequate. They invent moral and civilization-oriented ideals to cover up *(wen)* their inadequacies *(pu-tsu)*. Morality and civilization in this sense are basically hypocritical. It would be better simply to reduce our self-awareness and desire and return to the simplicity and wholesomeness of nature, as exemplified in undyed silk and uncarved wood.

20

---

1. Eliminate *(chüeh)* learning so as to have no worries[1]
Yes and no, how far apart are they?
Good and evil, how far apart are they?

1. Kao Heng and Ch'ih Hsi-chao think that the first line structurally resembles the last two lines in the preceding chapter, thus should belong to the end of that chapter (Kao Heng and Ch'ih Hsi-chao, 1974: 4). This is not a sound judgment. Moving this line to the end of the preceding chapter would destroy the rhyming pattern of the last four lines in that chapter. Rather than resembling the last two lines, this first line in thought content and sentence structure resembles the first line of the preceding chapter: Both begin with the character *chüeh* (to eliminate) to announce a position against consciousness and learning, thereby to serve as the key to the entire chapter.

2. What the sages *(jen)* fear,
I must not not fear.
I am the wilderness *(huang)*[2] before the dawn *(wei yang)*[3].

3. The multitude *(chung jen)* are busy and active,
Like partaking of the sacrificial feast,
Like ascending the platform in spring;
I alone *(tu)* am bland *(p'o)*,
As if I have not yet emerged *(chao)* into form.
Like an infant who has not yet smiled *(hai)*,
Lost, like one who has nowhere to return *(wu so kuei)*.

4. The multitudes *(chung jen)* all have too much *(yu yü)*;
I alone *(tu)* am deficient *(i)*.
My mind *(hsin)* is that of a fool *(yü)*,
Nebulous.

5. Worldly people *(su jen)* are luminous *(chao)*;
I alone *(tu)* am dark *(hun)*.
Worldly poeple are clear-sighted *(ch'a)*;
I alone *(tu)* am dull *(men)*,
I am calm like the sea,
Like the high winds I never stop *(chih)*.

6. The multitudes *(chung jen)* all have their use *(i)*;
I alone *(tu)* am untamable like lowly material.
I alone *(tu)* am different from others.
For I treasure feeding on the Mother *(mu)*.

General Comment

Chapter 15 describes the Taoist as self-effacing and self-regenerating in imitation of the dynamic non-being of Tao. This chapter is a mystic's self-portrayal. Amidst the hustle and bustle of the crowd glorying in the life of consciousness cut off

2. *Huang* 荒, the uncultivated or wilderness, has been interpreted to mean *huang* 慌, hurried, or *kuang* 廣, vast. In context it is better to take its literal meaning—"wilderness" or "uncultivated"—which accurately describes the Taoist's psychological state.

3. *Wei yang*, according to Lo Yun-hsien, means having no place of belonging (Kao Heng, 1956: 46) and is reiterated in the phrase *wu so kuei* in the last line of the next stanza. Chiang Hsi-ch'ang interprets *wei yang* as limitless or endless, taking *yang* to mean "end," as *The Book of Odes* (Ode 182) says: "What of the night? The night is not yet ended *(wei yang)*" (Cf. Waley, 1960: 191). Wing-tsit Chan points out that *yang* literally means "dawn," thus "not yet ended" means "not yet dawn," i.e., since the night has not ended, dawn has not begun.

from the unconscious, the Taoist mystic abides by the root of all beings. The six sections are variations on the same theme; in each the mystic contrasts those who dwell in the realm of distinction to his own psychological oneness with the Mother.

Detailed Comment

1. Learning brings knowledge; knowledge brings worries. Once Adam and Eve acquired the knowledge distinguishing between good and evil (yes and no), their life was burdened by toil. If we eliminate the consciousness of value opposites that comes from learning, we need worry no more. Since all differences and oppositions issue from the same ground and were originally one, how far apart can they be?

2. We take *jen* (a human being) to mean the Taoist sage, as contrasted to the *chung jen* (multitudes) in stanzas 3, 4, 6, and *su jen* (worldly people) in stanza 5. The Taoist does not fear the same things the multitudes and worldly people fear. Forgetful of the ground they pursue the path of consciousness and learning, keep themselves busy and active, pile up worldly goods, seek fame, etc. in an effort to stand apart. The Taoist, on the other hand, fears an independent life cut off from the ground of all.

Dawn is the time when things begin to be illumined by daylight. Tao as the womb of all is the darkness or night. *Wei yang,* not yet dawn, describes the psychology of the Taoist who hovers between the wilderness *(huang)* of the dark unconscious and the dawn of consciousness.

3. *P'o* in line 4 originally derived from *p'a*. In the *Shuo Wen p'a* means non-exertion or not doing anything, bland, or without distinction. *Chao* in line 5 according to the *Shuo Wen* signifies the breaking lines on the burnt tortoise shell in divination, i.e., an omen of the good or evil to come. As breaking lines *chao* is the beginning of distinction and separation, when a thing emerges into being to acquire its own identity. The Taoist mystic, bland and formless, has not acquired such identity.

Hai in line 6, meaning a child, was originally written *k'e*, meaning the smile of a baby (Kao Heng, 1956: 47). In the *Book of Rites* (Legge, 1967, I: 473) we read that when a child is three months old he receives his personal name from his father who smiles at him. Marcel Granet paints a vivid picture of this naming ceremony:

> But the child is not really in a position to possess a superior soul until it is capable of laughter. It is the father who teaches it to laugh and straightway gives it that personal name *(ming)* which the Chinese rites show to be identical with the superior soul, with destiny, and with life itself. At the third month the child, which up till then has been kept

in seclusion, is at last presented to the father who greets it with a smile. This solemn ceremony coincides with the first arrangement of the child's hair and with the mother's resumption of her place in the family, purified by three months of abstinence, from the bloody stains of child-birth

(1930: 324)

The infant who has not smiled has not attained the awareness of the self. The Taoist keeps himself in this state of the infant, without the determinations and limitations that come with receiving one's name.

Wu so kuei in the last line has usually been translated as "without a home." The homelessness of the Taoist is a religious homelessness. Like the formless and nameless Tao that is everywhere and nowhere, the Taoist eludes classification, thus is "without a home."

4. *Yu yü* (to have extra), to be surfeited with goods, is the condition of civilization. Nature is self-balancing: What has too much is taken away, what is deficient is replenished (ch. 77). To facilitate change and self-renewal, the Taoist maintains an inner emptiness (ch. 15). The multitude, however, always wants to be filled to the full, preventing self-renewal. They belong to being and having while the Taoist is one with becoming and renewing. The Taoist is one with the creative Chaos at the origin of the world, hence: "My mind is that of a fool, nebulous." Plotinus in a different context also speaks against the multitude's urge for worldly possessions:

You must turn appearances about or you will be left void of God. You will be like those at the festivals who in their gluttony cram themselves with things which none going to the gods may touch; they hold these goods to be more real than the vision of the God who is to be honored and they go away having had no share in the sanctities of the shrine.

(*The Enneads*, V.5.11)

5. *Men* 悶, dull-witted, is a state when mind *(hsin* 心 *)* is enclosed within the door *(men* 門 *)*, i.e., when consciousness is protected within nature. Its opposite is *ch'a*, clear-sightedness, when things are seen as distinct and separate. The character *tu*, the alone, describes Tao in chapter 25 as the lone creative Chaos before heaven and earth. In this chapter it appears six times to describe the psychology of the Taoist who, having withdrawn from the crowd, is alone with Tao. He is the alone with the Alone, which is familiar language in mysticism (Watson, 1968: 124; Plotinus, *The Enneads*, VI.9.11).

Alone with Tao the Taoist takes up the dynamic nature of the sea, symbol of the creative mother, and the ceaseless high winds, which as part of the atmosphere are present to yet transcend all particulars. Both the sea and the high winds, dynamic forces of nature, are root imageries of Tao. In the *Chuang Tzu* chapter 1, they become the Leviathan of the deep (sea) and the giant bird (winds) of the sky, powerful symbols of creativity, transformation, and freedom (Watson, 1968: 29–31).

6. In this concluding stanza we return to the chapter's opening line: "Eliminate learning so as to have no worries." Wang Pi interprets *i* as use. To the Confucian learning is for entrance to and advancement in officialdom, hence the saying: "The scholar who attains excellence becomes an official." The Taoist spurns such usefulness. Compared to the Confucian the Taoist is useless, like a wilderness or some untamable material. Instead of shaping himself into a useful vessel the Taoist prefers to draw sustenance from the inexhaustible creative power itself. He feeds on the mother, a practice which may have its model in prehistoric times. Marcel Granet says:

> The continuity of the royal lines was assured, and the agnatic right established from the moment that the son heroically had the courage to claim relationship with his father. Huang-ti, who was born on a Hill of the Owls, was able to sustain his emblematic genius by eating owls. It appears that it is a custom with owls to devour their mother. To feed on the flesh of one's mother (when the filiation is on the mother's side) is merely to confirm in oneself the virtues of one's race. The endo-cannibalism which permits a family to preserve its substantial integrity, is a perfectly simple duty of domestic piety.
>
> (1930: 217)

Let us note that when the Taoist feeds on the mother it is no longer an act of domestic piety, nor is it to assure the continuity of the royal line. We may call it an act of cosmic piety, for in this act humans acknowledge their filiation with the entire natural world.

21

1. The features *(yung)* of the vast *(k'ung)* Te,[1]
Follows entirely *(wei)* from Tao.

1. Wang Pi says *k'ung* means empty. Our translation follows Ho-shang Kung who takes *k'ung* to means vast.

2. Tao as a thing,
Is entirely illusive *(huang)* and evasive *(hu)*.
Evasive and illusive,
In it there is image *(hsiang)*.
Illusive and evasive,
In it there is thinghood *(wu)*.
Dark and dim,
In it there is life seed *(ching)*.
Its life seed being very genuine *(chen)*,
In it there is growth power *(hsin)*.

3. As it is today, so it was in the days of old *(ku)*, [2]
Its name goes not away *(ch'ü)*,
So that we may survey *(yüeh)* the origins of the many *(chung fu)*.
How do I know that the origins of the many are such?
Because of this.

General Comment

For effective contrast, this chapter is best read together with chapter 14. Both chapters call Tao the illusive and evasive *(hu-huang)*, i.e., the primal Chaos or Hun-tun described in chapter 25. In chapter 14 Tao recedes and becomes the nothing; here the same illusive and evasive Tao moves forward to become the realm of beings. There Tao is nameless; here Tao is the name that never goes away. There Tao is the formless form, the image of nothing; here Tao contains the seeds and images of all beings that are to be. The dominant character of Tao in chapter 14 is *wu*, nothing; in this chapter it is *yu*, being or having. The conclusion of chapter 14 traces Tao to the beginning of old; this chapter arrives at the realm of the many in the now.

Detailed Comment

1. There is an interesting story connected with these first two lines. Because *k'ung* is also Confucius's surname, and because *te* in Confucianism means virtue, *k'ung te* has been interpreted to mean the virtue of Confucius. The first two lines would

---

2. The first line in the Wang Pi text reads: *tzu ku chi chin*, "From the days of old till now." Other texts, including the Tang dynasty text and both versions of the recently unearthed Han Dynasty Ma-Wang Tui silk manuscripts read: *tzu chin chi ku*, literally, "From now to the days of old." Most commentators favor this reading because *ku* (old) rhymes with *ch'ü* (to go away) and *fu* (origin) in the next two lines. I have followed this reading but decided not to translate the line in the literal sense as "From now to the days of old," but in the sense I think it was intended, "As it is today, so it was in the days of old."

then read: "The appearance of Confucius's virtue, follows alone from Tao." To those Taoists convinced that Taoism preceded and influenced Confucianism, the above reading proves it. One *Hsiang Erh Commentary on the Tao Te Ching* has this to say:

> Tao is very great. It had taught Confucius. Yet later generations do not believe in the Taoist texts. They only exalt the Confucian books, considering them to contain the highest teaching. Therefore this text so states the case to enlighten and inform later worthies.

> (Shih-hsiang Chen: 54)

2. These lines give us four stages—*hsiang* (image), *wu* (thinghood), *ching* (germ), and *hsin* (growth power)—through which the illusive and evasive Tao prepares to become the world of concrete individual beings. The character *hsiang* is a key idea in the *Book of Changes* (*Hsi-tzu*, II: 1). The eight trigrams and sixty-four hexagrams are all images *(hsiang)* of change. In the *Tao Te Ching* *hsiang* appears also in chapters 4, 14, 35, and 41. In this chapter *hsiang* stands for the bare beginnings of things that are to be. Tao as the empty womb is no longer empty; it contains the images or archetypal forms of all beings. In the second stage the illusive and evasive Tao evolves into *wu*, not in its usual meaning as "a thing" but as the thinghood or essence of things that are yet to be. Indeed, in line 1 Tao, illusive and evasive, is already called a thing. In the third stage appears *ching*, germ or life seed—the extremely small, imperceptible seeds of all things reminding us of Leibniz's germs and animals souls (Lach). At the fourth and last stage, *hsin*—trust or growth power by which all beings attain their actuality—is present. In chapters 17, 23, 49, and 81, as well as in the *Four Texts of the Yellow Emperor* unearthed at the Ma-Wang Tui tomb in 1973, *hsin* means trust:

> Heaven holds the one by the three luminaries: the sun, its rising is trustworthy *(hsin)*, its setting is trustworthy *(hsin)*; the moon, its birth is trustworthy *(hsin)*, its death is trustworthy *(hsin)*. To advance and retreat with regularity *(ch'ang)*, this is the foundation of number. The stars all have their numbers so as not to lose their ranks. This is the foundation of trust *(hsin)*.

> (Cf. Jan Yun-hua, 1978)

In this chapter *hsin* as trust is extended to mean *shen*—to expand, grow, or advance forward—as attested in the *I-ching:*

> When the sun goes, the moon comes; when the moon goes, the sun comes. Sun and moon alternate; thus light comes into existence. When

cold goes, heat comes; when heat goes, cold comes. Cold and heat alternate, and thus the year completes itself. The past contracts *(ch'ü);* the future expands *(hsin)*. Contraction *(ch'ü)* and expansion *(hsin)* act upon each other; hereby arises that which furthers.

(R. Wilhelm, 1967: 338)

There is a direct connection between *hsin*, meaning trust or regularity, and *shen*, meaning the power to grow. Today, as we live most of our lives indoors, we rarely acquire trust from observing the movements of the sun, moon, and stars, but to the stargazers of antiquity the regularity of these heavenly bodies must have appeared to be a divine characteristic, inspiring trust and confidence in the ways of nature. Regularity or rhythm encourages trust and confidence, the prerequisite for life, growth, and expansion. The small seeds *(ching)* contained in the primal Chaos, endowed with the power to expand *(hsin)*, are now ready to come forward to become the world of many beings.

3. These last lines reflect not only to the first two lines of the chapter—the appearing world *(te)* traces to the hidden Tao—they also echo the last lines in chapter 14. Tao as the womb of all beings is still the origin of all beings today, thus it is the name that never goes away and all beings acknowledge Tao to be their source.

Yueh 閱 in line 3 is composed of the door 門 from which things issue forth 兌; it means to witness, inspect, or survey the coming out process of things. The door from which all beings issue is Tao (ch. 1.4). According to both Wang Pi and Ho-shang Kung, *chung fu—chung* meaning the multitudes (ch. 20) and *fu* beginning or origin—stands for Tao as the origin of the multitudes. *Fu* 甫, however, has been interpreted to mean *fu* 父, father, with *chung fu* then meaning the multitudes of fathers. Kao Heng says: "These fathers of all things all issue from Tao. Tao is that which produces the multitudes of fathers" (1956: 45). That which produces the multitudes of fathers is not a father. The *Chuang Tzu* says: "Well, there are clans and there are ancestors of clans. There may be the multitudes of fathers *(chung fu)*, but there may not be the father of the multitudes of fathers *(chung fu fu)*" (Cf. Watson, 1968: 129). A father of the multitudes of fathers, an *Urgrossvater*, would be Tao. Yet Tao is a mother (chs. 1, 6, 10, 20, 25, 52) or illusive evasive womb from which come the seeds that become the fathers of all beings.

If we equate the original Chaos with matter and consider the four stages (image, thinghood, germ, growth power) the gradual development of the forms of all beings from within the Chaos womb, then in the *Tao Te Ching* matter produces form. The life seeds of all beings that are to be are not introduced instantaneously from the outside, as in Plato, Aristotle, and the Western metaphysical tradition. These seeds slowly evolve from within the dark womb of matter itself. In the *Theogony* (104, 116) of Hesiod, we also find Chaos giving birth to Night, which gives birth to Day (Wheelwright: 26).

The sentence structure of the last two lines is also found in chapters 54 and 57. Wang Pi interprets these lines to mean: "How do I know that all beings begin from non-being? Because of what I have said above," i.e., since all beings originate from Tao, which as Chaos is non-being, all beings come from non-being.

22

1. Bent, thus *(tse)* preserved whole,
Unjustly accused, thus exonerated *(chih)*,
Hollow, thus filled *(ying)*,
Battered *(pi)*, thus renewed,
Scanty, thus receiving *(te)*,
Much, thus perplexed.

2. Therefore the sage embraces the One *(pao i)*.
He becomes the model *(shih)* of the world.
Not self-seeing, hence he is enlightened *(ming)*.
Not self-justifying, hence he is outstanding.
Not showing off *(fa)* his deeds, hence he is meritorious.
Not boasting *(ching)* of himself, hence he leads *(chang)*.
Because he is not contentious *(pu cheng)*,
Hence no one under heaven can contend with him.

3. What the ancients say: "Bent, thus preserved whole,"
Are these empty words?
Be preserved whole and return *(kuei)*.

General Comment

From the preceding chapter on ontology and cosmogony, this chapter arrives at an ethic of self-preservation and self-fulfillment by the central teaching of non-contention *(pu cheng)*. The way to fully develop one's potential is by avoiding the harmful influences that can shorten life, not, therefore, through struggle or warfare, but through humility and yielding. The Ho-shang Kung commentary considers the entire chapter the ethics of survival. It entitles this chapter "I Ch'ien," names of hexagrams 42 (I, Increase) and 15 (Ch'ien, Modesty) in the *I-ching*. The *Commentary on the Decision* of hexagram 15 gives the same message that humility leads to fulfillment:

> It is the way of heaven to make empty what is full and to give increase to what is modest. It is the way of the earth to change the full and to augment the modest. Spirits and gods bring harm to what is full and prosper what is modest. It is the way of men to hate fullness and to love the modest.
>
> (R. Wilhelm, 1967: 462)

The chapter moves from (1), a general observation of the dynamic interchange of opposites, to (2), an application of this dialectic of things to one's conduct in society, and to (3), a reaffirmation of the belief that true virtue imitates the ways of nature.

Detailed Comment

1. *Tse*, appearing in every line meaning "thus" or "then," indicates a transition to the opposite state of affairs in the dialectic of becoming. The first line "Bent, thus preserved whole" describes how a plant weathers a storm. The unbending will be mowed down but the bent will survive the destructive forces (ch. 76). This must have been the common wisdom of the time. The *I-ching, Hsi-tz'u,* II, chapter 5, says: "The measuring worm draws itself together for the sake of expanding forward [*hsin*, see ch. 21]. Dragons and snakes hibernate for the sake of preserving their lives" (R. Wilhelm, 1967: 338). Similarly "the hollow," like the valley (ch. 39), will be filled, the worn-out turns and becomes new (ch. 15), those with little shall receive more, but those who have much shall have their possessions taken away from them (chs. 36, 44, 77). This logic of reversion is even more eloquently expressed in the *Sermon on the Mount:*

> Blessed are ye poor, for yours is the kingdom of God.
> Blessed are ye that hunger now, for you shall be filled.
> Blessed are ye that weep now, for you shall laugh. . . .
>
> (*Luke* 6: 20–26)

While both texts can be construed today as preaching passive acceptance of a miserable fate with the promise of a better future—hence Marx's indictment against religion as the opium of the people—they differ as to the manner of fulfillment. The Gospel promises readjustment of justice in the next world, implying that affairs in this world are not amenable to change for the better. The *Tao Te Ching,* as the next stanza makes clear, is not meant to console but to teach the art of surviving intact and accomplishing what one sets out to do in this world without resorting to conflict or warfare. They are practical instructions on how to succeed in life.

2. *"Pao i,"* to embrace the one, or to live the vision of the round, also appears in chapter 10.1. The sage who is the model (*shih,* chs. 10, 28, and 65) of the world contains in himself all opposites in their dynamic union (embracing the one). The people of the world pursue one side of an opposition and are thus self-seeing, self-justifying, and boastful of their deeds; the sage is enlightened (ch. 33), outstanding, and a leader (*chang,* ch. 28) exactly because he does not contend. The same characteristics—that he is not full of self, does not show off *(pu ching),* and does not boast *(pu fa)*—are attributed in a speech by the legendary emperor Shun to his minister Yü, the legendary conqueror of the flood and founder of the first Chinese dynasty, the Hsia, in the chapter on "The Counsels of the Great Yü" (of doubtful authenticity) in the *Book of History:*

The sovereign said, "Come, Yü. The inundating waters filled me with dread; you accomplished all that you had represented and completed your task, thus showing your superiority to other men. Full of toilsome earnestness in the service of the country, sparing in your expenditure on your family—and this without being full of your self or elated—you again show your superiority to other men. You are without any prideful assumption *(pu ching),* but no one under heaven can contest *(cheng)* with you the palm of ability. You make no boasting *(pu fa),* but no one under heaven can contest *(cheng)* with you the palm of merit.

(Legge, 1971: 22–23)

This ethic of peace based on non-contention *(pu cheng)* (chs. 3, 8, 66, 68, 81), like the Christian teaching of turning the other cheek, is not in tune with the spirit of today's civil rights movement based on *cheng,* to claim one's rights against others or against the state. It seems that Huang Ti, the legendary first ruler of China, who gained his hegemony by many wars against other tribes, already had to abandon the ethics of non-contention *(pu cheng)* preached here. In the *Four Texts of the Yellow Emperor* discovered at Ma-wang-Tui, in the part called *Shih-ta Ching* (ten great classics) or *Shih-liu Ching* (sixteen classics, Tu, Wei-ming: 97, n.7), chapter 5, "On Tribal Struggle" *(hsing cheng)*, Huang Ti's ministers warn him: "If you are not contentious, you shall not succeed" (*Wen wu* 10 (1974): 37, T'ang Lan).

The last two lines are also found in chapter 66.4.

3. These lines reaffirm the chapter's theme. *Kuei* in the last line literally means "to return" (ch. 16): When a person dies he returns to the source of all. The last line is thus an injunction to live out one's full life span before one is called to return to one's source. This is to be accomplished by bending to avoid the harmful influences that shorten life.

23

---

1. Nature speaks *(yen)* little.
Hence a squall lasts not a whole morning,
A rainstorm continues not a whole day.
What causes *(wei)* these?
Heaven and earth.
Even [the actions of] heaven and earth do not last long,
How much less [the works] of humans?

2. Therefore one who follows Tao identifies with Tao,
One who follows *te* (nature) identifies with *te* (nature).
One who follows *shih* (loss) identifies with *shih*.
One who identifies with Tao is glad to be with Tao.
One who identifies with *te* is glad to be with *te*.
One who identifies with *shih* is glad to be with *shih*.

3. When you don't trust *(hsin)* (the people) enough,
Then they are untrustworthy *(pu hsin)*.

General Comment

This chapter, continuing the theme of non-contention in the preceding chapter, also introduces the idea of *shih* as loss of the original endowment of nature *(te)*. *Shih* is the way of consciousness. In the next chapter we shall see that when a person becomes fully conscious, he loses all his natural abilities.

Detailed Comment

Confucius, who regards speech and language as a holy medium, sometimes sounds like a Taoist: " 'I wish I could do without speaking,' said the Master. 'If you did not speak, Sir,' said Tzu Kung, 'what should we disciples pass on to others?' 'What speech has Heaven?' replied the Master. 'The four seasons run their courses and all things flourish; yet what speech has Heaven?' " (*Analects* 17: 19. Soothill: 195–196)

Literally the last two lines read: "Even heaven and earth do not last long/ How much less humans?" It is obvious that here the reference is not to heaven and earth themselves, since they do last long (ch. 7), but their works. Squalls and rainstorms as works or speech of heaven and earth do not last; once they are uttered, they are gone. Human rulers would do well to imitate heaven and earth. Having accomplished their deeds, they should retire without claiming merit, just as heaven and earth let go their works.

2. Here we are given three ontological states. Tao is the creative ground of all beings. *Te* as the natural world includes heaven, earth, and all creatures. *Shih* stands for the conscious works of human beings in alienation from the works of nature. While *te* literally means to receive (ch. 39), *shih* means to lose. Humans, through the development of value consciousness, step outside the safe limits of nature (ch. 24), thus becoming cut off from the life of the round (ch. 38). Wang Pi interprets *shih* as a condition of excess in contrast to *te* as a state of constant self-emptying: "*Te* (to receive) is due to being scanty. 'Scanty, thus receiving' [ch. 22.1], therefore it is said to receive. . . . *Shih* (to lose) is due to having too much. To have too much is to lose, therefore it is said to lose."

Te as the state of union with Tao and *shih* as the state of alienation from Tao mark two existential paths comparable to the Christian states of grace—when the soul is turned to God—and sin—when it is turned away from God.

3. The last two lines, returning to the theme in the opening line, already appear in chapter 17.2 with the same message. Nature speaks little. One who follows heaven and earth, trusting his people, also speaks little. Moral consciousness as *shih*, born from loss of the wholesomeness of nature, is self-validating: The ruler who belongs to *te* trusts his people and they thereby prove to be trustworthy; the ruler who belongs to *shih* distrusts his people and they thereby prove to be untrustworthy.

24

1. One who tiptoes cannot stand.
One who straddles cannot walk.
One who sees himself is not enlightened *(ming)*.
One who justifies himself is not outstanding.
One who shows off *(fa)* his deeds is not meritorious.
One who boasts *(ching)* of himself does not lead *(chang)*.

2. These to a Taoist are called:
Excess nature *(yü te)* and superfluous actions *(shui hsing)*,
Avoided *(o)* even by things.
Therefore the Taoist does not indulge *(ch'u)* in them.

General Comment

This chapter in the Ma-wang Tui texts follows chapter 21 and precedes chapter
22. I believe, however, that the existing arrangement is superior. Chapter 23
introduces the state of *shih* as consciousness' going beyond, thus losing, nature.
This chapter describes *shih* as the state when a person, being fully conscious, loses
all ability to do what nature easily accomplishes.

Detailed Comment

1. These lines present a contrast to chapter 22.2 showing, as Duyvendak puts it,
that "all excess is harmful" (1954: 64). Consciousness interferes with life's
smooth functioning. Commenting on the nature of "no-mind" in Buddhism
Suzuki says: "So long as there are conscious strivings to accomplish a task, the
very consciousness works against it, and no task is accomplished. It is only when
all the traces of this consciousness are wiped out that Buddhahood is attained"
(202).

2. Most texts have *yü shih*, excess food, in the second line. According to Liu
Ssu-p'ei, *yü shih* is to be read *yü te*, excess nature (Kao Heng, 1956: 59), i.e., moral
virtues in excess of the dynamic inner process of things (chs. 18, 38). Excess
nature parallels *shui hsing*, moral actions superfluous to the activity of natural
beings. Liu's reading becomes more persuasive in view of what the *Chuang Tzu*,
chapter 8, says:

Two toes webbed together, a sixth finger forking off—these come from birth but are excretions as far as nature *(te)* is concerned. Swelling tumors and protruding wens—these come from the body but are excretions as far as birth is concerned. Men overnice in the ways of benevolence *(jen)* and righteousness *(i)* try to put these into practice, even to line them up with the five vital organs! This is not the right approach to Tao and *te*. Therefore he who has two toes webbed together has grown a flap of useless flesh; he who has a sixth finger forking out of his hand has sprouted a useless digit; and he who imposes overnice ways, webs and forked finger, upon the original form of the five vital organs will become deluded and perverse in the practice of benevolence and righteousness and overnice in the use of his hearing and sight.

(Cf. Watson, 1968: 98)

25

1. There was something nebulous existing *(yu wu hun ch'eng)*,
Born before heaven and earth.
Silent, empty,
Standing alone *(tu)*, altering not *(pu kai)*,
Moving cyclically without becoming exhausted *(pu tai)*,
Which may be called the mother of all under heaven.

2. I know not its name,
I give its alias *(tzu)*, Tao.
If forced to picture it,
I say it is "great" *(ta)*.
To say it is "great" is to say it is "moving away" *(shih)*,
To say it is "moving away" is to say it is "far away" *(yüan)*,
To say it is "far away" is to say it is "returning" *(fan)*.

3. Therefore Tao is great,
Heaven is great,
Earth is great,

The king is also great.
In the realm there are four greats,
And the king is one of them.

4. Humans follow *(fa)* earth,
Earth follows heaven,
Heaven follows Tao,
Tao follows self-becoming *(tzu-jan)*.

General Comment

In content this chapter on cosmology and fundamental ontology is closely connected with chapters 14, 21, and 40. This chapter's most important contribution is in clearly delineating Tao's life as a four-stage cyclical movement corresponding to the four seasons of the year, again confirming Taoism as a nature mysticism, and the life of the divine in Taoism as the life and death of the divine in nature. This understanding of Tao is the key not only to this text but also to the *I-ching*, and the general mentality of the ancient Chinese.

Detailed Comment

1. The first character *yu*, meaning "being," "having," "there is," indicates that in this chapter Tao is being. *Hun*, meaning "to blend," "chaotic," or "nebulous," a state prior to the separation of heaven and earth when all is mixed with all (chs. 14, 15, 25), describes the initial state of Tao as being.

The last character in the first line *ch'eng* usually means "complete" or "formed" (chs. 2, 7, 34, 64). In this line it can mean neither. Form in Western philosophy means the essence of a thing or what determines a thing to be what it is. This nebulous something as the original stuff of the universe without any determination or form is like prime matter in Aristotle, but as the fertile ground that evolves to give rise to all forms and beings (ch. 21.3) it is also most unlike Aristotle's prime matter, which is devoid of any forms or creativity. Neither can we render *ch'eng* in this line as "complete" or "finished." As nebulous this something is most fluid and protean, neither complete nor finished. Since its being consists in its becoming, it is as much non-being as being. The function of the character *ch'eng* in this line is therefore to posit not the *essence* of this nebulous something as complete or formed, but the *existence* of this dynamic creativity as the origin of the world. In contrast to chapter 4, where Tao as the nebulous origin of all beings is said to be "so dark, it only seems to exist," here the existence of Tao is positively posited.

As *hun* and *ch'eng* this nebulous something has been identified with *Hun-tun*, the cosmogonic deity, in other Taoist texts (Girardot: ch.2). As primal being it is the Great Ultimate (T'ai-chi) of the *I-ching* issuing from the Unlimited (*wu-chi*, ch. 28.2); as standing alone it is the one born of Tao as zero (non-being, ch. 42); as silent and empty it is the ultimate emptiness (hsü-chi) of chapter 16 and the "great harmony" that "has hardly any sound" of chapter 41.

"Altering not" does not mean that Tao is a changeless stasis. Duyvendak perceptively explains "altering not" to mean "that it does not change its characteristic of alternating constantly" (1954: 66). The *I-ching* says:

> The Changes is a book
> From which one may not hold aloof.
> Its tao is forever changing—
> Alteration, movement without rest,
> Flowing through the six empty places;
> Rising and sinking without fixed law,
> Firm and yielding transform each other.
> They cannot be confined within a rule;
> It is only change that is at work here.

> (R. Wilhelm: 348)

The dynamism of the one qualifies it to be the mother of all beings. The Parmenidean Being, as the lone existent frozen in its immobility, cannot give birth to the many. Tao as the one is unceasing movement comprising its fertility and immortality.

2. Our translation of the third line, "If forced to picture it," follows the suggestion of Kao Heng. The Wang Pi text reads: "If forced to name it, I call it the Great." Since the author has just said "I know not its name" (see also chapter 1), it is unlikely that he immediately supplies not only one but four names of Tao. These four: great, moving away, far away, and returning are not names, but stages or states of Tao. Tao is not so much a being to be named as a becoming to be delineated in four stages.

In the face of the undeniably dynamic language of these lines, Wang Pi's comment is most disappointing. Perhaps due to Buddhist influence (Ho, Ch'i-min: 216–247, T'ang, Yung-t'ung, 1972), Wang Pi did not grasp these lines as portraying the movement of Tao. His comment on these lines shows that he grasps Tao rather statically as pervading and penetrating all things.

> Why I call it Tao is because I chose the greatest of all that can be used as a name. If you try to determine why the term Tao is used, it is because it is great. Yet whatever is connected with the great necessarily has divisions. Having divisions Tao would lose its position as the Ulti-

mate. Therefore, it is said, "If (reluctantly I am) forced to give it a name, I shall call it great."

"To move away" means to be in motion, which is not to hold on to the substance of the great. Tao operates everywhere and reaches everything. Therefore it is said to "move away."

To be "far away" is to reach the limit. Since it operates everywhere and nowhere does it not penetrate, it is not limited to just "moving away." Therefore it is said to be "far away." But even then it does not remain where it is, being in its substance independent. Therefore it is said to "return."

At best Wang Pi grasped Tao as a static non-being in the sense that it is neither one thing nor another, thus fiting none of these four states. Tao is reluctantly called the "great," which if spread out in space would allow division. It is tentatively called "moving away" because, present here and there, it is not confined to any specific location. It is called "far away" because it reaches the farthest corners. Finally it is called "returning" because, transcending all, it is purely itself. Wang Pi completely failed to grasp these four stages as the very life process of Tao, both its coming to be and perishing. Compared to the comment of Wang Pi, Kao Heng's comment is to the point: " 'If forced to picture it, I say it is great, moving away, far away, and returning,' means the substance of Tao is the greatest, the movement of Tao is cyclical" (1956: 61).

3. In these lines the central theme of the chapter, the nature or movement of Tao as the creative Chaos, is suddenly dropped. We are no longer discussing cosmogony because not only has the natural world come to be, the social world with its ruler is also well established. The topic now is on the four great forces in the realm of beings, and on how the three great powers—heaven, earth, and humans—imitate Tao's greatness.

The *I-ching (Book of Changes)* also speaks of heaven, earth, and humans as the three great powers manifesting the greatness of Tao or change. There are six lines in the hexagram; the top two represent heaven, the middle two represent the human ruler, and the bottom two represent earth (R. Wilhelm: 264). Change is effected through the interactions of the three primal powers of heaven, earth, and humans, thus the *Hsi-tz'u,* I: 2, says: "The movements of the six lines *(yao)* contain the ways *(tao)* of the three primal powers" (R. Wilhelm: 289).

4. *Fa,* meaning the law, also means to imitate, to take after, or to follow, as the *I-ching* says: "Therefore in following *(fa)* and imaging *(hsiang)*, none are greater than heaven and earth" (Cf. R. Wilhelm: 319). For both the *Tao Te Ching* and the *I-ching* the greats are arranged in the following hierarchy: The king is great by following the earth, the earth is great by following heaven, and heaven follows Tao, which is a sponteneous creativity *(tzu-jan)*. Such a worldview

does not grant humans with their thinking power any special privileges. Humans join the ranks of the great only to the extent they image earth and heaven, which image Tao or spontaneity.

26

---

1. The heavy *(chung)* is root *(ken)* to the light *(ch'ing);*
The tranquil *(ching)* is master *(chün)* to the agitated *(tsao).*

2. Therefore the sage travels all day,
Without leaving *(li)* his baggage wagon *(tzu chung).*
Although he has glorious palaces *(yung kuan),*
He avoids its sumptuous apartments *(yen-ch'u).*
How could the Lord of ten thousand chariots,
Conduct himself lightly in the world?

3. One who acts lightly loses his foundation *(pen);* [1]
One who is agitated loses his master *(chün).*

General Comment

Chapter 25 concludes by saying that the ruler, one of the greats in the realm of being, follows the earth. This chapter explains what it means to follow the earth.

1. The *Han Fei Tzu* commentary, carried away by its political analogy, changes this line: "One who acts lightly loses his foundation *(pen)*" to "One who acts lightly loses his ministers *(ch'en)*" (Liao, I: 209), the dialectic between the ruler *(chün)* and the minister *(ch'en)* being topmost in the mind of a political strategist like Han Fei. The Ho-shang Kung text follows the Han Fei text. My translation follows the Wang Pi text for the following reasons. Notwithstanding Han Fei's concern, there is in this chapter no reference to the relationship between minister *(ch'en)* and ruler *(chün)* (Ma Hsü-lun, 1965: 90–91). Also, it is the Tao Te Ching's style to recapture the message of the opening lines in the concluding lines. This is the case here: *Pen* (foundation) and *chün* (master) in the last two lines reflect *ken* (root) and *chün* (master) in the first two lines. Indeed, *pen* (foundation) is a variant of *ken* (root). Further, both versions of the recently discovered Ma-wang Tui texts belonging to the Huang Lao tradition, have *pen* (foundation), confirming my conviction that the Wang Pi version is the more original one, and that the change to *ch'en* (minister) in the Han Fei Tzu text is unwarranted.

The ancient Chinese were grateful to the earth for patiently bearing up the weight of all beings. The *Doctrine of the Mean* says: "The earth before us is but a handful of soil; but in its breadth and depth, it bears the load of mountains like Hua and Yüeh without considering them heavy *(chung),* it carries the rivers and seas without letting them leak away, thus it holds up all things" (Cf. Chan, 1963a: 109).

The ruler who follows the earth does likewise. While Plato's aspiration is to mount up and lift off from the earth, and while the *Chuang Tzu* leads us soaring into the clouds, the *Tao Te Ching* is earthbound. In today's space age, humans travel far into space and celebrate what Joseph Campbell calls the "earthrise," meaning that the earth, though ponderous, is agile in her own way. The message here is still valid: Humans must not attempt journey in flight without earth as the starting point and final destination. If we lose touch with the heavy (the earth), we shall lose our base.

More practically, this chapter speaks of the burden of the Taoist ruler who carries the weight of his society on his shoulders (ch. 78.3).

Detailed Comment

1. Since the light and the agitated belong to consciousness, while the heavy and tranquil belong to the unconscious, this chapter harks back to chapter 24, which warns against a consciousness cut off from the unconscious. The Taoist abides by the heavy which sustains the light, and the tranquil which underlies the agitated.

2. Just as an infant does not depart from the safety of its mother (ch. 52), and the fish does not depart from the deep (ch. 36), the ruler must not leave (*li,* ch. 28.1) his baggage waggon, which is his state and his burden.

In the *Han Fei Tzu,* chapter 21, entitled: "Illustrations of the *Lao Tzu*" these lines receive a Legalistic twist. "Baggage wagon" now means the power base a ruler must never relinquish or else put his life in danger. A historical example is given of a ruler who abdicated in favor of his son. His residence was then surrounded and he was starved to death (Liao, I: 209–210). Here, the Taoist cut off from the holy Tao courts death; in legalism the ruler who relinquishes his political power loses his life. Here, political thought flows directly from religious vision; thus the obvious message of this chapter is the role of the ruler who, by following the earth that follows heaven and Tao (ch. 25.4), ensures harmony between society and cosmos. In Legalism the goal of politics is no longer the seamless continuity between human society and cosmic change. The goal now is to consolidate and perpetuate the ruler's power (E. M. Chen, 1975). Compared to Legalism, which deals with *real politik,* the political philosophy of the *Tao Te Ching* remains on the ideal plane.

The term *kuan* has come to mean Taoist temple. In ancient times it meant a palace (ch. 1.3). *Yen-ch'u,* swallows' nests high above the trees, refer to the apartments of princes and concubines. The ruler rejects such frivolous pursuits belonging to the light for the serious business of the state, which is his weight.

3. With its predilection for the technique of immortality, the Ho-shang Kung commentary takes *chün* (the master or ruler) to mean the semen. Its commentary on these two lines reads: "If the king is light-minded and excessive, he will lose his ministers; If the ascetic is light-minded and excessive, he will lose his semen."

27

---

1. Good *(shan)* running leaves no tracks,
Good speech has no flaws,
Good counting uses no counters,
A good lock uses no bolts yet cannot be opened,
A good knot uses no rope yet cannot be untied.

2. Hence the sage is always good at saving people,
Therefore no one is rejected.
He is always good at saving things,
Therefore nothing is rejected.
This is called following the light *(ming).*

3. Therefore the good person,
Is the not-good *(pu-shan)* person's teacher.
The not-good *(pu-shan)* person,
Is the good person's capital.
One who does not honor *(kuei)* the teacher,
Or love *(ai)* the capital,
Is greatly confounded though knowledgeable *(chih).*
This is called the important mystery *(miao).*

General Comment

This chapter, containing the character *shan* (the good) eleven times, is on the nature of the good.

Detailed Comment

1. The character *shan*, the good or perfect, begins every line here to qualify a particular activity, whether it is running, speaking, counting, closing the door, or tying a knot. When an activity reaches perfection it discards the ordinary mode of execution. This means the really perfect is ineffable like Tao. Good running, good speech, and good counting, do not leave any trace of their activities. One who imitates Tao and participates in the goodness of Tao acts in the same manner.

2. A goodness that accepts the good and rejects the not good is a second-order goodness—it leaves tracks, it has flaws, it is calculating, it can be opened and untied. The goodness of the sage, like the goodness of Tao, rejects no one. The character *ming*, enlightenment or mystical vision, is composed of the sun and the moon and symbolizes the unity of opposites.

The *Tao Te Ching* definitely rejects the notion of election or predestination taught in some religions. The moral war, deadly serious though it is, is fought only on this side of existence. When Jesus said to let the wheat and weeds grow together until harvest time when the wheat will be gathered into the barn and the weeds burnt, he spoke of the kingdom of God as this world's ultimate achievement. Taoism shows that there is yet a deeper vision in which wheat and weeds are both gathered into the bosom of Tao, their sharp differences softened and blended into one (ch. 4).

3. When we resolve moral opposites into natural opposites, we shall see that the good requires the not good just as much as the not good requires the good. Saints are models or teachers for sinners, while sinners are working capital for saints; without sinners saints would have no one to do good to. This is why Aristotle, for whom independence or self-sufficiency is the highest value, considers the moral life, which requires others as objects of its activity, inferior to intellectual life, which we can perform, so he thought, continuously and independently of others (*Nicomachean Ethics*, 1178: a25–b23). According to the *Tao Te Ching*, however, the nature of existence is such that all beings are interdependent. The proper relationship between the good and the not good, therefore, is one of mutual fulfillment. While the not good should honor or exalt *(kuei)* the good, the good should love or care *(ai)* for the not good.

Han Fei's illustration of these lines is an example of the extent to which the *Tao Te Ching* teaching can be distorted in legalism. In the view of the *Han Fei Tzu* love (as indulgence) encourages disobedience and leads to disregard for law and authority, calling down punishment for the violators; hence, to love someone means to lead that person to ruin. A good politician therefore loves the not good, his enemy, with a view to his eventual downfall. The story is told of King Wen (a good king) giving Fei Chung (a bad minister) carved jade plates so that Fei Chung could advance his career under the tyrant Chow and finally come to ruin

(Liao, I: 227). One can think of no more sinister love than this. Indeed, if the story of King Wen is historically accurate he may be called a good king, but certainly in this act he was not a good person. It is clear that the gap between the *Tao Te Ching* and legalism is unbridgeable. The profoundly religious vision of the *Tao Te Ching* is incomprehensible to a legalist whose dedication to political expediency has purged him of any remnant of love except the most sinister kind.

28

1. To know *(chih)* the male,
But to abide *(shou)* by the female *(tz'u)*,
Is to be the valley *(ch'i)* of the world.
Being the valley of the world,
And departing *(li)* not from the everlasting power *(ch'ang te)*,
One again returns to the infant *(ying erh)*.

2. To know *(chih)* the white *(pe)*,
But to abide *(shou)* by the black *(heh)*,
Is to be the model *(shih)* of the world.
Being the model of the world,
And deviating *(t'eh)* not from the everlasting power,
One again returns to the unlimited *(wu-chi)*.

3. To know *(chih)* the illustrious *(yung)*,
But to abide *(shou)* by the obscure *(ju)*,
Is to be the valley *(ku)* of the world.
Being the valley of the world,
One's everlasting power *(ch'ang te)* being full,
One again returns to the uncarved wood *(p'u)*.

4. The uncarved wood disperses to become vessels *(ch'i)*,
To be used *(yung)* by the sage as officials.
Therefore a great institution does not mutilate *(ko)*.

General Comment

This chapter, besides continuing the theme of the unity of opposites discussed in chapters 26 and 27, echoes chapter 10 on many topics, among them, the priority of the famale *(tz'u)*, the return to the infant *(ying erh)*, and the injunction against departing *(li)* from the everlasting creative power *(ch'ang te)*.

Detailed Comment

1. The female being prior and giving rise to the male (chs. 6, 10)—"to know the male, but to abide by the female"—means that the creature, having come from Tao, returns to and abides by Tao the mother. This is what chapter 10.1 means when it exhorts us to embrace the one without ever departing from it. *Li*, also the name of hexagram 30 in the *I-Ching*, represents the state of consciousness (ch. 12.4) when all beings, standing out from the ground, perceive one another. According to the *Tao Te Ching* death begins with the separation *(li)* of the male from the female[1] or the creature from the ground. Only the infant, containing in itself both the male and female (ch. 55) and drawing directly from the mother's life-giving power (ch. 52), is free from death. Returning to infancy is therefore returning to the unity in the primal female, which alone contains immortality.[2]

2. *Chi* in the last line means the extreme boundary, limit, or perfection (ch. 68). *Wu-chi* as the negation of all boundaries or limits means the unbounded, unlimited, or infinite.[3] If t'ai-chi (Supreme Ultimate) in the *I-Ching* (R. Wilhelms, 1950: 318–319) is the ultimate reality of the *via affirmativa*, wu-chi as ultimate non-being is the ultimate reality of the *via negativa*. It is equivalent to the hsü-chi (ultimate emptiness) in chapter 16.1. When we transcend the extreme boundary of being, we arrive at nothingness *(wu)* or emptiness *(hsü)*.

3. The illustrious *(jung)*, such as official ranks, belong to culture, while the obscure or ignoble *(ju)* stands for the crude conditions of nature. One who knows the illustrious but abides by the obscure is one with the low-lying valley and the simplicity of uncarved wood *(p'u)*.

4. This last stanza, reflecting on how the one nature breaks itself up into

1. Norman O. Brown (133) quotes this chapter to support his thesis that death begins with the distinction of sexes.

2. In religious Taoism this means that Lao Tzu, being the male that has returned to the female, is his own mother. See Schipper: 363–364.

3. Wing-tsit Chan says that the term *wu-chi*, an important metpahysical concept in Neo-Confucianism, appeared for the first time in the *Tao Te Ching* (1963: 149). Chan's translation of wu-chi as non-ultimate, however, conveys the impression that it is not the ultimate.

the many so that instruments of various usages become available to the sage, seems to be a commentary on what has gone before. It introduces us to the next chapter on how to govern society from within the Taoist unitive vision. Like the three pairs of opposites above (male-female, white-black, illustrious-obscure), *p'u*, the uncarved wood, and *ch'i*, a formed vessel, are opposites in contrast. The uncarved wood *(p'u)*, standing for the condition of nature untouched by culture, is nameless (chs. 32 and 37). Vessels *(ch'i)*, on the other hand, are already shaped to serve specific purposes. When Tao becomes the world of ten thousand things, each with its specific form and name, the one universal becomes the many limited particulars. Yet, unless the universal is curtailed and limited, it cannot serve any function. As the male returns to the female, the white returns to the black, and the glorious returns to the obscure, the named *ch'i* (vessels) also return to dynamic union with the nameless *p'u* (uncarved wood). As long as the sage uses the natural endowments of his officials without mutilating their nature, human society is in harmony with nature's reversive process.

29

1. One who desires to take the world and act *(wei)* upon it,
I see that it cannot be done.
The world *(t'ien hsia)* is a spirit vessel *(shen ch'i)*,
Which cannot be acted *(wei)* upon.
One who acts *(wei)* on it fails,
One who holds on to it loses *(shih)*.

2. Therefore things either move forward or follow behind;
They blow hot or blow cold;
They are strong *(ch'iang)* or weak;
They get on or they get off.

3. Therefore the sage gets rid of over-doing,
Gets rid of extravagances,
Gets rid of excesses.

General Comment

This chapter develops the theme of the last line in the preceding chapter—
"Therefore a great institution does not mutilate"—and is an excellent manifesto
for today's theology of nature. The central message is *wu wei*, do not act against.
Not only is the natural world a spirit vessel with a sacred life rhythm coming from
Tao, every creature, as the preceding chapter points out, is also a vessel of Tao
not to be tampered with by unholy acts of human desecration. Our role is to
conserve the earth, not to dominate or mutilate it.

Detailed Comment

1. *T'ien hsia* (under heaven) in lines 1 and 3, translated as "the world," can be
taken to mean the natural world, the natural environment, or the state, the
empire. In context it is obvious that this chapter is about the ruler's relationship
with his state or his people. Duyvendak says that by spirit vessel *(shen ch'i)* "is
probably an allusion to the nine sacred bronze vessels, which were symbolic of
the royal power over the nine divisions of the 'empire' " (1954: 74). The Ho-
shang Kung commentary interprets *shen ch'i* to mean the people: Since "the
people are the spiritual beings in the empire" the ruler must not disturb them
in their peace and quietude. "To act" *(wei)* means to impose an order on things
alien to their inner rhythm. "To hold on to" means to keep the world immobile
according to human wishes. Since the world has an inviolable life of its own such
efforts are doomed to failure. The body politic is an integral part of and is
endowed with the same inviolable life force as the natural world. The ruler,
entrusted with this sacred vessel, exercises extreme caution lest he violate its
sacred character.

   The conviction that human beings cannot destroy nature's integrity, beauty,
and harmony with impunity, is shared by American Indians and ancient Greeks
(Lovelock) and starkly contrasts to the traditional Judeo-Christian view of the
relationship between humans and the natural world. *Genesis* (1: 28) tells how
humans were created in God's image and so have "dominion over the fish of the
sea, and over the birds of the air, and over the cattle, and over all the earth, and
over every creeping thing that creeps upon the earth." In Taoism humans do not
dominate the earth, they follow it (ch. 25).

   The last two lines also appear in chapter 64.

2. These four lines describe the way things are, always in the process of
change: rising or falling, coming out or going back, getting on the carriage in the
procession of beings, or falling off from the carriage of being to enter into the
oblivion of non-being.

3. The sage is sensitive to the rhythm of the world and follows its contours

of change. He takes care not to disrupt the cosmic procession of beings. His job is to dismantle the works of consciousness called overdoing, extravagance, or excess (ch. 24) from the viewpoint of a self-regulating nature.

30

1. One who assists the ruler with Tao,
Does not overpower *(ch'iang)* the world by military conquests.

2. Such affairs have a way of returning *(huan):*
Where armies are stationed,
Briars and thorns grow,
After great campaigns,
Bad years are sure to follow.

3. The good person is resolute *(kuo)* only,
But dares not *(kan)* take the path of the strong *(ch'iang)*.
Be resolute *(kuo)* yet do not boast *(ching)*,
Be resolute yet do not show off *(fa)*,
Be resolute yet do not be haughty,
Be resolute because you have no choice,
Be resolute yet do not overpower *(ch'iang)*.

4. When things are full grown, they age.
This is called not following Tao.
Not following Tao they perish early.

General Comment

While the preceding chapter serves as the basis of a theology of nature, this chapter provides the rationale for a theology of peace. It carries the theme of non-action or non-domination in the preceding chapter to international relations. If humans are not supposed to dominate other creatures, neither should they dominate fellow humans. This chapter is a critique of military power *(ch'iang)* specifically against wars, which are instruments of death.

It is commonly misunderstood that certain parts of the *Tao Te Ching* teach military strategy or that certain chapters came from the military school (Chan, 1963b: 222). In those chapters discussing warfare or the military (30, 31, 57, 67, 68, 69, 73, 76, 78) only five chapters (30, 31, 67, 68, 69) treat warfare as a fact of life. All of them are pacifist, condemning war as an evil to be avoided by all means. Indeed, none of the so-called military chapters deal with military strategy or instruct how to kill one's enemies successfully. They all advise against use of military power except in dire necessity for self-defense.

Detailed Comment

1. *Ch'iang*, the strong and overpowering, defines a manner of being not conducive to long life (chs. 55.3 and 76). He who assists the ruler with Tao avoids the path of the strong.
2. "Such affairs have a way of returning *(huan)*" suggests the notion of *karma*, the law of retributive justice insuring that whatever we do will reap its effect in the future. *Huan*, however, does not necessarily mean to recoil upon the doer; it can simply mean to return or repeat. Disasters have a way of perpetuating themselves. Thus, one year's bad harvest because the planting season is missed in the heat of a military campaign repeats its consequences in the years afterward in the depletion of manpower, poor land fertility, bad weather, and so on.

In our own day the lesson of things returning has been driven home in the ecological crisis. The insecticides and toxic wastes that we have released into the environment have come back to shorten our own lives; what we do to the environment we do also to ourselves. This is particularly the case now. The aftereffects of nuclear war are such that what the victor does to his enemy he does to himself.

3. Kao Heng (1956: 71) interprets *kuo* as to win by killing one's enemies); thus, he who is good in military affairs is good at killing although he does not boast or show off. This interpretation of *kuo*, violating the spirit of the chapter on the evils of military conquest, is unacceptable. *Kuo* in this chapter means the resolute determination to resist the strong and fight for one's life. While emphasizing the soft and yielding as the way to life, while teaching the winding or bending *(ch'ü)* way to ward off the world's destructive forces (chs. 22 and 45), the *Tao Te Ching* allows wars of self-defense. *Kuo* is a resolve, in fear and trembling, to avoid death by facing death, which ensures the survival of the defending party (chs. 69 and 73). Such wars, born of the respect and love for the life in all beings, are not fought for the sake of self-glorification or conquest and thus are conducted without the boasting or showing off of provocative bravado *(ch'iang)*.

Ching, to boast, and *fa*, to show off, both products of a consciousness that has cut itself off from Tao, and both leading to conflicts and struggles, also appear in chapters 22 and 24.

4. These concluding lines on how the strong deviates from the path of Tao and so meets its end quickly returns to the theme in the opening lines. The same lines also conclude chapter 55.

31

1. Military weapons are implements *(ch'i)* of ill omen,
Avoided *(o)* even by natural creatures *(wu)*.
Hence the Taoist does not indulge *(ch'u)* in them.

2. The princely person *(chün-tzu)* in dwelling honors the left,
In military campaigns honors the right.
Hence military weapons are not implements of a princely person.

3. Military weapons, being implements of ill omen,
Are to be employed only in dire necessity.
Better to regard them with lack of interest.
Do not admire *(mei)* them.

4. If one admires *(mei)* them,
One would be rejoicing in the killing of people.
But whoever rejoices in the killing of people,
Will not be successful *(chih)* in the world.

5. Therefore in joyful affairs the left is honored,
In mournful affairs the right is honored.
The Second-in-Command takes the place of the left,
The Commander-in-Chief takes the place of the right,
Meaning that this is his place in the funeral rite.

6. When many people have been killed,
Wail them with sorrow and lamentations.
When victorious in battle,
Mark the occasion with the rite *(li)* of funeral.

General Comment

The theme of this chapter is the same as that of the preceding chapter: the tragedies of war.

Most commentators consider the text of this chapter garbled. We do not have Wang Pi's comment on this chapter (or on ch. 66). Some say that this is because Wang Pi did not consider this chapter part of the text (Rump: 94–95). Others suggest that his comment has been mixed up with the text, resulting in its repetition. The Ma-Wang Tui texts, while antedating the Wang Pi commentary, are not substantially different from it, apart from having more connective characters between sentences, making for better reading and more organically connected lines. This means that Wang Pi simply did not comment on this chapter. My translation of this chapter mainly follows the Ma-wang Tui texts.

Detailed Comment

1, 3, 4. What is said in (1) is reiterated in (3): wars, being evil, are to be fought only in dire necessity and are never to be welcomed or pursued. The conviction that only those rulers who refrain from killing will be admitted to the secrets of heaven is echoed in the *I-ching:*

> In this way the sages purified their hearts, withdrew, and hid themselves in the secret. In good fortunes and bad they shared with the people. Their spiritual power enabled them to foreknow the future; their wisdom enabled them to store up the past. Who were they that could do all these? Only those ancients who were intelligent, discerning, powerful in spirit and body, and *yet who did not kill.* [1]

2, 5. The left is the honored place in affairs of life; the right is the honored place in affairs of death (Granet, 1975: 37; R. Needham). In peacetime the princely person honors the left but in wartime, when death prevails, the right side becomes the honored place (ch. 79). The following texts from the *Li-chi (The Book of Rites)* show that the left stands for heaven, life, male, east, the strong, and the flourishing; the right stands for earth, death, female, west, the weak, and the perishing:

> When they have entered the door, the host moves to the right, and the guest to the left, the former going to the steps on the east, and the latter to those on the west.
>
> (Legge, 1967, I: 72)

1. Cf. R. Wilhelm, 1950: 316–317. Wilhelm failed to translate the italicized portion of the last sentence and so missed more evidence of the close relationship between the *Tao Te Ching* and the *I Ching* that he, among sinologists, was the first to point out.

On the march the [banner with the] Red Bird should be in front; that with the Dark Warrior behind; that with the Azure Dragon [symbolizing heaven] on the left; and that with the White Tiger [symbolizing earth] on the right . . .

(*Ibid.* I: 91)

In all salutations of males, the upper place was given to the left hand. In all salutations of females, the upper place was given to the right hand.

(*Ibid.* I: 479)

When leaving the city, in mounting a war chariot, the weapon was carried with the point in front; when returning and entering it again, the end. The left was the place for the general and officers of an army; the right, for the soldiers.

(*Ibid.* II: 77)

On the last quoted passage Ch'en Hao commented this way:

In marching out the weapon is carried with the point in front means the blade is pointed toward the enemy. When returning, the weapon is pointed toward the back, meaning that they do not point the blade at their own state. The left is *yang,* the path of life; the right is *yin,* the path of death. The Left General is the commanding general. In the procession of the officers they all honor the left, expressing the wish that there may be no defeats; the procession of the soldiers honors the right, showing their determination to die.

(II: 196).

6. Does this suggest fear of the dead? To borrow the observations of Frazer and Freud on aboriginal cultures: Is the funeral rite a remnant of a past expiatory rite to prevent slain enemies from troubling their slayers? (Frazer: 249–250; Freud: 62)

I offer an alternative interpretation. The character *li* (rite) appears only in one other place (ch. 38) in the text where *li* is said to be the mere flowering of Tao. Whether the author was an expert on *li* is a matter of scholarly debate (See Introduction, "Lao Tzu's Meeting with Confucius"). This chapter reveals a deeper meaning of *li: Li* is rooted in the tragedy of life, thus it involves death. If the essence of Tao is *tz'u* (ch. 67)—the benevolence and compassion of the creative principle for all beings—this benevolence or compassion also includes sorrow, since what lives must die, and in the case of war many lives are cut short. The deepest essence of *li* is the external expression of deep-seated sorrow and mourning over the passing of life and, in the context of this chapter, over the violent destruction of life in wars. The killing of one's enemies is an occasion for mourning, since all come from the same womb of Tao.

32

1. Tao everlasting *(ch'ang)*
is the nameless uncarved wood *(p'u)*.
Though small,
Nothing under heaven can subjugate it *(mo neng ch'en)*.
If kings and barons can abide by *(shou)* it,
All creatures will arrive as guests *(pin)* to a banquet.

2. Heaven and earth unite,
To send down the sweet rain.
Without being commanded by the people *(mo chih ling)*,
It falls evenly *(chün)* by itself.

3. At the beginning of institution names come to be.
Once there are names,
One must know when to stop *(chih chih)*.
One who knows when to stop does not become exhausted *(pu tai)*.

4. Tao in the world is like
Valley streams flowing into rivers and seas.

General Comment

In contrast to the preceding chapters on the devastations of wars this chapter, presenting a harmonious natural world under the sway of Tao, returns to the theme of the sacredness of the natural world (ch. 29).

Detailed Comment

1. The key idea in this stanza, in sentence structure and message similar to chapter 37.1, is *shou*, to abide by. The advice to rulers is to abide by the everlasting Tao. Nameless, unadorned, and small, Tao does not dictate from above but allows all beings to develop according to their own inner rhythms. The world, left to its own spontaneity, is a harmonious realm. If rulers and governments do the same, all beings will flock to them as they flock to Tao.

Tao as undifferentiated and nameless is *p'u*, the uncarved wood. When the *p'u* disperses into various individual forms, it becomes the many vessels to be employed by the ruler as officials to serve in various functions (ch. 28.4). Although it is small Tao cannot be subjugated to carry out orders like a minister carries out the orders of a ruler *(mo neng ch'en)*. Rather, all beings are naturally drawn to Tao (ch. 35) and to Tao all beings submit. The conclusion is that the ruler needs only to abide by *(shou)* Tao to rule successfully.

2. Heaven and earth are benevolent forces treating all beings equally and without prejudice. The sweet rain, signifying the union of heaven and earth to benefit all creatures, falls evenly *(chün)* on all.[1] Just as Tao cannot be ordered around *(mo neng ch'en)*, heaven and earth are not commanded *(mo chih ling)* by anyone. Everything happens spontaneously.

3. The *Chuang Tzu* in chapter 2 enumerates four stages of knowing (Watson, 1968: 41). The most perfect knowing is unaware that things exist. This is Tao prior to the coming of the world of ten thousand things. Then there is the knowing that things exist but there are as yet no boundaries between them. This is the state of nature as nameless uncarved wood, when all things are still indistinguishable from one another. The third stage is the knowing that there are boundaries. Here names come to be and natural distinctions are made. While Tao is nameless, its creatures have names that imply natural distinctions. At this stage the many do not yet war against each other; nature as a multiplicity is still in the unity of Tao and its life process is unending. The last stage is the knowing that distinguishes between the right and the wrong or the good and the evil. At this moment the spontaneity, harmony, and unity of nature are lost. This is the moment when discord and death enter the world.

The last line, "One who knows when to stop does not become exhausted" (ch. 44.3), grasped in the light of these four stages of knowing, bids us to stop at the third stage when names come to be without entering into the fourth stage when conscious distinction between good and evil arises. While there is continuity, reversion, and spontaneity from the nameless Tao to the ten thousand beings with ten thousand names, to go beyond naming to moral consciousness would

---

1. According to the *Shuo Kua* (ch. 11), *chün,* meaning fair, equal, level or even-handed, is the characteristic of K'un, the hexagram of earth, the mother (R. Wilhelm, 1950: 275).

result in human alienation from the everlasting Tao. This is *tai*, becoming exhausted when one is cut off from the unending life of the round.

4. These two lines give us an analogy of the relationship between Tao and its creatures. The question is: Which is like the valley streams and which is like the rivers and seas? Most commentators understand these lines to mean that the creatures are like the valley streams flowing toward Tao as rivers and seas. Wang Pi's comment is representative:

> Valley streams seek rivers and oceans. Not that rivers and oceans summon them. They return on their own without summons or entreaties. Those who practice Tao in the world obtain equality *(chün)* without commanding it, receive [the allegiance of the people] without seeking for it. Therefore it is said that he is like the rivers and seas to the valley streams.

Wang Pi's interpretation seems confirmed in chapter 51.2, which also tells how all beings spontaneously pay homage to Tao, chapter 35, which compares Tao to a banquet at which all creatures partake, and chapter 66, which speaks of the rivers and seas as lords of the valleys. However, the analogy should be turned around. The central message in this chapter is that Tao, the small, is benevolently present in the world to sustain all beings. This stanza is a refrain of (1) and (2). Just as the rain falls spontaneously and evenly to nourish all beings (2), Tao is like the valley streams that, in meandering downward to the rivers and seas, fertilize the lands by which they flow.

33

---

1. One who knows *(chih)* others is knowledgeable *(chih)*;
One who knows *(chih)* the self is enlightened *(ming)*.

2. One who overcomes others has physical might;
One who overcomes the self *(tzu sheng)* is strong *(ch'iang)*.

3. One who knows contentment *(chih tsu)* is rich;
One who acts strongly *(ch'iang)* has will power *(chih)*.

4. One who does not lose where one belongs lasts long;
One who dies without perishing *(wang)* has longevity.

General Comment

This chapter, organically connected to chapters 22 and 24, develops the line in the preceding chapter: "One who knows when to stop does not become exhausted." The first six lines give three pairs of contrasting situations: one who abides in and is contented with his situation is at peace with the world and lives long, but one who squanders life's energies in contests against others shortens his life. The last two lines focus the chapter's message: Humans must not lose sight of where they belong. They don't have a destiny separate from the world; their goodness and spirituality do not mark them as independent of the rest of nature but rather integrate them with the all.

Detailed Comment

1. Here we are given two forms of knowing, *chih* 知, a pure form of awareness, and *chih* 智, knowledge of the external world. Knowing the external world is merely being worldly wise. Knowing oneself and where one belongs is called enlightenment (*ming*, ch. 27.2). Knowing others sets one against others; knowing the root brings peace and contentment.

    2. Usually *ch'iang*, the strong, means violence (ch. 30), which invites early death (chs. 42, 55, and 76). Its opposite, *jo*, the weak, gentle, and yielding, is the way of the everlasting Tao (ch. 40). However, in the line "One who overcomes the self *(tzu sheng)* is strong" and in chapter 52.3, *ch'iang* does not mean brute force but inner strength conducive to long life. The weak and gentle bend and survive (ch.22.1); therefore, they are really strong and long lasting. There are thus two ways of being strong. Those who are strong in overcoming others have mere physical might, but those who overcome their own self-will by being gentle and bending, hence life preserving, are truly strong. This is not the Nietzschean self-overcoming that as an example of the will to power leads to perishing. Following spontaneity *(tzu jan*, ch. 25) and the uncarved wood (*p'u*, ch. 32), and reverting the self to its root, the strength of the Taoist comes from abiding by the unending life of the mother (ch. 52).

    The Ho-shang Kung commentary interprets self-overcoming in the religious sense of overcoming one's passions and desires, a self-overcoming that requires great willpower.

    3. The first line is also found in chapters 44.3 and 46.2. These lines again represent two opposing situations. "One who knows contentment" is at peace with the world, while "one who acts strongly" is at war with the world. The *Tao Te Ching* is for the former but not the latter.

    Confucian commentators (Chiao Hung) and even the legalistic commentary in the *Han Fei Tzu* (Liao, I: 226) interpret the second line as a statement in praise of one who has strong willpower to achieve a goal, like what is said in the *Doctrine of the Mean:* "If another man succeeds by one effort, you will use a hundred efforts. If another man succeeds by ten efforts, you will use a thousand efforts. If one really follows this course, though stupid, he will surely become intelligent, and though weak, will surely become strong" (Chan, 1963a: 107).

This is not the position here. To have such a strong will *(chih)* the mind must so constrain the vital energy *(ch'i)* that it cannot flow freely (chs. 3 and 55.3). Such a will leads to early death. It is not the way of Tao.

4. The message of the first line is the same as that in chapters 10.1 and 54.1. For Plato, when the soul is fixed in its vision of the immortal and unchanging absolute ideas, it wanders no more but becomes confirmed in immortality and changelessness. By clinging to Tao without ever letting go, the Taoist is also one with the ever changing and living Tao.

The last line in the Wang Pi text reads literally: "One who dies without being forgotten *(wang)* has longevity." This has caused other Confucian commentators to say that the Taoist idea of immortality is, after all, not very different from the Confucian one as presented in the *Tso Chuan* (Duke Hsiang, 24th year) (Chan, 1963a: 159). There we read that immortality consists in the establishment of virtue, deeds, and words while one is alive to ensure that one is not forgotten by later generations after death. There is no hint of such an idea here. Even Wang Pi did not interpret this line in such a manner. In his commentary he equates *wang,* to forget, with its homophone *wang,* to perish: "Whoever dies, but whose Tao by which he lived does not perish *(wang),* completes his longevity. The body is gone, but the Tao still exists."

In the final analysis, longevity means not to stand apart from Tao. One who identifies his individual life with the universal life of Tao is as long living as the everlasting Tao.

34

---

1. The great Tao floods over,
To the left, to the right.

2. Ten thousand beings live by it,
And it does not reject them.
Work is accomplished *(ch'eng),* yet it has no name.

It clothes and nourishes ten thousand beings,
But does not lord over them.

3. Always without desire,
It may be named the small;
Ten thousand beings return *(kuei)* to it,
Yet it does not lord over them,
It may be named the great.

4. Because it never considers itself great,
Therefore it can accomplish *(ch'eng)* its greatness.

General Comment

In this and the next chapter Tao is portrayed as the principle of plenitude diffusive of itself. Like the Good of Plato (*Timaeus* 29, 33) it does not envy anything, therefore it brings forth all beings.

Detailed Comment

1. Chapter 25 describes Tao's cyclical movement in four stages: It is the "great" that "moves away" to become the "far away" that "returns." As the "far away" Tao is non-being. This non-being in its reversive movement "returns" and becomes being. The "great" is Tao as the creative fertility flooding over to pour out a world of ten thousand beings.

2. Tao is great by virtue of its giving rise to the world. Yet, Tao itself is characterized by the "not": It rejects nothing, it has no name, it lords over nothing. Name and power belong to the realm of being. Tao as the support and substratum of all beings has no name or power. In clothing and nourishing all beings Tao is the nursemaid of beings but does not lord over them. It is the mother (ch. 25) who gives rise to her children but herself remains dark and withdrawn. Thus even while Tao pours forth to become the world of beings, Tao itself remains the not or non-being.

3. In chapter 1.3a the desireless is the hidden or non-being whereas being or the appearing world comes from desire. In itself Tao is without desire and is therefore named the small (ch. 32). Yet, because Tao gave rise to all beings, it is truly the great. The greatness of Tao is in its effects—ten thousand beings all come from Tao and return *(kuei)* to Tao on their own.

4. Consciousness limits the creative act. Being unconscious, Tao's creativity is limitless. Tao is not aware of itself as the great, therefore it is truly the great.

35

1. Hold aloft the Great Image *(hsiang)*,
The whole world will go to it.
Going to it, they will meet with no harm,
Only safety, peace, and contentment *(an p'ing t'ai)*.

2. When music and dainty dishes are offered,
The passers-by stop.

3. Tao, when it is uttered by the mouth,
Is so bland it has no flavor.
When looked at, it is not enough to be seen.
When listened to, it is not enough to be heard,
When used *(yung)*, it is inexhaustible.

General Comment

This chapter continues to sing a hymn to Tao as the peace and benediction of the world. The central theme of our commentary is peace *(t'ai p'ing)*, which appears in this chapter in the words *an p'ing t'ai*, safety, peace, and contentment.

Detailed Comment

1. The great image, says the Ho-shang Kung commentary, is Tao. When the ruler holds the great image, i.e., when he governs the world by Tao, he is no longer harmful to the people (ch. 60.2). For Tao is a benevolent power (ch. 81.3), the ground of harmony of all beings. The whole world flocks to it to have safety, peace, and contentment.

2, 3. Because in (3) Tao is said to be flavorless, invisible, and inaudible, most commentators interpret music and dainty dishes as distracting the faithful from the path of Tao. Wang Pi says:

A man hears these words about Tao. They are not like music and dainties which are timely and pleasing to the human heart. While music and dainties can stop the passers-by, words about Tao, how bland and flavorless they are!

Lu Hsi-sheng says:

Music pleases the ear; dainty dishes satisfy the mouth. Thus passers-by
tarry and indulge in them. But these are not their true abode and they
must not stay long.

(Chiao Hung)

I disagree with the above interpretations. Notwithstanding the diatribes
against the five musical notes and five flavors in chapter 12.1, the *Tao Te Ching*
is not against life's simple pleasures and teaches no asceticism. The only sensual
pleasures frowned upon are those that alienate humans from their oneness with
nature. The sage ruler empties the minds but fills the bellies of his people (chs.
3.2 and 12.4). Like music that nourishes the soul and good food that nourishes
the body, Tao is a nurturing principle at whose table all passers-by stop to feed.
Although Tao is flavorless, invisible, and inaudible, it is an inexhaustible fountain
dispensing safety, peace, and contentment.

In its last three lines this chapter is organically connected with chapter
14, which is also on Tao as the great image. Chapter 14 speaks of Tao as non-
being "moving away" from the world of beings. This chapter speaks of Tao as
benevolently present in the world, though it is present by a kind of absence.
In the realm of full actuality of beings, the divine whose goodness and creativity is inexhaustible (ch. 6) is to be looked for in the small, minute, and self-
effacing.

36

1. What is to be reduced,
Must first be expanded.
What is to be weakened,
Must first be made strong *(ch'iang)*.
What is to be abolished,
Must first be established.
What is to be taken away,
Must first be given.
This is called the subtle illumination *(wei ming)*.

2. The soft and weak overcome the hard and strong.
Fish must not leave the stream.
Sharp weapons *(ch'i)* of a state,
Must not be displayed.

General Comment

The two preceding chapters present Tao as the benevolent power in the world. This chapter shows us the cyclical process of things. If we take the first part to be an observation on the rise and fall of political fortunes, we may take the second part also as a political statement against the show of military force.

Through Han Fei's interpretation this chapter has been grasped exclusively in the legalistic light as advocating devious tactics. The unfair criticisms by Chu Hsi (Chan, 1963b: 17, 1975a), Chien Mu (1957: 116–117), and their followers are typical examples (Fung, 1952, I: 183ff). The main burden of our comment here is to distinguish between the positions of the *Tao Te Ching* and legalism and to vindicate this chapter as part and parcel of the total vision of the text.

Detailed Comment

1. These lines give us a very subtle *(wei)* insight into the reversive workings of things. Knowledge of this cyclical process of events liberates one from the blindness of a one-sided view. One who knows that all fortunes have their rise and fall knows that what is called a fortune today may turn out to be a calamity and what is a calamity today may yet prove to be a blessing (ch. 58). This insight cures him of greed and power hunger, turning him into a pacifist.

Legalists throughout history have availed themselves politically of this keen observation in a different direction from its intention. To them these lines teach how to topple one's enemy; for example, by pampering an ambitious enemy one prepares for his downfall. The *Han Fei Tzu* tells a story illustrating the point. Like the *Chan-kuo ts'e* (*The Strategy of the Warring States*, 22: 1b), it attributes these lines to the *Chou shu (Book of Chou)*:

> Chih Po requested land from Wei Hsüan Tzu (Prince of Wei). Wei Hsüan Tzu refused. Jen Chang (his minister) said: "Why not grant him the land?" Hsüan Tzu said: "He has no legitimate reasons to make the request. Therefore I refused." Jen Chang said: "To request land without legitimate reasons, he must alarm the neighboring states. Since his desires are insatiable, the whole world will have fear. If you grant him the land, Chih Po will certainly be full of pride and underestimate his enemies. His neighboring states, on the other hand, will certainly be alarmed and become united. Now when the united armies face a state

that underestimates its enemy, Chih Po's life will not last long. The *Book of Chou* says:

He who is to be vanquished,
Must first be installed.
He who is to be dispossessed of,
Must first be given"

(Liao, I: 230).

In the *Tao Te Ching* the rise and fall of political fortunes means that politics is subject to the cyclical process governing all events. The spirit is one of non-action *(wu-wei)*. The spirit in the *Han Fei Tzu,* as the above story illustrates, is to deviously use, by human action, this natural process as a tactic to bring about the desired result. Thus, what is a holy natural process is secularized in the *Han Fei Tzu* to become an instrument for statecraft.

Wang Pi's comment shows the legalistic influence though he is also aware of the *Tao Te Ching*'s pacifist stance and spirit of non-action. He takes these lines in the Huang Lao spirit of resting with the people:

If you desire to eliminate the strong, the violent, the cruel and the rebellious, rely on these four sayings. Follow the nature of things themselves. Do not use punishment to eliminate those that one is about to eliminate. Let them destroy themselves. This is called the subtle illumination.

2. The first line, "the soft and weak overcome the hard and strong," is the chapter's main theme, giving meaning to what precedes and follows it. In the *Tao Te Ching* and even more often in the *Chuang Tzu* (Watson: 80, 87, 88, 163, 295), Tao sustains all beings as water sustains fish. "Fish must not leave the stream" means that creatures must not stand apart from Tao. For the same reason the ruler must not exhibit the sharp weapons of a state. The power to punish and kill resides in Tao (ch. 74). To parade one's military might is to arrogate the power of punishment to oneself, which is to court death. Because the proud will be put down (ch. 24), and because the strong and violent do not die natural deaths (ch. 42), do not invite harm to the state by parading sharp weapons which, being instruments of death, are to be used only in dire necessity (ch. 31). Here it is not a matter of hiding the sharp weapons but of not employing them at all (ch. 80). This chapter fully agrees with chapters 30 and 31, which speak against military conquests. "The soft and weak overcome the strong and violent" because, as chapter 76 observes, they are "companions of life."

In the *Han Fei Tzu* Tao as the water that sustains all now becomes the power, position, and influence, instruments that the ruler wields to control his ministers. While the *Tao Te Ching* says never depart from Tao or else end your spiritual as well as physical life, the *Han Fei Tzu* says never allow yourself to be stripped of power, position, and influence, or else end your political and physical life. (Liao, I: 211). The *Han Fei Tzu* interprets the term "baggage wagon" *(tzu chung)* in chapter 26.2 to mean the ruler's power and influence which, once lost, can never be regained. In the same vein "sharp weapons of a state" means the ruler's power to reward and punish, and "must not be displayed" means that the ruler alone holds these powers, never delegating them to his ministers. The last three lines mean that the most lethal, state-of-the-art weapons of a nation must not be made public knowledge. Exposure means losing leverage. Just as "fish must not leave the stream" or else perish, the "sharp weapons of a state must not be displayed" or else the state perishes. Thus interpreted the *Tao Te Ching* becomes a manual on devious tactics *(yin mou)* for domination and control of one's subjects internally and overpowering one's enemies externally.

37

---

1. Tao everlasting *(ch'ang)* does not act *(wu wei)*,
And yet nothing is not done *(erh wu pu wei)*.
If kings and barons can abide by *(shou)* it,
The ten thousand things will transform by themselves *(tzu hua)*.

2. If in transforming desire *(yü)* is aroused,
I shall suppress it by the nameless uncarved wood *(p'u)*.
With the nameless uncarved wood,
There shall be no desire *(wu yü)*.

3. Without desire there is thus quietude *(ching)*. 1
The world shall be self-ordered *(tzu ting)*.

1. The first line in the Wang Pi text reads *"pu yü i ching"* (not desiring there is thus quietude). We have translated the line according to the Tang Dynasty inscription *"wu yü i ching"* (without desire there is thus quietude), following directly from the line above.

General Comment

This is another inspiring chapter affirming the peace and dynamism found in nature. In thought and sentence structure it can be regarded as an explication of chapter 32.1. In the first stanza we are given the contrast between human actions *(wei)* and natural transformations *(hua)*. The second stanza concerns the contrast between human desire *(yü)* and the simplicity of nature *(p'u)*. The two concluding lines look forward to peace in the world when humans outgrow their unnatural desires.

Detailed Comment

1. If we look at the world as a static realm with humans the only active agents, then humans carry the burden of responsibility for the world, giving them a sense of superiority and the right to dominate the world. This view characterizes Western consciousness from Descartes to Sartre, as well as Hsün Tzu's brand of Confucianism. Taoism does not regard humans as the only active agents. Nature untouched by civilization is a dynamic realm while human action *(wei)* only interferes with and stifles the natural processes of things. Tao lets all beings operate on their own, accomplishing everything by doing nothing *(wu wei)*. The action that characterizes Tao is called *hua*, transformation, or *tzu-hua*, self-transformation. Human action *(wei)*, imposing an order on nature, is disruptive and destructive; transformation *(hua)* is the process by which natural beings unfold according to their inner rhythm. When the ruler imitates Tao by a policy of *wu wei* he allows peace to prevail among humans and between humans and the natural world.

   For the meaning of *wu wei erh wu pu wei*, "Not doing and yet nothing is not done," in the first two lines, see chapter 48.

2. Self-transformation *(hua)* is the way all natural beings operate. Humans in their infancy (the state of *te*, ch. 55), are at peace with all and participate in the self-transformative process of all beings. At a certain stage, however, they become conscious of themselves as distinct from the rest of the natural world. Desire *(yü)*, arising from self-awareness and the feeling of a lack, prompts humans to act *(wei)* in the world, to appropriate the world for the self. Nature prior to the arousal of desire is called the nameless uncarved wood *(p'u)*, directly identified in chapter 32 with Tao. Chapter 32.3 also advises the ruler to stop at the appearance of names without proceeding further to conscious distinction between good and evil, which requires human action to uphold good and correct evil. This chapter recommends the ruler not only to stop at the stage of names but also to keep his people in the condition of the nameless uncarved wood *(p'u)* prior to self-awareness and the arousal of desire. As consciousness of self *(chih)*

gives birth to desire *(yü)*, producing action *(wei)*, in turn disrupting the self-transformative process of nature, in the nameless uncarved wood there is neither desire nor action to disturb world peace (see also ch. 3).

3. Darwin sees the natural world as a battlefield where only the fittest can survive. Taoism sees the world purged of human desire and action as a peaceful order wherein the fit and the unfit, the good and the not good, are in harmonious symbiosis (ch. 27). St. Augustine defines peace as the tranquillity of order (*The City of God*, XIX.13) fully attainable only in heaven; he believes that on earth, weighed down by original sin, there can be no lasting peace. The Taoist believes that whatever happens in nature is self-ordering (ch. 23) and self-balancing (ch. 77). *Ching* (quietude) is the peace of earth free from disturbances caused by human desire and action. When humans outgrow the desire to dominate and to conquer leading to wanton aggression and destruction, peace on earth will prevail.

38

1. A person of high *te* is not *te*,
Therefore such a person has *te;*
A person of low *te* does not lose *(shih) te*,
Therefore such a person has no *te*.

2. A person of high *te* does not act *(wei)*,
For such a person has no cause for action;
A person of low *te* acts,
For such a person has cause for action.

3. A person of high *jen* (humanity) acts,
Yet such a person has no cause for action;
A person of high *i* (righteousness) acts,
For such a person has cause for action.

4. A person of high *li* (priopriety) acts,
Yet finding no response,
Proceeds to bare the arms and throw a rope.

5. Therefore when Tao is lost *(shih),* then there is *te.*
When *te* is lost, then there is *jen* (humanity).
When *jen* is lost, then there is *i* (righteousness).
When *i* is lost, then there is *li* (propriety).

6. As to *li,* it is the thin edge of loyalty and faithfullness,
And the beginning of disorder;
As to foreknowledge *(ch'ien shih),* it is the flowering of Tao,
And the beginning of stupidity *(yü).*

7. Thus a great person, abiding in the thick,
Does not dwell in the thin;
Abiding in the kernel,
Does not dwell in the flower.
Therefore such a person leaves that and takes this.

General Comment

The theme of non-action in the preceding chapter now takes a central position in this first chapter of the second part of the *Tao Te Ching* known as the "Te Classic." This chapter is also important in delineating the descending order from Tao (the creative ground) and *te* (nature), to the struggles and warfares of the moral sphere, through the stages of *jen* (universal humanity), *i* (group righteousness), and *li* (ritual or propriety). Entrance into the moral sphere is fittingly called *shih,* loss of Tao and *te,* the original carefree state of nature. This chapter, an anti-Confucian polemic, has Wang Pi's longest commentary.

Detailed Comment

1. Here are two main ideas: Reversion is the way to being and consciousness leads to loss. To attain being one must transcend oneself to one's root; only in doing so is one's being solidly anchored (ch. 52.1). Here the character *pu* (not; also ch. 5) is used much in the fashion of Hegelian dialectic. This "not" does not merely negate but negates to transcend, and thereby truly preserves that which has been negated. "High *te* is not *te*" because high *te,* through self-abnegation, transcends itself and becomes one with Tao; by negating itself and reverting to the root, it preserves itself.

The second main idea here is that consciousness leads to loss: to become conscious of something is to lose hold of that very thing one has become conscious of. When nature is perfect (high *te*), it is unconscious of itself. As soon as nature becomes conscious it falls below itself (low *te*). A person of low *te* works at not losing *te*, yet because this person's activities are characterized by conscious effort, they fall short of their goal (ch. 24).

It is obvious that *te* (nature), which comes after Tao (creativity), is a fluid concept. High *te*, unconscious of itself, transcends itself to become one with Tao; low *te*, conscious of itself, can not even preserve itself. Low *te* is indeed not nature but virtue. In the *Tao Te Ching* virtue (low *te*) means the loss of nature's (high *te*) original perfection.

2. In this stanza the unconscious high *te* is distinguished from the conscious low *te* by its non-action *(wu wei)*. A person of high *te*, at one with Tao and the movement of all beings, does not act or toil. There is no cause for action. A person of low *te*, standing apart to judge the world, relying on the self and doing everything consciously, is burdened with toil.

3. The moment human action is introduced into the world humans step out of nature into virtue. *Jen* 仁, composed of two 二 and a human being 亻, means humanity or human-heartedness (ch. 5). In its high form, which, according to Wang Pi, is universal, benevolent, all-loving, impartial and selfless, *jen* transcends itself to reach the freedom of *te*. Thus, although we enter the sphere of morality with *jen*, in its high form *jen* reverts to *te*. The person of high *jen*, at one with the harmonious self-ordering nature *(te)*, has no cause for action.

The next stage, *i* (righteousness 義), when the self 我 is subordinated to the common good represented by the king 王, is a more restricted form of morality. While *jen* stands for universal humanity or love, *i* is the morality of a group or the obligation between ruler and subjects. A person of high *jen* finds no cause for action. A person of high *i* finds much to do in the world.

4. *Li* in its etymology means religious sacrifice. The value of *li* as holy rite in Confucianism has made up a good part of the recent discussion on Chinese ethics from Herbert Fingarette onwards (Cua). Though the character *li* appears only in this chapter and in chapter 31.6, the idea of sacrifice and ritual is present also in chapters 5, 29, and 54. Traditionally the author Lao Tzu was an instructor of rites.

The *Tao Te Ching*'s overall attitude toward *li* is negative. In this chapter *li* as ritual coming after *jen* (universal human solidarity) and *i* (group solidarity) occupies the last stage of moral development such that it actually marks human alienation from the divine. Ritual behavior externally manifests an inner awareness of one's separateness from the divine, thus, one treats the Holy as the Other, with reverence and awe. In the deepest sense rituals are designed to reconnect us to the divine. Standing on their own, however, they are mere appearance without substance or solidarity. The religion of ritual is the religion of the Pharisees, bordering on irreligion.

As social behavior *li* is the gentleman's code characterizing awareness of one's status as different from that of others. Hsün Tzu, the philosopher of *li*, sees it as a means of maintaining social order, believing that each individual, by accepting and playing his distinctive family and social role, contributes to the harmony of the whole (Watson, 1963b: 89–111). To the *Tao Te Ching* this kind of order through distinction and separation is precarious at best. True piety does not distinguish or divide, which gives cause to quarrels and wars. When I observe all the rules of propriety I demand that others do likewise. When they fail I feel justified in making claims and waging war. To bare one's arms and to throw a rope (Kao Heng and Ch'ih Hsi-chao, 1974: 6) are acts showing determination prior to engaging in combat (ch. 69). History chronicles many stories of warfare due to non-observance or violation of ritual (Walker: 80–81, 94).

Because *li*, a holy rite, is the way of the sage for Confucians, they usually interpret the last two lines to mean: "Even if the sage practicing *li* does not find a corresponding courtesy, he, not becoming angry, would persist in (conducting himself according to) *li* and guide his people to *li*" (Ma Hsü-lun: 118).

5. This passage sums up the progression from Tao (the creative ground), to *te* (the created world), to *jen* (humanity), to *i* (righteousness as group morality), and finally to *li* (ritual behavior), as the steady process of loss *(shih)*, sacrificing a greater and more inclusive unity to a narrower and more restricted consciousness. Tao and high *te*, being unconscious, are reversive and harmonious (chs. 40 and 65). From low *te* down to *jen, i,* and *li* we fall from the reversive process of Tao and *te* (nature) to the non-reversive rigidity of conscious human actions. Moral consciousness as a permanent rupture from the world issues in actions aimed at changing the shape of the world. Human action is warfare waged by humans against nature. The *Chuang Tzu*, chapter 9, has an excellent commentary on these lines:

> Therefore in a time of perfect *te* the gait of men is slow and ambling; their gaze is steady and mild. In such an age mountains have no paths or trails, lakes no boats or bridges. The ten thousand things live species by species, one group settled close to another. Birds and beasts form their flocks and herds, grass and trees grow to fullest height. So it happens that you can tie a cord to the birds and beasts and lead them about, or bend down the limb and peer into the nest of the crow and the magpie. . . .
>   Then along comes the sage, huffing and puffing after *jen* (humanity), reaching on tiptoe for *i* (righteousness), and the world for the first time has doubts; mooning and mouthing over his music, snipping and stitching away at his *li* (rites), and the world for the first time is divided. . . . If Tao and *te* had not been cast aside, how would there be any call for *jen* and *i?* If the true form of the inborn nature had not been abandoned, how would there be any use for rites *(li)* and music?

> (Cf. Watson, 1968: 105)

People in the state of nature are virtuous because they do not know what virtue is. Moral virtues are called forth due to the loss *(shih)* of nature. It is due to the loss *(shih)* of a more inclusive virtue *(jen)* that narrower forms of virtue *(i, li)* also become hard to maintain. The important thing is to preserve the original wholeness. Then all will be well.

6. *Ch'ien shih*, foreknowledge, is knowledge through the art of divination. According to one theory both Taoism and Confucianism developed from the ancient diviners (Hu Shih, 1931: 28). The *I-ching*, the most sacred Confucian text, is a book on divination. The *Doctrine of the Mean* (ch. 24), another Confucian text, also takes the power of divination to be the mark of a holy person.

> It is characteristic of absolute sincerity to be able to foreknow. When a nation or family is about to flourish, there are sure to be lucky omens. When a nation or family is about to perish, there are sure to be unlucky omens. These omens are revealed in divination and in the movements of the four limbs. When calamity or blessing is about to come, it can surely know beforehand if it is good, and it can also surely know beforehand if it is evil. Therefore he who has absolute sincerity is like a spirit.
>
> (Chan, 1963a: 108)

According to the *Tao Te Ching* divination is necessary only when humans have lost direct access to Tao. It is better to never depart from Tao and *te*, never acquire any moral consciousness, and thus never need recourse to the art of divination, which is but "the flowering of Tao, and the beginning of stupidity."

7. Nature or the unconscious is the thick, while virtue or consciousness is the thin. The Taoist's choice is the thick hidden kernel where life resides, not the thin flower pertaining merely to appearance. The last line also appears in chapters 12 and 72.

39

---

1. Those of old that attain the One:
Heaven attains the One thus is clear,
Earth attains the One thus is peaceful,
Spirits attain the One thus are efficacious,

Valleys attain the One thus are replenished,
Ten thousand beings attain the One thus come to be,
Princes and barons attain the One thus are exalted in the world.
All because they attain the One.

2. Heaven, without that which renders it clear, might crack,
Earth, without that which renders it peaceful, might explode,
Spirits, without that which makes them efficacious, might cease,
Valleys, without that which replenishes them, might become empty,
Ten thousand beings, without that which sustains them in existence,
    might become extinct,
Barons and kings, without that which exalts them to high positions,
    might be toppled.

3. Therefore the exalted is rooted in the humble,
The high has the low for foundation.
Therefore barons and kings call themselves orphaned, widowed and
    unworthy.
Is this not taking the humble for one's root? Is it not?

4. Therefore the most famous has no fame.
Do not tinkle like jade,
Or chime like stones!

General Comment

The central theme in the preceding chapter—in order to be what it is a being must revert to its origin—is elaborated in this chapter. Every being becomes what it is by returning to the one from which it comes. The chapter has two parts. (1) and (2) are on ontology, while (3) and (4) are reflections on ethics and politics based on the ontological foundation provided in (1) and (2). A similar pattern will be seen in chapter 42, where ontology in (1) is followed by ethical and political reflections in (2) and (3).

Detailed Comment

1. The one as the ontological foundation of all beings appears in five chapters. In chapter 42, where we shall more thoroughly examine its meaning, the one is the beginning of being born of Tao as non-being. In chapter 14 the one is the extremely small origin bordering between being and non-being. In chapters 10 and 22 it is that to which the Taoist or the sage clings as the source and model of his being. In this chapter the one is what endows everything with its specific

nature so that it is what it is. Just as among numbers the number one is the smallest and yet the beginning and foundation of all numbers, the one is Tao, the creative ground, coming forth as the small to become the world, which is the great. The meaning of the one is consistent throughout: It is the humble and small born of the nothingness of Tao to serve as the ground of all beings. The Ho-shang Kung commentary calls the one the child of Tao.

The one as the beginning of beings is the state of *te* as the small. The *Chuang Tzu*, chapter 12, says: "There was the One but there was yet no form. It is that by the obtaining of which things are born. This is called their nature *(te)*" (Watson, 1968: 131). The one, born of Tao as non-being, is the seed of all beings by determining all beings to be what they are. All the great creative forces in the world become what they are by attaining and preserving the one as the core of their being—heaven is clear, earth is peaceful, spirits are efficacious, valleys are replenished, all beings come to be, and rulers bring order to their states. This dynamic, organic, rich, and actively transforming world has its secret and origin in the smallest of all, the one.

2. As what endows all beings with their specific natures, the one reminds us of the life seed *(ching)* in chapter 21.2. The loss of the one spells ruin for all: Heaven will crack, the earth will explode, spirits will cease, ten thousand beings will perish, and rulers will topple.

3. Since the social political order is an extention of the natural order, the application on ethics and politics is clear. Those who occupy high positions (kings and barons) must embrace the small and humble (the one) if they are to be ontologically grounded. To be "orphaned" or "widowed" is the most miserable fate. This is how a ruler refers to himself to show that he embraces the humble within himself. A king referring to himself as *pu ku*, meaning he is not worthy of his title, is like a Christian ruler calling himself a sinner.

4. The first line in the Wang Pi text has 輿 the Ho-shang Kung text has 車 a simplification, both meaning carriage. Waley makes a lot of the idea of carriage, translating *i*, the one, as "the whole," to better agree with the problem of the part and the whole in King Malinda's story in Buddhism (1958: 191–192, Conze, 1959: 146–161). I agree with I Shen-ting, Ma Hsü-lun, and Chiang Hsi-ch'ang that 輿 is a corruption of 譽 fame or praise, thus the first line reads: "Therefore the most famous has no fame." Chapter 17 says the best government is not praised by its people, only the second best is. Instead of advertising oneself, it is better to hide among the fameless. The *Chuang Tzu*, chapter 18, says: "Perfect happiness knows no happiness, the most famous has no fame" (Watson, 1968: 191). The first line, "Therefore the most famous has no fame," parallels the first line in (3): "Therefore the exalted is rooted in the humble" leading to the next two lines: Do not chime forth loudly like jade and stone pieces in musical bells. The sage covers up his jade under coarse garments (ch. 70).

40

1. Returning *(fan)* is the movement *(tung)* of Tao.
Weak *(jo)* is the functioning *(yung)* of Tao.

2. Ten thousand things under heaven are born of being *(yu).*
Being is born of non-being *(wu).*

General Comment

This chapter presents the *Tao Te Ching*'s theology in a nutshell. Chapters 38 and 39 speak of reversion to the source as the movement by which a being fulfills itself. This chapter identifies reversion as the very life of Tao itself. Reversion in this chapter is not the creature's return to the source but the return of the source to the world. Tao is a nothing that returns to give rise to the world of beings.

After this chapter on fundamental ontology and cosmogony the reader would do well to proceed directly to chapter 42.1, which is on cosmogony.

Detailed Comment

1. A number of terms express the notion of reversion, a key concept in the *Tao Te Ching*: *fan* (ch. 40), to return to the world; *fu* (ch. 16), to recover, repeat, or return; *kuei* (ch. 28), to return to the ground or source; *chou* (ch. 25), to move round and round; and *huan* (ch. 30), to come back or to retribute, to name a few. *Fan* as used here and in chapter 25 ("To be far away is to return *[fan]*") and 65 ("The dark *te* clarifies and moves far away, then it returns *[fan]* with things") means movement back to the world of appearance. What has disappeared from the world will return.

In the *I-ching* hexagram 24, Fu, embodies this return to the world. The Commentary on the Decision says: "In the hexagram of Return (Fu) we indeed see the heart of heaven and earth!" (Cf. R. Wilhelm, 1950: 505) The promise of life returning to earth in the spring after the trials and tribulations of winter is the hope of the world. To the ancient Chinese this return, a promise that never fails, was the heart of heaven and earth. Thus, even in the midst of death and despair there is hope of new life.

The early Christians also expected the imminent return of the Messiah, who is the heart of heaven and earth. As the apocalyptic vision was delayed, the faithful reinterpreted the coming of Christ to mean it was "already" and "not yet." Still, the coming of the Messiah remained an object of expectation and waiting (Pelikan: 126).

Wang Pi's comment on this line, like his comment on chapter 25.2, shows his tendency to interpret the dynamic portrayal of Tao in static logical terms. He interprets *fan*, Tao's return as the creativity of the world, to mean that logical opposites depend on each other. Thus, Tao is the opposite of all beings just as the high and low, noble and ignoble, being and non-being, are opposites. The Ho-shang Kung commentary, on the other hand, grasps the dynamic aspect of this line: "To return is to return to the root. The root is Tao, which is always in motion. In motion it generates the ten thousand beings. Those that turn their backs (on Tao) perish."

Tao as the creativity of the world is gentle and weak *(jo)*. Indeed, Tao is so weak that its very existence seems to be in question (ch. 4).

2. For Johannes Scotus Erigena, the nothing out of which all things come to be is the divine goodness. For Whitehead there are "four creative phases in which the universe accomplishes its actuality. . . . The action of the fourth phase is the love of God for the world" (1969: 413). We have seen in chapter 25 that Tao's cyclical movement consists of four stages: the great, the disappearing, the far away, and the returning. In returning *(fan)*, the fourth phase of Tao's movement, Tao gives rise to the world.

If we look upon these four stages as two opposite poles, Tao's reversive movement is the rhythm from non-being to being, back to non-being, and forth again to being. Non-being, out of its own inner necessity, generates its opposite, being. Being is not external to non-being but is generated from within the womb of non-being.

The Ho-shang Kung commentary identifies being *(yu)* with heaven and earth, the named aspect of Tao, as in chapter 1.2. From the union of heaven and earth all beings come to be (Yü, 1981).

41

1. When a superior person *(shan shih)* hears Tao,
He diligently practices it.
When a middling person *(chung shih)* hears Tao,
He hears it, he doesn't hear it.

When the inferior person *(hsia shih)* hears Tao, he roars.
If Tao were not laughed at,
It would not be Tao.

2. Therefore, established sayings *(chien yen)* have it this way:
"The illuminating *(ming)* Tao appears *(jo)* dark,
The advancing Tao appears retreating,
The level Tao appears knotty *(lei)*.

High *(shan)* te appears like a valley,
Great whiteness *(po)* appears spotted *(ju)*,
Expansive *te* appears insufficient,
Well-established *te* appears weak,
The genuine in substance appears hollow.

Great *(ta)* square has no corners,
Great vessel *(ch'i)* is late in completion,
Great voice *(yin)* has hardly *(hsi)* any sound,
Great image is formless,
Tao is hidden and without name."

3. Yet it is Tao alone,
That is good in lending help and fulfilling all.

General Comment

This chapter continues to dwell on Tao as the non-being that gives rise to and
nurtures all beings. It describes Tao mystically as the coincidence of opposites
eluding the grasp of ordinary consciousness. The chapter concludes by reasserting
the goodness of Tao.

Detailed Comment

1. Tao is so hidden from the vulgar ways of the world that only those endowed
with deep spirituality follow it diligently. Those falling in the middle will receive
Tao in a half-hearted manner, and if you mention Tao to the inferior person you
only invite scorn. To them Tao's unobtrusiveness betrays either its lack of power
or lack of existence.

Is the inferior person *(hsia shih)* here the Taoist counterpart of the fool in
the Bible who says in his heart there is no God? The inferior person who laughs
at Tao would not laugh at an all-powerful biblical God. Tao is described as dark,

weak, passive, indeed a nothing. All these perfections of Tao are imperfections according to ordinary consciousness.

2. This long quotation on the nature of Tao can be divided either by the rhyming pattern at the end of each line or by the subject term at the beginning of each line. Since the rhyming is lost in translation I have divided it roughly according to the subject terms, thus, the first (a) group of three lines has Tao as the subject term, the second (b) group of five lines has *te,* and the third (c) group of five lines has *ta,* the great or maximum that exceeds ordinary measure, as the opening character of each line. Every line in this quote brings out the hidden nature of Tao, explaining why Tao is so neglected by the ordinary consciousness. We shall comment on the quote line by line.

(a) The illuminating *(ming)* Tao appears *(jo)* dark—*Ming,* the light that illuminates at night, is the opposite of *kuang,* the bright light belonging to day. *Ming* is the mystical light of the round, illuminating both the coming out and the return of all beings (chs. 4.2, 52.3, 56.2, and 58).

The advancing Tao appears retreating. Wang Pi comments on this line by quoting from chapter 7.2: "Therefore the sage puts his body last and his body is first, regards his body external and his body is preserved." It is better to illustrate this line describing Tao, not the Taoist, from chapter 14.2: "Its coming up is not light, its going down is not darkness" and 14.3: "Come toward it one does not see its head, follow behind it one does not see its rear."

The level Tao appears knotty *(lei). Lei* means knots in the silk strand. Taoism teaches an ethics of peace, not war. Tao's very levelness lies in the bumps and windings it patiently takes with things. This is the meaning of chapter 45: "Great straightness appears bent" and the *Chuang Tzu,* chapter 4: "I walk in curves, lest I injure my feet."[1] Wang Pi's comment here is excellent: *"Lei* means bumpy. Since the great level Tao follows the nature of things without insisting on a flatness that cuts through things, its flatness cannot be discerned, thus it appears bumpy and uneven."

(b) High *te* appears like a valley. *Shan,* translated in the first line of this chapter as "superior," is translated as "high" in this line to agree with the same term in chapter 38.1. This line again illustrates what chapter 78 says: "Straightforward words appear to be their opposite" *(cheng yen jo fan).* What possesses *te* in the fullest degree is hollow like the low-lying valley (ch. 6).

Great whiteness *(po)* appears spotted *(ju).* This refers to the quality of jade. By the opening character *ta* (great) this line belongs to the third group. Obviously it is here due to the sound of its last character *(ju),* which rhymes with lines in this group. We have seen that in chapter 28 *po* (white) is the opposite of *heh*

---

1. Watson's translation (1968: 66): "I walk a crooked way—don't step on my feet" is inaccurate and misses the intention of the author.

(black), and *ju* (defilement, disgrace) is the opposite of *yung* (glory, honor). In the *Chuang Tzu* (Cf. Watson, 1968: 308), Lao Tzu uses this and the next line (not as *kuang te,* but as *sheng te*) in lecturing Yang Tzu Chü on the need to be humble.

Expansive *(kuang) te* appears insufficient. Tao's power and creativity overflows, yet it appears small and deficient (ch. 34). Rather, it is Tao's economy (which appears deficient) that allows its power and creativity to be expansive (*kuang,* ch. 67.3).

Well-established *te* appears weak. Kao Heng interprets the first character to mean "healthy" and the last character to mean "weak." Wang Pi interprets the last character to mean "accompanying": a person well anchored in Tao is at peace with the world. Such a person, a good companion to others, may give the appearance of weakness.

The genuine in substance appears hollow. This is another way of saying that what is full appears empty, or what is most genuine, being unpretentious, appears lacking in inner quality.

(c) The logic of these lines is the same as in chapter 45.1. The first character *ta,* the great, means the greatest or maximum, what the medievals called the transcendentals. What operates here, however, is not the logic of perfection of an Anselm or an Aquinas of the fourth way, but the logic of the coincidence of opposites of a Nicholas of Cusa: Tao is the smallest as well as the greatest (ch. 34).

Great *(ta)* square has no corners. The Chinese consider the earth square and heaven round. Since the origin and destiny of earth is in heaven, the greatest square is resolved into the round, which has no corners.

Great vessel *(ch'i)* is late in completion. Whatever has a specific nature for a specific function is called a vessel *(ch'i).* In becoming a vessel a thing becomes useful, but there is both a value and disvalue in becoming a vessel. Restricted to a specific function, it is useless otherwise. A vessel of great versatility would take a long time to complete. Tao, the greatest vessel, never reaches completion. Chapter 29.1 calls the world "a sacred vessel." This sacred vessel, like the consequent nature of Whitehead's God, never reaches completion because it is always transcending itself.

Great voice *(yin)* has hardly *(hsi)* any sound. Chapter 25.1 speaks of Tao as silent and empty. Chapter 14.1 says: "What is listened to but not heard, is named the extremely faint *(hsi)*." That the absolute is most eloquently present in the world by its silence is again the familiar language of mystics. St. John of the Cross (1542–1591) speaks of the harmony of silence in his *Spiritual Canticle* (114–115).

Great image is formless. Chapter 25 informs us that Tao is at best only an image of the absolute. Chapter 35 says: "Hold the great image, the whole world will go to it." Since the absolute is without form or being Tao as the great image is the image of nothing (ch. 14.3).

Tao is hidden and without name. This line sums up the message of the quote on the self-effacing nature of Tao. Meister Eckhart (1260–1327) says that Jesus has no name; Bodhidharma (c. 470–503) says that Buddha has no name.

3. These concluding lines show that the chapter as a whole is meant as an encomium to Tao. The most hidden and passive Tao is the world's most benevolent force.

42

---

1. Tao gives birth to one,
One gives birth to two,
Two gives birth to three,
Three gives birth to ten thousand beings.
Ten thousand beings carry *yin* on their backs and embrace *yang* in their front,
Blending these two vital breaths *(ch'i)* to attain harmony *(ho)*.

2. What people hate most,
Are to be orphaned, widowed and unworthy.
Yet kings and dukes call themselves by these.
Thus things are either decreased so as to be increased,
Or increased *(i)* so as to be decreased *(sun)*.

3. What others teach,
I also teach:
"The strong and violent *(ch'iang liang)* do not die a natural death."
This I shall hold as the father *(fu)* of my teaching.

General Comment

Stanza (1) on cosmogony and cosmology belongs with chapter 40, as is the case in the Ma-wang Tui silk manuscript. Version A does not contain chapter 41 while version B has chapter 41 preceding chapter 40, which is then followed directly by this chapter.

This chapter's structure resembles that of chapter 39. Stanza (1), on cosmogony and cosmology, is followed by ethics in (2) and (3). The unifying theme in chapter 39 is the concept of the one as the small and humble. In this chapter the unifying theme is found in the last character in (1)—*ho*, meaning harmony. As all beings come to be through the harmony of *yin* and *yang* (1), it is through harmony that all beings are preserved (2) and long lasting (3).

Detailed Comment

1. The one, the beginning of being, comes from non-being (ch. 40.2). Tao is this non-being or "neither being nor name" giving rise to the one, the beginning and foundation of all beings (ch. 39). In the *Chuang Tzu*, chapter 12, the one is also said to arise from non-being *(wu):* "In the very beginning there was non-being *(wu).* It has neither being *(yu)* nor name. It is that from which the one arises" (Cf. Watson, 1968: 131).

In the context of chapters 39 and 40, both concluding with a reflection that the great must be grounded in the small, the one can be fittingly interpreted microcosmically as the extremely small beginning of being issuing from the nothingness of Tao (ch. 21). However, the one is also the macrocosmic lone existent prior to the existence of heaven and earth. This one cosmogonically is the "something nebulous *(hun-ch'eng)* . . . standing alone, altering not" in chapter 25. The Ma-wang Tui text, both versions A and B, specifically identifies the one with the dynamic movement in chapter 14: "As to the one, its coming up is not light, its going down is not darkness. . . ." Such a one is the votex, the whirling creative energy at the beginning of the world. In the *I-ching* this is the T'ai-chi (Supreme Ultimate) that bifurcates into two poles: "Therefore there is in the Changes the Supreme Ultimate which generates the two primal forces" (Cf. R. Wilhelm, 1950: 318).

Microcosmically the two and three are stages in the growth of the one to become all beings in the world. If we identify the one with the seed in chapter 21.2, two and three are the growth power *(hsin)* exhibited in the seed. In the macrocosmic sense the two is born when the whirling vortex or cosmic egg separates into two opposite poles—heaven and earth—whose interactions produce the co-creative forces *yin* and *yang* which unite (the three) to produce all things. That *yin* and *yang* are products of the dynamic interactions of heaven and earth is clear even in the Confucian text *Li Chi (Book of Rites),* chapter on Li Yun (On the Revolution of Rites): "Rites certainly are rooted in the "T'ai-i" (aboriginal one) which separates to become heaven and earth, which rotate to produce *yin* and *yang*" (Cf. Legge, 1967, I: 386–387).

Yin and *yang* can be regarded as cosmogonic principles transcending the ten thousand beings, or as constitutive principles dwelling within the ten thousand beings. In the line "Ten thousand beings carry *yin* on their backs and embrace *yang* in their front" 萬 物 負 陰 而 抱 陽 they are constitutive principles. Every being that comes from the three (the union of *yin* and *yang*) is the unity of a duality thus embracing both *yin* and *yang* in its being.

In the Ho-shang Kung text, however, this line undergoes a major change to read: "Ten thousand beings turn their backs towards *yin* and their face towards *yang*" 萬 物 負 陰 而 向 陽 . Read this way *yin* and *yang* are no longer the constitutive principles of all beings, but *yin* is their origin or where they come from while *yang* is their destiny or where they are heading. Since *yin* is mother or earth and *yang* is father, heaven, or sky, all beings, like flowers and plants sprouted from the earth, face toward *yang* (father, heaven) with their backs toward *yin* (mother, earth). Is this not the life of Eros as the universal image of all beings in Plato's *Symposium?* Plato gives us to understand that Eros, when he arrives at his father (plenty), shall discard his mother (poverty). This is also the desideratum in religious Taoism, to which the Ho-shang Kung text belongs: *yin* is identified with death while *yang* means eternal life. In the *Tao Te Ching* *yin* and *yang,* blending harmoniously, are inextricable constitutive principles in all beings. The child does not turn toward the *yang* as to the father; the child is the *yang* born of Tao as *yin,* and even as the *yang* it carries the *yin* on its back. The primary image is the mother and child (chs. 1, 20, 25, 52), not the father and son.

Yin and *yang* as cosmogonic principles are called *ch'i,* air or breath. From Tao as non-being to particular individuals through the union of *yin* and *yang* we witness the movement from nothing to vapor to particular individuals. The more determined an entity, the less dynamic or mobile it is. The original creative fertility of the world is conceived as a pure becoming without residue. As empty *(hsü)* and nothing *(wu)* it is most dynamic *(ch'ung)* and inexhaustible (ch. 4). One, two, and three as cosmogonic principles are vapors representing the forward going stages of the creative evolution. Eventually *yin* is identified with the heavy vapor that sinks down and solidifies to become the earth, while *yang* is the light vapor ascending to become the bright heaven. As procreative agents representing heaven and earth *yin* and *yang* are dynamic airs or breaths *(ch'ung ch'i)* blending harmoniously to become all beings.

2. The first three lines, teaching the familiar lesson of humility, echo chapter 39.3. The last two lines reflect chapter 36. From observing facts of nature, the fact that opposites generate each other, we arrive at ethical truth: A humble person shall be exalted while a puffed-up person will be put down. The proper behavior for kings, barons, and others occupying high positions is humility. Like *yin* and *yang* blending to produce harmonies in the world, the humility of the

ruler, representing harmony in his person, produces peace and harmony in his realm.

Sun (to decrease) and *I* (to increase) in the last two lines are names of hexagrams 41 and 42 in the *I-ching*.

3. While humility is the way to peace and long life, asserting one's strength leads to violent early death. This part on the evils of strength and recalcitrance serves as a transition to the next chapter on the benefits of gentleness.

The third line, "The strong and violent do not die a natural death," is here acknowledged to be the teaching of others. In the *Shuo-yüan (Collection of Discourses)* compiled by Liu Hsiang (77–6 B.C.), this line is contained in an inscription on a metal statue in the imperial ancestral temple Confucius visited (Kao, 1956: 98; Chan, 1963b: 177, note 1, SPTK 10/16b–17a). This teaching must be very old for it to have been appropriated by both the Confucian and Taoist schools.

The character *fu*, the father, appears only in this chapter. The *Tao Te Ching* refers to the mother (non-being) as the ultimate source of all beings, while the father (being) is the source of particular types of beings (ch. 21.4).

43

1. The softest *(chih jou)* in the world,
Gallops *(ch'ih ch'eng)* in the hardest *(chih chien)* in the world.
That which is not penetrates that which has no crevice
(wu yu ju wu chien).

2. I thereby know the benefit of no-action *(wu-wei)*.
The teaching without words,
The benefit of no-action,
Hardly anything in the world can compare with them.

General Comment

This chapter is similar in content to chapter 78, so much so that Duyvendak, following the suggestion of Ma Hsü-lun, transposes the first part of chapter 78 to this chapter in his translation. Both chapters extol the virtues of gentleness and yielding which are yet the most powerful weapons in the world, weapons that conquer without injuring either themselves or their enemies.

Detailed Comment

1. *Ch'ih ch'eng,* meaning to gallop on horseback, implies great freedom of movement without resistence. This is the freedom of non-being *(wu yu).* Sartre also equates non-being or nothing with freedom. In Sartre's case the seat of negation is in consciousness. In Taoism, negation is the very nature of the absolute. Tao alone is the absolute nothingness that penetrates all beings. Beings are able to penetrate other beings only to the extent that they approximate nothing or contain in themselves some degree of nothing. The account of the successful butcher in the *Chuang Tzu,* chapter 3, illustrates the Taoist concept of freedom.

> When I first began to cut up a bullock, I saw only the bullock. Now I meet the bullock with my spiritual *(shen),* not physical, eye. Senses only know immobility but spirit follows the movement. Conforming to nature's *(t'ien,* heaven) own reasoning my knife slices through the great crevices and glides through the great cavities, moving along [the bullock's] own structure, avoiding the tendons and particularly the great bones. . . . Now at the joints [of bones and tendons] there are interstices. Yet the edge of my chopper [is so sharp that it] has no thickness. To insert what has no thickness into what has crevices *(wu hou ju yu chien),* certainly there is plenty of room to move about.

> (Cf. Watson, 1968: 50–51)

Wu yu ju wu chien (that which is not penetrates that which has no crevice) in this chapter becomes *wu hou ju yu chien* (that which has no thickness penetrates that which has crevices) in the *Chuang Tzu.* The best a blade can do is approximate non-being by having almost no thickness. Since even when it has almost no thickness it still has some thickness, it can only penetrate beings that have crevices. Now it happens that all beings, since they issue from non-being, are accompanied by non-being (ch. 11); thus, there are crevices even in what seems most impregnable. A blade that has almost no thickness will find plenty of room to move in the cavities of bone joints in a bullock.

2. From the observation that in nature the softest substances, like water and air, penetrate the hardest substances, like rocks, the sage learns that the art of ruling consists of doing nothing and saying nothing. On the benefit of teaching without words see chapters 2, 23, 56, and 73.

44

1. Your name and your body *(shen)*, which is dearer?
Your body and material goods, which is more abundant?
Gain and loss, which is illness?

2. Therefore in excessive love one necessarily goes to great expenses,
In hoarding much one necessarily loses heavily.

3. Knowing contentment *(chih tsu)* one does not suffer disgrace,
Knowing when to stop one does not become exhausted *(tai)*.
This way one may last long.

General Comment

This chapter concerns how to promote long life. Its immediate object is to warn rulers and nobility of the futility of gathering wealth, which, as far as conserving one's life energies, is more a liability than an asset.

Detailed Comment

1. The Confucian lives for name and fame. Confucius said: "The gentleman considers it ill to end his days without his name being famous" (*Analects*, 15: 19). According to Hobbes success and power, elevating often in the forms of fame and wealth, promote health and long life (*Leviathan*, I, ch. 10). The Taoist believes otherwise. Success and power elevating oneself while putting down others, merely feeding individual pride. The Taoist treasures his body, the seat of his life, more than any of life's accoutrements, including fame or wealth. He also suspects that acquiring fame and wealth shortens life; chapter 42.2 says: "Thus things are either decreased so as to be increased, or increased so as to be decreased."

2. The rich go to great trouble and expense to acquire and protect their treasured objects, but as chapter 9 says: "To fill the hall with gold and jade, there is no way to guard them."

3. When a person is contented with what he has he does not push his luck to the limit that invites the turning of fortune, like the fisherman and his wife in Grimm's fairy tale. Also, he does not push himself to the brink of destruction *(tai)*, often the fate of the over-ambitious. To live humbly, to be at peace

with oneself and the world, to not squander life's energies are ways to long life. This primordial trust in the goodness of life and the world reflects chapter 13.

45

1. Great perfection appears lacking *(ch'üeh)*,
Its use is unending.
Great fullness appears empty,
Its use is inexhaustible.
Great straightness appears bent,
Great ingenuity *(ch'iao)* appears crude,
Great eloquence *(pien)* appears inarticulate.

2. When agitation *(tsao)* wins *(sheng)*, the cold arrives,
When tranquillity *(ching)* wins *(sheng)*, the hot arrives.
Clear and tranquil the world is in the right mode *(cheng)*.

General Comment

The first part offers a theology of the coincidence of opposites (ch. 41.2). The second part gives a theology of the round whose center is at rest.

Detailed Comment

1. It is clear that all these lines refer to Tao: Tao as non-being is the great perfection that appears as privation; Tao's inexhaustible creativity appears empty; Tao is a great straightness that does not impose itself on others but follows the contours of all beings patiently and thus appears bent (ch. 41.2a); Tao is the great artisan whose wonderful workmanship appears crude; Tao works silently to accomplish all, thus its great eloquence *(pien)* appears inarticulate; and so on.

2. My translation of the first two lines follows the Ho-shang Kung interpretation. They literally read: "Agitation overcomes the cold, tranquillity overcomes the hot." Since they don't make much sense commentators have tried

rearranging the characters. According to Ma Hsü-lun the first line, "The agitated *(tsao)* overcomes the cold," should read "The cold overcomes the agitated," paralleling the second line, "The tranquil *(ching)* overcomes the hot." Chiang Hsi-ch'ang, citing chapter 26.1—"The tranquil *(ching)* is the master of the agitated *(tsao)"*—thinks that the first two lines should read: "The tranquil *(ching)* overcomes the agitated *(tsao)*, the cold overcomes the hot." Both Chiang and Ma believe the tranquil and cold are superior to and so should overcome the agitated and hot.

Such maneuvering is quite unnecessary. The message here is not that one opposite should overcome another but that their turning constitutes the round. Here the Ho-shang Kung commentary, by inserting a comma after the character *sheng* (to overcome, to win) in both lines, produces a most admirable effect. Reading them as "When agitation wins, the cold arrives; when tranquillity wins, the hot arrives" (my translation) Ho-shang Kung comments:

> To win *(sheng)* means to reach the extreme. In spring and summer the Yang air moves quickly upwards, and all things flourish and grow big. After the extreme has been reached, the cold sets in. With cold there is decline and death. This means that humans ought not to become agitated. In fall and winter all things lie quietly under the yellow springs. After the extreme has been reached, heat sets in. With heat there is the source of life.

This is to read Tao in its dynamic process through the progression of four seasons (ch. 25). Agitation characterizes the frantic life activities building up from spring to summer, when things develop to their full. This building up of life's activities at the same time dissipates energy; thus when it reaches its zenith a decline or cooling down sets in preparing for fall and winter, when life comes to a standstill. Likewise, when tranquillity, the conservation of energy, reaches its zenith, heat or life is generated. After the decline of fall and the stillness of winter, when all things are buried underground, heat generates to produce new life. This rhythm from the tranquil to the agitated and back to the tranquil is the rhythm of life. The same rhythm is found in chapter 15.3, where the cycle of life is captured in the alternating activities of water. Tranquil water is clear but becomes muddied when life stirs. Thus, it moves from clarity to muddiness and back to clarity.

The tranquillity called the right mode or equilibrium *(cheng)* of the world is not a sterile end. Tranquillity is the pivot of the life realm, the still point most busily preparing for the appearance of new life. Tao as the coincidence of opposites, described in (1), is the tranquillity that produces this beautiful and harmoniously balanced natural world.

46

1. When the world practices Tao,
Fast horses are used for their dung.
When the world does not practice Tao,
War horses give birth at the borders.

2. Among offenses *(tsui)*, none is greater than having what is desirable.
Among calamities *(huo)*, none is greater than not knowing contentment.
Among blames *(chiu)*, none is greater than the desire for gain.
Therefore the contentment that comes from knowing contentment
Is a long lasting contentment.

General Comment

From discussing the peaceful life of the round in the preceding chapter, this chapter returns to the theme of chapter 44 and reflects on the root of war as due to the ruler's insatiable desire for acquisition. Plato in the *Phaedo* says, "The desire of getting wealth causes all wars" (66B), but Hobbes, for whom desire is conterminous with life, supplies us with the best commentary on this chapter:

> I put for a general inclination of all mankind, a perpetual and restless desire of power after power, that ceaseth only in death. And the cause of this, is not always that a man hopes for a more intensive delight he has already attained to; or that he cannot be content with a moderate power: but because he cannot assure the power and means to live well, which he hath present, without the acquisition of more. And from hence it is, that kings, whose power is greatest, turn their endeavours to the assuring it at home by laws, or abroad by wars. . . .
>
> (64)

Detailed Comment

1. Peace reigns in the world when Tao is practiced. Military horses, idle in peace time, are used on the farm, their dung fertilizing the fields. When the world does not practice Tao war erupts. Then, even female horses are used for combat and stationed at the front, thus the phenomenon of giving birth at the borders.
   2. These lines give the same message as found in chapters 33.3 and 44.3. Conscious desire *(yü)*, following upon the knowledge *(chih)* of values, is a symp-

tom of discontent. All religions see desire or craving as the root of suffering and an obstacle to union with the divine. Originally Christianity also opposed material acquisitions. Christ told his followers to part with material goods in order to follow him. The demand for high yield in the parable of the talents (*Matthew* 25: 14–30) was meant in the spiritual sense; in its missionary spirit we may call Christianity spiritual capitalism.

The Taoist teaching against the desire for gain, on the other hand, is not based on the opposing claims of the spirit and flesh or of God and the world. The choice is between the peace of nature and the wars humans wage against one another for the possession of desirable goods. The *Chuang Tzu*, chapter 12, says: "Therefore it is said, those who shepherded the world in ancient times were without desire and the world was satisfied, without action and the ten thousand things were transformed. They were deep and silent and the hundred clans were at peace" (Watson, 1968: 127).

47

1. Without stepping *(ts'u)* out the door,
Know *(chih)* the world.
Without looking out the window,
See *(chien)* the Tao of Heaven.
The farther one comes out,
The less one knows.

2. Therefore the sage knows *(chih)* without travelling,
Names *(ming)* things without seeing *(chien)* them,
Accomplishes *(cheng)* without work *(wei)*.

General Comment

This chapter presents a theory of knowledge, particularly, a theory on how to know the Tao of heaven, but its underlying motive is the same as that in chapter 46—the importance of being contented and at peace with the world. Chapter 46 concerns the futility of accumulating desirable objects. This and the next chapter concern the futility of accumulating knowledge about the world of things.

Detailed Comment

1. These lines claim that for a knowledge of Tao one can dispense with experience of the world. To experience things is to move in the direction of their coming out. For a knowledge of the root we must follow their return. The knowledge of particular things in the world is not the unitive saving knowledge. Indeed, the more we accumulate knowledge of particulars, the less we know Tao. Chapter 81 says: "One who knows (Tao) does not accumulate knowledge, one who accumulates knowledge does not know (Tao)." Taoism's supposed connection with the development of Chinese science notwithstanding, the *Tao Te Ching* is not pro-science in spirit, and would disagree with the cosmological argument of Thomas Aquinas, for whom human knowledge of God is through knowledge of the world, hence the importance of science for the vision of God.

2. Is the Taoist process perhaps akin to the Augustinian conversion and introspection—the soul withdrawing from the world of the many to its interior self finally rises beyond itself to the one source of all beings? The answer is again no. While repudiating the knowledge of the many as not conducive to the knowledge of the one, the *Tao Te Ching* yet holds the world to be the seat of truth from which humans must humbly learn to gain insight into the truth of Tao. In the down-flowing water (ch. 8), the yielding of the tender and pliant plants (ch. 76), and so on, we learn the truth of Tao.

It seems then that we are talking of two kinds of empiricism. The empiricism of modern western science is based on the spirit of conquest by division: The unruly material world is to be disciplined, nature is to be tortured piece by piece so that it may be conquered. Taoism preaches a religious empiricism witnessing Tao's presence in the world. Its withdrawal from the world is not out of disdain for the world, but is the expression of a quiet at-homeness in the world. Taoists are so much at home that they have no wanderlust (ch. 80). The Taoist does not venture outdoors because he has no intention of conquering the world. In Taoism nature needs no disciplining. While Western scientific empiricism is an instrument for human transformation of the world, Taoist religious empiricism results in *wu wei*, doing nothing to disturb the spontaneous flow of things. This is how the Taoist "accomplishes without work."

Wang Pi's comment on these lines again shows his Confucian predilection. For him these lines speak of the power of the mind. The mind can dispense with the knowledge of the external world because in much of what it knows, it is its own source of truth, particularly the truths of right and wrong.

Knowing where things are heading, therefore (the sage), without travelling, can by thinking come to know them; recognizing the Source of things, therefore (the sage), without seeing them, can name the principle *(li)* of right and wrong; enlightened of the nature of things, by merely following them, (the sage), without acting on them, accomplishes them.

48

1. To pursue *(wei)* learning one increases daily.
To pursue *(wei)* Tao one decreases daily.
To decrease and again to decrease,
Until one arrives at not doing *(wu-wei)*.
Not doing *(wu-wei)* and yet nothing is not done.

2. Always take the empire when there are no businesses.
If there are businesses,
It is not worthwhile to take the empire.

General Comment

This chapter repeats the theme of the preceding chapter on the distinction between the coming out process and the return process. When the sage returns to Tao, he also returns the world to Tao.

Detailed Comment

1. To pursue learning is to increase the stock of our knowledge of the many. To pursue Tao, on the other hand, is to give up what has been accumulated so that one can return pure to the pure, what Plotinus calls the alone to the alone. Simone Weil says that if God's process of making the world is creation, our process of going back to God is uncreation.

Buddhist commentators take the third line, "To decrease and again to decrease," to be two stages of shedding what has been acquired. Kumarajiva interprets this to mean the removal of the consciousness of both good and evil:

To decrease, it is to leave no defilement unremoved, such that evil is forgotten. Then again to leave no subtle thoughts unremoved, such that good is forgotten. Evil is negative; good is positive. First cut off the negative, then again cut off the positive. Therefore it is said "To decrease and again to decrease." Having forgotten both the positive and the negative, having cut off both feelings and desires, one's nature *(te)* conforms to Tao, thus one reaches non-action *(wu-wei)*.

(Chiao Hung)

Han-shan Te-ch'ing, on the other hand, takes this line to mean the deactivation of both the faculties of feeling and thinking in the belief that once feelings are completely purged, thinking loses its function and thus subsides.

First you get rid of your feelings by your thinking. This is called "to decrease." When feelings are forgotten, thinking also ceases to activate. This is called "again to decrease." In this way the mind has neither thinking nor feeling. All selfish desires are purged. Such is to reach the state of non-action *(wu-wei)*.

(Ibid)

2. These lines apply the psychology of the sage in (1) to the style of his government. Duyvendak, following the suggestion of Ma Hsü-lun, moved them to chapter 57, calling it "an ideal case of text-correction." The fact is that these lines are integral parts of the chapter. When added to chapter 57 they are completely redundant.

In the West humans reorganize the world according to their own reasoning principle. Thomas Aquinas says that irrational beings do not go to God by themselves, but rational beings do (S.Th., I, 65,2., Dondeyne: 39). The very salvation of the world, therefore, depends on its reorganization by humans. According to Hegel, nature is to be transformed into spirit through human agency. Learning or the scientific project has as its goal the transformation of the world to bring it closer to God.

Taoism disagrees with both the presupposition and procedure of such a standpoint. The Taoist views as superfluous all human activity in the world; they cover up the face of the divine already present in the world. The whole process of learning should be dismantled so that Tao can again become manifest in the world. This fundamental disagreement between Taoism and the Western view is due to two fundamentally different notions of the natural world. The Taoist world is not inert with material things extended out there, as Descartes saw it, but is alive and self-regulating without humans meddling with it to increase the amount of business in it. Human learning with resulting modifications in the world does not bring either the natural world or humans themselves closer to the divine. To move closer to Tao humans need to take the opposite direction, to drop their projects one by one until there is nothing for them to do. The proper human role is to respond to the inner dynamism of things and be a part of their flow, not to superimpose on them an order disturbing their pre-established harmony. This is to practice *wu-wei,* the imitation of Tao. Tao, as chapter 37 says, "is always not doing *(wu-wei)* and yet nothing is not done."

49

1. The sage has no set mind *(ch'ang hsin),*
He takes the mind of the people as his mind.

2. The good *(shan)* I am good to them,
The not good I am also good to them.
This is the goodness of nature *(te).*
The trustworthy *(hsin)* I trust them,
The not trustworthy I also trust them.
This is the trust of nature *(te).*

3. The sage in the world,
Mixes *(hun)* the minds *(hsin)* of all.
The people lift up their eyes and ears,
The sage treats them all like children.

General Comment

This chapter, on the learned ignorance of the sage, continues the theme of the preceding chapter. In its discussion on the nature of the good it recalls chapter 20 and will be echoed in chapters 62 and 79. The ideal is to return to the original chaos womb before the emergence of distinctions and values marking the loss of original unity. The sage, by returning to the mind of the infant, not distinguishing between the good and the not good, re-educates his people to become like children again.

Detailed Comment

1. The Taoist sage, being selfless (chs. 7, 22), has no set mind or determined will *(ch'ang hsin)* of his own. Like Tao his way is a bending one (chs. 22, 45), taking the mind of his people as his own mind and the work of his people as his own work.

2. The good that repudiates the bad is not better than the bad, since it operates on the principle of exclusion. Only the good that embraces both the good and the bad is truly good. Such is the goodness and trust of nature *(te)* that follows upon Tao (ch. 21). The sage who follows nature's way does likewise.

This deep religious insight, that the ground of all beings accepts both the good and the not good, both the trustworthy and the untrustworthy, was beautifully expressed by Jesus:

> You have heard that it was said, thou shalt love thy neighbor and hate thy enemy. But I tell you, Love your enemies, do good to those who hate you, pray for those who persecute and insult you, that so you may be true children of your Father in heaven, who makes his sun rise on the evil and equally on the good, his rain fall on the just and equally on the unjust. . . . But you are to be perfect, as your heavenly Father is perfect.
>
> (*Matthew* 5: 43–48)

Generally, Confucians teach a graded love—love for family, friends, and strangers should be kept distinct. When Confucius said: "Within the four seas all men are brothers" (*Analects* 12: 5), however, he was pronouncing a religious conviction. An anecdote in the *Han shih wai chuan* confirms this deeper teaching within Confucianism.

> Tzu-lu said, "If a person is good to me, I will also be good to him. If a person is not good to me, I will not be good to him."
>
> Tzu-kung said, "If a person is good to me, I will also be good to him. If a person is not good to me, I will try to enlighten him, getting closer or more remote depending on the situation."
>
> Yen Hui said, "If a person is good to me, I will also be good to him. If a person is not good to me, I will still be good to him."
>
> The three disciples, holding different positions, asked Confucius about it. Confucius said, "The position of Yu is that of the Man and Mai barbarians; the position of Tz'u is that of friends; the position of Hui is that of family."
>
> (Hightower: 295–296)

The Ho-shang Kung commentary on these lines shows its usual moralistic overtone. It reads line 2 to mean "The not good I shall make them good." Taking *hsin* in lines 4 and 5 to mean faith instead of trust, line 5 reads: "The faithless I shall make them have faith." The sage shall make good those who are not good; the sage shall give faith to those without faith (in the Taoist religion). While the *Tao Te Ching* wants us to rise above the moral to the mystical level, forgetting the distinction between good and not good, trustworthy and untrustworthy, the Ho-shang Kung commentary, representing religion on a different plane, enthusiastically works at converting the not good into the good and the faithless into the faithful.

3. The character *hun* indicates the state of the chaos womb *(hun-ch'eng)* in chapter 25. In the *Chuang Tzu*, chapter 7, we have the story of the death of Hun-tun who died upon acquiring eyes and ears, along with other sense organs, which opened him to a world of distinctions (Watson, 1968: 97). In closing the eyes and ears of his people the sage is not manipulating them like a dictator, as some critics have charged (see chs. 36 and 65), but is restoring them to the infant's innocence, oblivious to the distinction between good and evil. Such a state also describes his own psychological condition: He has himself returned to the nebulous *(hun)* state of the infant, before it learned to smile (ch. 20).

50

1. From coming out to life to going back to death:
Those companions *(t'u)* of life,
They are one-third *(shih-yu-san);*
Those companions of death,
They are one-third;
Those living but moving toward the place of death,
They are also one-third.
Why?
Because of the intense *(hou)* life-producing activity.

2. I have heard that one who knows how to nourish life,
On land meets no tigers or wild buffaloes,

In battle needs to wear no armors or weapons,
A wild buffalo has nowhere to butt its horns,
A tiger has nowhere to sink its claws,
A weapon has nowhere to enter its blade.
Why?
Because such a one has no place of death.

General Comment

The first stanza concerns ordinary mortals who die; the second describes those who are deathless. What is deathless is the unceasing life-producing activity. The person at one with this unceasing creativity is immortal.

Detailed Comment

1. The phrase *shih-yu-san* (ten-with-three), appearing here three times, has been given varied interpretations. In the *Han Fei Tzu* (233 B.C.), chapter 20, it is taken to mean the four limbs and nine orifices of the body; by gaining or losing their functions a person is born or dies. This is supposedly the most ancient interpretation. Other commentators, however, take it to mean "three-out-of-ten," a rough way of saying one-third. The path from life to death may be divided into three segments: those in the first segment, being young and tender, are companions of life; those in the last segment, being old and stiff, are companions of death; those in the middle are moving from being companions of life to being companions of death. This interpretation finds support in chapter 76: "Therefore the hard and unyielding are companions of life, the tender and yielding are companions of death."

What we have in this passage is the life of the round, constituted by this dynamic process of coming to be and ceasing to be. Life and death are opposites that alternate with each other; what has life pushes on toward death so that new life can come to be. Death is therefore just the other side of life. Since life and death accompany and succeed each other, it is better not to worry about the matter. The point is not to dwell on either life or death, but to transcend both to the life of the one; as the *Chuang Tzu*, chapter 22 says:

Life is the companion of death, death is the beginning of life. Who understands their workings? A person's life is a coming-together of breath. If it comes together, there is life; if it scatters, there is death. And if life and death are companions to each other, then what is there for us to be anxious about?

The ten thousand things are really one. We look on some as beautiful because they are rare or unearthly; we look on others as ugly because they are foul and rotten. But from the foul and rotten the rare and unearthly are born, and the rare and unearthly upon death turn into the foul and rotten. So it is said, You have only to comprehend the one breath that is the world. The sage never ceases to value oneness.

(Cf. Watson, 1968: 235–236)

The last line, "Because of the intense life-producing activity" *(i ch'i sheng sheng chih hou)* answers the question: "Why this movement from life to death?" The same line can also mean "Because of the intense activity to keep on living." Read this way death is due to an overeagerness to live. Thus, the more a person tries to cultivate techniques for long life, the sooner he dies. Chapter 55.3 says: "To help life along is to bring ill portend." Chapter 75 proposes "People take death lightly, because they are in thick pursuit of life *(ch'iu sheng chih hou)*" and concludes "One who has nothing to pursue in life, is wiser than one who values life."

2. This stanza describes either the Taoist immortal or the immortal process of life itself. The key is provided in the last line. The immortal "has no place of death."

The interpretation of *shih-yu-san* in the *Han Fei Tzu* as the four limbs and nine orifices, parts, and organs of the body, appears to be more relevant here. For the individual coming to life is due to the possession of the body and its functions, ceasing to be is due to loss of the body and its functions, and the very process of moving from life to death is also due to the activities of the body and its organs. Therefore, whatever has a body is moving toward its place of death; only one who transcends the body has no place of death.

Death is a phenomenon from the individual's viewpoint. Cut off from the life of the round and standing alone, an individual faces his opponents and arrives at the place and time of his death. However, in the round, which is the eternal life process, productive, and embracing all opposites, there is no death. There is only intense life-producing activity. A person who transcends his individuality, identifying himself with the eternal life process that has no place of death, also has no place of death. Such a person "On land meets no tigers or wild buffaloes, in battle needs to wear no armors or weapons," and so on.

In chapter 55 we shall see that the power of the Taoist immortal who is immune to weapons and attacks by wild beasts is naturally possessed by the infant; being one with the ground the infant is unconscious of the division of opposites. So that all may live long is the reason why the sage in the preceding chapter makes himself and his people into little children who do not distinguish between the good and the not good, the trustworthy and the untrustworthy.

51

---

1. Tao gives birth,
Te rears *(hsü)*,
Things *(wu)* shape,
Circumstances *(shih)* complete.

2. Therefore the ten thousand things,
None do not respect Tao and treasure *te*.
Tao is respected,
Te is treasured,
Not by decree *(ming)*,
But by spontaneity *(tzu-jan)*.

3. Therefore Tao gives birth,
Te keeps, grows, nurtures, matures, ripens, covers and buries.

4. To give birth without possession,
To act *(wei)* without holding on to,
To grow *(chang)* without lording over,
This is called the dark *te*.

General Comment

This chapter concerns the providential powers of Tao and *te* in the life cycle of every being, especially *te* as the ever-supporting and yet self-effacing presence in the world.

Detailed Comment

1. Tao is the creative principle that gives birth. *Te* means nature either as a universal power or the power inherent in each individual being. As a universal power *te* is the resident creativity in the natural world, the presence or providence of the non-appearing Tao in the world of ten thousand beings. As the power inherent in each individual being determining its unfolding from within *te*

corresponds roughly to the formal cause in Aristotle. Tao as non-being and formless gives birth to all beings endowed with their specific forms.

In addition, beings are molded by fellow creatures *(wu)* as well as by circumstances *(shih)*—the larger formative forces in nature such as the weather, atmosphere, terrain, soil condition, etc. In the case of human beings *shih* also includes the social political conditions that determine the formation of humans even more powerfully than natural circumstances. These natural and social environments finalize the concrete actualization of all beings.

2. Of these four conditions or causes Tao and *te*—as what gives birth to and preserves and unfolds all beings—are internal determining principles, while fellow creatures *(wu)* and circumstances *(shih)*, facilitating or frustrating the actual unfolding of beings, are external determining conditions. A being stands to Tao and *te* as to source and ground. Its relationship to other beings and circumstances, however, is one of equal rank and competition. This is the familiar problem of the one and the many: The many issue from the one; among themselves they struggle. Tao and *te*, as the internal determining principles of all beings, enjoy privileges not accorded to things *(wu)* and circumstances *(shih)*. Being internal to all beings they are respected and treasured by all spontaneously and unconsciously.

3. While Tao's function is giving birth, *te* accompanies all beings throughout their careers; thus, *te* keeps, grows, nurtures, matures, ripens, covers, and buries.

In the Wang Pi and Ho-shang Kung texts we have *"yang chih fu chih"* for the last two functions, meaning that a thing, having grown to full size, is nurtured and sheltered from harm. Such an interpretation equates Tao or *te* with the benevolent power responsible for the coming out, growth, and maturing process of things. Like father and mother it has creative and preservative, but not destructive, functions. *The Book of Odes* (Ode 202) says: "Father begot me, Mother reared me, let me, kept me, raised me, nurtured me, watched over me, tended me. . . ."

The coming out process, however, is incomplete without the going back process. After maturing and ripening, a being's natural process is to fade and self-destruct. This reversive movement, as it governs Tao (chs. 25, 40), governs every being in the world. In this phase also we must not exclude the presence and efficacy of *te*. After the decline and self-destruction of beings, the function of *te* is to cover and bury them, not as punishment following upon a moral judgment, but because its function is to be the receptacle and resting place of all that have exhausted their life force or, as Whitehead says, that have attained their objective immortality. The Tang dynasty text has *"kai chih fu chih,"* literally, "to cover and to bury." *Te*'s kindness as a mother is in caring for the whole cycle of the life process, including the phase of covering and burying her children. The *Lü Shih Ch'un Ch'iu,* I, Book 3, chapter 5, entitled "On the Round Tao" describes the cycle of all beings: "When things are activated they emerge. Emerging they are born. Having been born they grow. Growing they become big. Being big they are completed. Being complete they decline. Declining they perish. Having perished they become hidden. This is the round Tao."

4. These four lines also appear at the end of chapter 10, as ethical reflections concluding the mystical vision of Tao and *te.* In this chapter these same lines depict the very nature of Tao itself, insofar as its presence can be experienced in the world. My comments here are addressed to the ontological rather than the ethical aspects of these statements.

The *yu* in the first line "to give birth without possession *(yu)*" means to have or to own. Tao is the Nothing *(wu)* that has given rise to all beings (chs. 40 and 42). Having given birth to all beings, however, Tao itself remains nothing. Tao is the inexhaustible creativity that does not claim ownership of any being. "To give birth without possession" is the gift of an absolute that is nothing in itself.

The second line says Tao accomplishes all things "without holding on to" what it has accomplished. The very idea of Tao as change means that Tao, always moving forward, never remains at one set point. Thus if Tao accomplishes all things, it lets go of all things. This does not mean that Tao abandons what it has accomplished to move on to new things, like the Bergsonian *elan vital* that leaves behind the species it has produced to replicate by themselves in order that it may progress to ever new heights of evolution. Tao "acts without holding on to" means that Tao, being an ever living creativity, does not impede the self-development of the beings it has created. This is meant to contrast with the human tendency to hold on to what they have accomplished, refusing to let go, thus frustrating the inner dynamisms of the processes they have helped shape.

Chang in the third line means to expand, to grow (in years), thus to govern (one who has grown in years, supposedly also in wisdom, is qualified to govern— see ch. 10). Implied in the idea of governing is the power to inspire growth. *Chang* as the power to govern also includes *tsai,* the power to judge and execute. Tao, however, is a power that inspires growth without killing. The function of Tao and *te* in all aspects of life is to enhance and nurture.

These concluding lines sum up the nature of Tao and its dark mystical presence in the world as *te:* it gives birth without possession, acts without holding on to, and grows without lording over. Such a conception of the absolute is the complete opposite of the jealous God. Tao and *te* are powerful not because they dominate the beings they have produced and nurtured, but because having produced and nurtured them they make no demands on them.

52

1. The world *(t'ien hsia)* has an origin *(shih)*,
Which is the world's *(t'ien hsia)* mother *(mu)*.
Having reached the mother,
(We) know her child.
Having known the child,
Return and abide by its mother.
(In this way) one loses the body without becoming exhausted.

2. Stop the apertures *(tui)*,
Close the doors,
(In this way) one's whole life *(shen)* is without toil *(ch'in)*.
Open the apertures,
Going about the affairs,
(In this way) one's whole life *(shen)* cannot be saved.

3. To see the small is called illumination *(ming)*.
To abide by the soft is called strength.
Use the bright light *(kuang)*,
But return to the dim light *(ming)*,
Do not expose your life *(shen)* to perils,
Such is to follow *(hsi)* the everlasting *(ch'ang)*.

General Comment

This chapter supplies the profound religious voice needed to heal the rift between humans and nature so that the life of both may be long lasting. Stanza 1, on the close relationship between the world and Tao, continues the theme from the preceding chapter. Stanza 2, on the art of long life, reverts to the theme of chapter 50. In view of the term *t'ien hsia* (the world or empire) in the first two lines of the chapter, this chapter is on the art of prolonging not so much the life of the individual as of the state (ch. 59) or the world. The overall message is the importance for consciousness to revert to the unconscious as its source. Only that form of life which is rooted in the source or mother is truly illumined *(ming)* and long lasting *(ch'ang)*.

Detailed Comment

1. In chapter 1, the *shih*, origin or *arche*, and *mu*, mother, are distinguished. In itself as origin *(shih)* of heaven and earth Tao is nothing *(wu)* or nameless *(wu ming)*; as the mother *(mu)* giving birth to the ten thousand things Tao is being *(yu)* or the named *(yu ming)*. In this chapter the nameless origin *(shih)* and the named mother *(mu)* combine; the nameless origin has given birth to the world and is therefore named mother of the world.

The relationship between Tao and the world in Taoism is much more intimate than the relationship between God and the world in Christianity. In Christianity the Son was begotten, not made, hence the intimate relationship between the Father and the Son who are indeed of the same substance (consubstantiation). The world was made, not begotten: God and the world do not share the same substance. The Taoist world, however, is indeed begotten by Tao: Tao gives birth to the world as a mother gives birth to her child. Still the Taoist world does not have the same substance as Tao. Tao as mother has no substance, it is nothing *(wu)*. The world begotten by Tao is the very substance or body *(shen)* of Tao. This is the importance of the word *shen*, body or life, throughout this chapter. The world of beings as the child, the concrete embodiment of Tao, derives its body and its life from the mother (as Tao) and is sustained by the mother (as *te*) in all its phases (ch. 51). The mother alone is everlasting (chs. 4, 5, 6, and 25). When the child abides by the mother, its life force is also unending.

The need to return to and abide by the source is also a familiar theme in Western religious thought. In Neo-Platonism the effect must return to the cause as to its father in order to confirm itself in being and to be fertile itself in turn: Thus Nous must return and contemplate the One to confirm itself as Nous, and to produce Soul as the next hypostasis (Plotinus, *The Enneads*, V.1.5; V.3.11; VI.7.16; and VI. 7.17; Gersh, ch. 3). This is also Augustine's notion of a human being in God's image; he must revert to God if he is to fulfill himself (*Soliloquies*, I.1.2). But again there is an important difference between Taoism with its mother-child symbolism and Neo-Platonism or its Christian version with its emanation theory. In Taoism the symbol of eternity is the circle or the round in which the beginning is joined to the end; thus the mother gives birth to the child who returns and abides by the mother. In Neo-Platonism the symbol is not the circle in which the end joins the beginning; it is rather a descending scale of being with matter at the end. Matter, being devoid of form, is forever banished from the divine, never to return to the source.

The last line is identical to the last line in chapter 16.

2. *Tui* (aperture) in line 1 is the name of hexagram 58, the Joyous, Lake, in the *I-Ching*. In the *Shuo Kua (Discussion of the Trigrams)*, the eighth wing of the *I-Ching*, chapter 9, in which the Trigrams are identified with various parts

of the body, Tui is said to be the mouth (R. Wilhelm, 1950: 279), which is related to speech or the opening to consciousness. The Ho-shang Kung commentary identifies the character *tui* in line 1 with the eye and *men* (door) in line 2 with the mouth.

In Taoism apertures and doors, eyes and mouths, lead to awareness of the external world and represent the birth of consciousness introducing death into the world. The *Chuang Tzu,* chapter 7, tells us of the death of Hun-tun (Chaos):

> The emperor of the South Sea was called Shu (Brief), the emperor of the North Sea was called Hu (Sudden), and the emperor of the central region was called Hun-tun (Chaos). Shu and Hu from time to time came together for a meeting in the territory of Hun-tun, and Hun-tun treated them very generously. Shu and Hu discussed how they could repay his kindness. "All men," they said, "have seven openings so they can see, hear, eat, and breathe. But Hun-tun alone doesn't have any. Let's bore him some!"
>
> Every day they bored another hole, and on the seventh day Hun-tun died.
>
> (Watson, 1968: 97)

Hun-tun, the god of the center, leads a carefree life prior to acquiring its openings. One with the unconscious, it draws on the inexhaustible life of the mother (ch. 6). Distinctions and divisions bombard Hun-tun (Chaos) once its apertures and doors are open. Its original unity lost, it shrivels and dies.

In the biblical story of the fall, Adam and Eve were condemned to a life of toil and death when they, disobeying God's command, acquired the knowledge distinguishing between good and evil. The carefree life in the garden of Eden before the fall is comparable to the blessed life of Hun-tun (Chaos) prior to his acquiring sense openings. In the biblical story, however, knowledge of the distinction between good and evil is presented as a divine possession. This constitutes the temptation—the desire to possess what God has—and it is inevitable, since humans were created in the image of God, that they should desire such knowledge. In the biblical story the fall represents humans departing from nature to approach God who transcends nature; this is why Hegel hails the fall as the first step in the ascent of humans. In Taoism the divine is Hun-tun, the sacred Chaos. Knowledge of good and evil is not a sacred possession. The journey toward value consciousness is not due to a desire to emulate the mother. On the contrary, it represents a departure from the sacred unity in the mother to the fragmented existence of an independent consciousness. Henceforth the child strikes out on its own, no longer protected by the mantle of the mother. Consciousness, cut off from the life-sustaining unconscious, quickly perishes.

If we apply these lines to the art of ruling the message is clear. The ruler should enlighten neither himself nor his people. The more laws are promulgated, the more lawbreakers are created (chs. 3 and 18). The busier a ruler is about the affairs of his state, the more he has to do. But, if he lets nature take its course, all shall be well (chs. 58 and 65).

3. To see the small and abide by the soft is to live the life of the round or *ming*, the union of the sun with the moon or the bright with the dark. Consciousness, which courts the bright and strong, is destructive to nature and life. Only that form of consciousness that abides by the unconscious, that sees the small and abides by the soft, is capable of long life. Such a form of consciousness knows the child, but returns and abides by the everlasting mother.

53

---

1. If I have a little *(chieh-jan)* knowledge *(chih)*,
To walk the great path (Tao),
I shall fear this:
The great path (Tao) is very flat and easy,
Yet others *(jen)* are fond of bypaths.

2. The courts are very neat,
The fields are very weedy,
The granaries are very empty.
Wearing embroidered clothes,
Carrying sharp swords,
Being surfeited with foods and drinks.
To accumulate wealth and treasures in excess,
This is called robbery and crime.
This is not to follow Tao.

General Comment

In the spirit of *p'u* (the uncarved wood), Taoists are physiocrats who favor farming as the economic basis for the state. They like to see wealth spread among the people. A splendid court and undue accumulation of wealth by the ruling class signify an empty granary and state treasury.

Detailed Comment

1. The *Tao Te Ching* is generally against governments that rule by knowledge *(chih)* (ch. 65). The government's aim is to restore the people to a state of "no knowledge and no desire" *(wu chih wu yü)* (ch. 3). In this chapter, however, *chih* means the reversive knowledge of the round that inspires in the ruler a holy fear of Tao.

The last line in the Wang Pi and Ho-shang Kung texts have *erh min hao chin* with *min* meaning the common people, as opposed to the rulers. I have followed the Tang dynasty text that has *jen,* meaning others (ch. 20), i.e., other rulers. Obviously, the author is not referring to the people here, but to the rulers who are fond of bypaths.

2. It seems that the fields are neglected and the granary is empty because labor has been conscripted to maintain the court in top condition. While the ruling class wallows in luxury the people are impoverished. The *Tao Te Ching* here endorses Proudhon's famous dictum that "property is theft," though it accuses the government (or ruler) rather than wealthy citizens.

54

---

1. One who is well established is not uprooted,
One who embraces firmly cannot be separated from,
Thus sons and grandsons shall perform sacrifices without interruptions.

2. In cultivating this in one's person,
The person's *te* becomes genuine;
In cultivating this in the family,
The family's *te* has more to spare *(yü);*
In cultivating this in the village,
The village's *te* grows strong;
In cultivating this in the state,
The state's *te* becomes abundant;
In cultivating this in the world *(t'ien hsia),*
The world's *te* becomes universal.

3. Therefore observe *(kuan)* the person by the person,
Observe the family by the family,
Observe the village by the village,
Observe the state by the state,
Observe the world by the world.
How do I know such is the case in the world?
Through this.

General Comment

If we take this chapter to concern the importance of cultivating virtue *(te)* and being sacrificed to by one's descendants after death, its outlook appears Confucian. The *Han Fei Tzu* takes this chapter to concern how to maintain political power for oneself and one's descendants. In its context, however, this chapter is directly linked to chapters 52 and 55—how to restore the social world to the long-lasting natural world.

Detailed Comment

1. The first two lines continue the familiar theme in chapters 10, 39, and 52 on the intimate relationship between Tao and the world. The appearing world must be rooted in the hidden Tao if it is to prosper. The third line, however, shows clearly that the topic here is how the ruler may hold on to his political power. In ancient China only the ruling family could sacrifice to its ancestors. Once a state was conquered members of its royal household were no longer permitted to perform sacrifices to their ancestors. To ensure a long life for his state, thereby a long life for himself in the hereafter, the ruler must be firmly rooted in Tao and *te*. The same sentiment is expressed in chapter 17 of the *Doctrine of the Mean:*

> Confucius said, "Shun was indeed greatly filial! In virtue *(te)* he was a sage; in honor he was the Son of Heaven; and in wealth he owned all within the four seas. Temple sacrifices were made to him, and his descendants preserved the sacrifices to him. Thus it is that he who possesses great virtue *(te)* will certainly attain to corresponding position, to corresponding wealth, to corresponding fame, and to corresponding long life. . . .
>
> (Chan, 1963a: 102)

2. This holding on to the root is to become a spiritual practice on every level of existence. The five-stage progression from the individual *(shen)* to the family *(chia)*, to the village *(hsiang)*, to the state *(kuo)*, to the whole world *(t'ien hsia)*

has a familiar ring. An identical five-stage progression can be found in both chapters 1 and 2 of the ancient economic treatise, *Kuan-tzu* (after Kuan Chung).[1] A four-stage progression is found in the Confucian text *The Great Learning:*

> . . . when the *personal life* is cultivated, the family will be regulated; when the *family* is regulated, the state will be in order; and when the *state* is in order, there will be peace throughout the *world*. From the son of Heaven down to the common people, all must regard cultivation of the personal life as the root or foundation.

> (Cf. Chan, 1963a: 86–87)

In Confucianism *te* means moral perfection achieved through one's effort *(wei)* to overcome the promptings of selfish desires; thus virtue marks humanity as superior to the rest of nature. In the *Tao Te Ching te* has the more primitive meaning of the power of life and rejuvenation in all beings, human and non-human (E. M. Chen, 1973b). *Te* stands for the original endowment of nature prior to moral distinctions and conscious effort *(wei)*. Thus *te* is possessed in the fullest only in the infant (ch. 55). What is discussed in these lines, the growth and expansion of *te* from the individual through the family, village, state, until it floods the whole world, is no less than the growth and expansion of the Taoist kingdom of grace.

The *Han Fei Tzu* commentary on this chapter expands the meaning of *te* (natural endowment) in the secular sense as communal wealth. *Te* is not merely individual or spiritual, it is also social and economic. Just as the individual depends on his life force *(te)* to flourish, the family prospers by its wealth. "*Te* in the individual is the stock of his life force *(ching)*; in the family *te* is its wealth and property; in the village, the state and the empire, their *te* is their people" (Cf. Liao, I: 205). *Te* is the condition of peace and prosperity in society when the population increases and the people acquire wealth.

3. *Kuan*, in chapter 16 meaning the Taoist "mystical vision," appears here five times, making it the key idea. Taking a hint from chapter 47: "Without stepping out of the door, know the world," Wang Pi takes these lines to mean that the truth is not far to seek. The standard of each being is contained within itself. Thus you need only observe yourself to know whether you are holding on to your *te;* you need only observe the family to know whether it is holding on to its *te;* and so on.

1. Translation of chapter 1 is found in 1954, of chapter 2 in 1965: 141. In order to see the parallel between the texts of the *Tao Te Ching* and the *Kuan-Tzu* the reader must consult the Chinese texts directly. The two translations listed in the bibliography under Kuan Chung, not being literal renderings, do not show the parallels in the original texts.

55

1. One who contains *te* in fullness,
Is to be compared to an infant.
Wasps, scorpions, and snakes do not bite it,
Fierce beasts do not attack it,
Birds of prey do not pounce upon it.

2. Its bones weak, its sinews tender,
But its grip is firm;
Knowing not the union of the female and male animals,
Yet its organ stirs.
Such is the perfection of its life-force *(ching)*.
Crying all day, yet it does not get hoarse.
Such is the Perfection of its harmony *(ho)*.

3. To know harmony is to know the everlasting *(ch'ang)*;
To know the everlasting is to be illumined *(ming)*.
To help life along is to bring ill portend;
To use mind *(hsin)* to direct the life breath *(ch'i)* is called the strong
    (ch'iang).

4. When things are full-grown they become old,
It is called not following the Way (Tao).
Not following the Way one dies early.

General Comment

This chapter defines the meaning of *te* in Taoism as a state prior to the rise of
desire or action (ch. 37), when all beings self-transform *(tzu-hua)* in synchronicity
(Jung 1960). This chapter is also a paean to infancy against the stiffness and
inflexibility of old age. I take the message spiritually. Spiritually some young
persons are already stiff and inflexible, while some old persons are as supple and
gentle as infants.

Detailed Comment

1. The Taoist believes that harmony is the original state of things; discord is due
to departure from the original state. Humans in their earliest condition were also

in harmony with all beings in nature. The *Chuang Tzu* portrays this idyllic state of affairs:

> Therefore in a time of Perfect *te* the gait of men is slow and ambling; their gaze is steady and mild. In such an age mountains have no paths or trails, lakes no boats or bridges. The ten thousand things live species by species, one group settled close to another. Birds and beasts form their flocks and herds, grass and trees grow to fullest height. So it happens that you can tie a cord to the birds and beasts and lead them about, or bend down the limb and peer into the nest of the crow and the magpie.
>
> (Watson, 1968: 105)

In the infant the principle alienating humans from the rest of nature has not yet developed. Since the infant is not perceived by anything as a threat, it is not an object of attack. Wang Pi comments: "The infant asks for nothing and desires nothing. Since it does not offend against anything, poisonous creatures also do not offend against it. One who contains *te* in fullness does not offend against anything, therefore nothing will harm its integrity."

Han-shan Te-ch'ing (1546–1623) comments:

> The infant neither knows nor recognizes anything. Its life force being full it exists in forgetfulness *(wang)*. One who forgets things is also forgotten by things. Thus it mingles with the animals without disturbing their groupings; it mingles with birds without disturbing their flights. Even ferocious creatures do not harm it, as it does not have a vulnerable spot. Such is the fullness of its life force.

2. The infant enjoys this special blessing because it is both internally and externally unified. Its internal unity is due to the perfection of its life-force *(ching)*; its external unity is due to the perfection of its harmony *(ho)* with all. To begin with the infant's bones are soft and its sinews tender. Since the soft and tender belong to life while the hard and strong head toward death (ch. 76), the infant has a firm grip on life.

Although the infant is either male ("its organ stirs") or female, because its knowledge distinguishing male from female is not yet explicit, the infant may be said to contain both sexes without separation. *Ching*, literally the semen (ch. 21.2), also means the power of life in a person. The infant, not the grown male or female, contains the full power of life *(ching)*. The division of sexes may be good for the perpetuation of the species; in the individual, sexual activity signals the transmission of life's reserve and thus a prelude to death.[1]

That the infant can cry all day without getting hoarse shows that whatever it does it does without ill effects. Its crying is neither the expression of a Nietzschean will to power aimed at overcoming others, nor what Sartre calls an act of bad faith veiling its own impotence while putting others in the wrong. The infant is not intentional. Its crying is spontaneous, like a tempest full of sound and fury while raging but, once subsided, restoring the earth to calm (ch. 23). The infant may cry all day but it is in harmony *(ho)* with all.

3. The third line literally means: "To help life along is to bring good portend." Wang Pi's comment: "Life cannot be artificially prolonged. To do so is to cut it short" shows that the original text meant just the opposite. Philosophical Taoism, preaching non-action *(wu-wei)*, looks upon conscious effort as detrimental to life (ch. 24). The *Chuang Tzu,* chapter 5, also says: "Always follow nature and do not try to help life along" (Cf. Watson, 1968: 75–76). Religious Taoism, on the other hand, has devised various ways to help life along, including breathing exercises, sexual hygiene, herbs, and immortality pills. Among the manuscripts unearthed at Ma-wang Tui (T'ang Lan, 1975b), there is a fragment illustrating breath control techniques and health-inducing animal postures referred to in the *Chuang Tzu,* chapter 15:

> To pant, to puff, to hail, to sip, to spit out the old breath and draw in the new, practicing bear-hangings and bird-stretchings, longevity the only concern—such is the life favored by one who practices circulating the Tao *(tao-yin)*, the person who nourishes the body, who hopes to live to be as old as P'eng-tsu.
>
> (Cf. Watson, 1968: 167–168)

In line 4 *ch'i*—air, breath, or vital force keeping the body alive—is unconscious and spontaneous. The infant is all *ch'i* but no mind *(hsin);* thus it is soft and in harmony with all (ch. 10). When the mind is allowed to overpower *ch'i,* it constricts the flow of the life breath in the body, resulting in early death. The Taoist ruler "empties the minds of his people" (ch. 3). In the *Chuang Tzu* this is called "fasting the mind," an important part of a Taoist's spiritual training (Watson, 1968: 57–58).

4. To grow old means to become hard and rigid, the prelude to death. Tao is the ever old which is yet ever young (ch. 14). The secret of long life then lies in the imitation of Tao. We must change our direction; our goal is not to grow away from, but toward the infant.

1. This must have been the theoretical foundation for the sexual technique of recirculating the semen in religious Taoism. See Ch'en Kuo-fu: 366–369, 436–437.

56

---

1. One who knows does not speak,
One who speaks does not know.

2. Stop the apertures,
Close the door;
Blunt the sharp,
Untie the entangled;
Harmonize the bright,
Make identical the dust.
This is called the mystical identity *(hsüan t'ung)*.

3. Therefore with this person you cannot get intimate *(ch'in)*,
Cannot get distant,
Cannot benefit,
Cannot harm,
Cannot exalt
Cannot humiliate.
Therefore such person is the exalted of the world.

General Comment

Most commentators take "the exalted of the world" in the last line as referring to a ruler. We may regard the whole chapter as giving us the psychology of the Taoist ruler/mystic. The coming out process is one of speech, distinction, partiality, and strife. The ruler/mystic takes the world back to Tao. The knowing without speech suppresses distinctions and so removes the cause for partiality and strife. By giving up speech and distinctions the ruler mystic returns all to the dark undifferentiated ground, thereby reestablishing the mystical identity of all beings in Tao.

Detailed Comment

1. Mystical experience is non-verbal or ineffable (ch. 1.1). When it comes to Tao, silence is more eloquent than speech (ch. 5.3).
    2. The first two lines characterizing the carefree state of the Taoist are found in chapter 52.2. The next four lines are found in chapter 4.2 as the function of Tao blending all in its own nothingness. Here they describe the psychology of

the ruler/mystic. The secret to successful governing lies in keeping a vision of unity and solidarity in the realm of the many, thereby establishing the peace of the ground amidst seeming conflict. By playing down the distinctions among things and individuals the ruler/mystic removes the causes of their conflicts. Wang Pi's comment on (1) and (2) is to the point:

"One who knows does not speak" means that such a person follows the natural path *(tzu-jan)*. "One who speaks does not know" means that such a person complicates matters. To "stop the apertures, close the door; blunt the sharp, untie the entangled" is to abide by the original state of things so that the causes of disputes are eliminated. To "subdue the bright" means if things do not stand out from one another, they can make no special claims which cause disputes. . . ."

3. Like Tao, the ruler/mystic functions now as a universal. The distinctions between close relatives *(ch'in,* ch. 79.3) and unrelated persons, between benefit and harm, glory and humiliation, for example, which operate in the realm of particular beings, count as nothing for one who abides in the source. Like Tao the ruler/mystic accepts all, blends and harmonizes all.

57

---

1. Govern a state by *(i)* the normal *(cheng);*
Conduct warfare as *(i)* the abnormal *(ch'i);*
Take the empire when *(i)* there is no business.

2. How do I know such should be the case? By the following:
In an empire with many prohibitions,
   People are often poor;
When people have many sharp weapons,
   The state is in great darkness *(tzu hun);*
When persons abound in ingenuity *(ch'iao),*
   Abnormal *(ch'i)* objects multiply *(tzu ch'i);*
When laws are abundantly promulgated *(tzu chang),*
   There are many thieves and brigands.

3. Therefore the sage says:
I do not act *(wei)*,
  Hence the people transform by themselves *(tzu-hua)*;
I love tranquillity *(ching)*,
  Hence the people are normal by themselves *(tzu-cheng)*;
I have no business,
  Hence the people grow rich by themselves;
I have no desire,
  Hence the people are like the uncarved wood by themselves *(tzu-p'u)*.

General Comment

This chapter on political philosophy provides the philosophical foundation for the *laissez faire* policy of "resting with the people" that produced wealth and prosperity during the early Han dynasty.

Detailed Comment

1. These three lines have been interpreted to represent policies of three different schools of thought. If we take *cheng* to mean "to rectify" and read the first line to mean "Govern a state by rectification," it represents the teaching of the Confucian School (*Analects* 12: 17: "To govern is to rectify"). If we interpret *ch'i* in the second line to mean "surprise tactics," it represents the strategy of the military school. Only the third line represents the Taoist position.

To us these three lines all represent the Taoist position. *Cheng*, meaning the normal or natural condition, the state of peace, and *ch'i*, meaning the abnormal condition or the state of war, form a pair of opposites in this and the next chapter. The Taoist governs a state by following nature, the normal condition, and treats wars as abnormal occurrences to be undertaken with great reluctance. If other rulers take wars to be the normal business of the state, the Taoist ruler accepts rulership only when there is no business to conduct.

2. These lines are typical of the *Tao Te Ching's* primitivistic stance. Governmental restrictions impair the livelihood of the people; sharp weapons (ch. 36) among the people encourage fighting and riot; love of invention results in the abundance of strange *(ch'i)* objects; the more laws, the more lawbreakers; the more sophisticated the citizenry, the more corrupt the society. We live dangerously when we depart from nature's normalcy *(cheng)*. Today our fear of genetic engineering's potential to infest the world with monstrosities *(ch'i)* echoes the same fear (Rifkin).

3. There are two types of government. An eager government intent upon improving its people's lot will introduce legislations, issue edicts, multiply laws.

Such a meddling government prevents its people from unfolding the activities inherent in their own natures, resulting in a restless, intractable, and poor population. The Taoist ruler, by doing nothing *(wu-wei)*, allows his people to develop themselves. *Ching* is the peace or tranquillity of nature or of the female (ch. 61) which begets the motions of life *(tung)* (ch. 15). Nature is ever peaceful and tranquil, yet ever active and productive (ch. 45.2). The policy of "resting with the people" produces the best results.

Ssu-ma Ch'ien must have had these lines in mind when he concluded the biography of Lao Tzu in the *Records of the Historian* this way: "Li Erh taught non-action, to make room for self-transformation; he abided in clarity and tranquillity, to allow for the process of self-equilibrium *(tzu-cheng)*" *(Shih chi,* 63: 3b).

58

---

1. When the government *(cheng)* is dull,
Its people are wholesome;
When the government is efficient *(ch'a)*,
Its people are deficient *(ch'üeh)*.

2. Calamities *(huo)* are what blessings depend on,
In blessings are latent calamities *(huo)*.
Who knows where is the turning point *(chi)?*

3. Because there is no longer the normal *(cheng)*,
The normal reverts and appears as the strange *(ch'i)*,
The good reverts and appears as the uncanny.
Rulers *(jen)* have lost their way,
For a long stretch of days.

4. Therefore the sage is square but not cutting *(ko)*,
Sharp but not injurious,
Straight but not overreaching,
Bright *(kuang)* but not dazzling.

General Comment

This chapter follows the preceding chapter in both terminologies and ideas. The tone is somewhat pessimistic. It extols the virtues of an inactive government, which, alas, had become rare.

Detailed Comment

1. The *Tao Te Ching* believes that the development of intelligence results in the loss of the original goodness of nature. A dull and sleepy government does not encourage its citizens to sharpen their wits, thus preserving them in the wholesomeness of nature. A smart and efficient government awakens its citizens to competition, envy, and struggle; thereby they become deficient in natural goodness. In this way a supposedly desirable event (development of intelligence) results in something regrettable (loss of the original goodness of nature).

2. The turning of the round can be illustrated even in political matters. What seems to be a misfortune (dull government) brings about a blessing (wholesome citizens), while what seems to be a blessing (efficient government) actually leads to misfortune (deficient citizens). Thus the wheel of fortune turns. What appears a blessing at the moment may turn out to be a misfortune, while what appears to be a misfortune now may prove later a blessing in disguise. Chapter 18 of the *Huai-nan Tzu* tells the story of an old man at the border who, armed with the insight that blessings and misfortunes have a way of turning into each other, met both with equanimity (SPTK, 18/6a).

3. Some translators have found these seemingly enigmatic lines unintelligible. If we connect them with the preceding chapter (57.1) the meaning is quite clear. The *Tao Te Ching* laments that things have come to such a state that what is normal (a dull and peaceful government) is now perceived as abnormal, while what is abnormal (government engaged in constant warfare) is now accepted as normal. *Jen* here means rulers. Thinking that they must enlarge their territory, institute new laws, inspire the people to revolutionary zeal, etc., they have lost their way.

4. Only the sage encompasses the opposites within himself. Embracing in himself both heaven (round) and earth (square), he is a square whose corners do not cut (ch. 41), a sharp knife that does not injure, a straightness that curls itself up so that it is not overreaching (ch. 45), and a brightness that abides in the dark Tao (ch. 41). The sage, by holding on to both poles, is able to avoid harming his people (ch. 60).

59

1. In governing people and serving heaven,
Nothing is better than being sparing *(se)*.

2. Being sparing,
Is called early adherence [to Tao].
Adhering early,
Is called being heavy with accumulated *te (chung chi te)*.

3. To be heavy with accumulated *te*,
Then [such a person is] all overcoming.
Being all overcoming,
Then there is no knowing the limit *(chi)*.

4. Not knowing the limit,
One may rule a state.
Having the mother of a state,
It may last long.
This is called being deeply rooted and firmly founded,
The way to long life and enduring vision *(chiu shih)*.

General Comment

Like chapter 54 this chapter is on the art of long life for the state. The idea of
te is grasped here as nature's rootedness in Tao. The imagery is a plant with its
roots stretching deep into the soil. Just as the individual who abides by Tao lives
long, the society that draws its strength from nature *(te)* will also last long.

Ho-shang Kung interprets the entire chapter as the way to conserve one's
semen and life breath and so to attain long life. Waley translates *chiu shih*
(enduring vision) in the last line as "fixed staring," a yoga practice. We stress that
the main issue of the chapter, stated in the opening line, concerns "governing
people and serving heaven," i.e., how society may last long.

Detailed Comment

1. According to the *Shuo Wen, se* (嗇), translated as "sparing," follows *lai* (來),
to come, and 回, to collect, meaning to come and collect the grains (*se* 穡), which

is how the farmer gathers in the harvests lest they are lost. Han Fei interprets *se* as sparing in expenditure, which results from quietude *(ching)*, as opposed to the wastefulness of agitation *(tsao,* chs. 26.1 and 45.2). *Se,* meaning sparing in the expenditure of energy that preserves one's life force, is another word for *chien,* frugality, in chapter 67 one of the three treasures of the Taoist.

2. Early adherence to Tao means that there is no departure from Tao at all. Being sparing one conserves one's life energies. One is like an infant in full possession of the original endowment of life. In the process of growing up this life stock can be depleted and dispersed. The Taoist recoups his life force. This is called heavy with accumulated *te.*

3. When a person is heavy with accumulated *te* he becomes as invincible as an infant (ch. 55). These lines recall chapter 28.2, that says one who is like the infant, who never departs from the everlasting *te,* becomes the model of the world, and as such returns to Tao as the unlimited *(wu-chi).*

4. Such a person at one with Tao is fit to be a ruler. For only that society which is deeply rooted in Tao has a lasting life.

60

1. Governing a great state,
Is like cooking small fish.

2. If you rule the world by Tao,
The ghosts *(kuei)* will lose their spiritual *(shen)* power.
Not that the ghosts lose their spiritual power,
But their spiritual power will not harm the people.
Not that their spiritual power will not harm the people,
But neither does the sage harm the people.

3. Since both are harmless,
Te flows back and forth [without impediment].

General Comment

Here and in chapter 39 we learn that the Taoist world consists of spirits, ghosts, rulers, and people, as well as myriad creatures of earth, and that their natures *(te)* are mutually implicated. The sage as ruler mediates the smooth functioning of the whole universe. By following Tao and thus not harming the people with his over-ambitious programs, he keeps the harmful powers of the spirits and ghosts in quiescence.

Detailed Comment

1. This is a familiar refrain now couched in a fresh analogy. One should take the empire when there is no business (chs. 48.2 and 57.1). In cooking small fish not much labor though great care and delicate touch are required.

2. There are two harmful forces in the world. In the visible world the ruler is the source of harm while in the invisible world spirits and ghosts are the source of harm. Of these two, the ruler's position is pivotal. When the sage does not sharpen the minds of his people or stir them to activities violating the nature of things, he brings peace not only to the social political order but also to the spiritual realm. Spirits and ghosts harm the people only when there are transgressions. When the sage rules the world by Tao there will be no transgressions and no occasions for spirits and ghosts to manifest their harmful powers.

There is a hint of ancient shamanism in speaking of the sage as having this power to harm the people. Like the spirits and ghosts, the sage as ruler or chieftain irradiates the power *(te)* of the noumenal, and, like them he possesses the power *(mana)* to harm. Anyone who encounters him is in the presence of a harmful demonic power just as if he were in the presence of a spirit or ghost. At the same time the *Tao Te Ching* shows itself already freed from shamanism's fear of the uncanny in spirits and ghosts. There is a fundamental harmony between the visible and the invisible. The demonic powers of spirits and ghosts become destructive only when the sage does not abide by Tao. When Tao prevails in the world, all harm is removed. Beings on different planes of existence will vibrate sympathetically to one another.

3. Now *te* as the life force informing every being in the world will flow unimpeded from one realm to the other. This mutual influx of *te* is the peace and harmony of the world.

61

1. A large state is down stream *(hsia liu)*.
Where the rivers under heaven *(t'ien hsia)* converge,
Is the female *(p'in)* under heaven.
The female always wins the male *(mou)* by stillness *(ching)*,
By stillness it is low-lying *(hsia)*.

2. Therefore, by being low-lying *(hsia)* to a small state,
A large state acquires *(ch'ü)* a small state.
By lowering *(hsia)* itself to a large state,
A small state acquires a large state.
The one acquires by being low-lying *(hsia)*,
The other acquires by lowering *(hsia)*.

3. A large state without overstepping its boundary *(pu kuo)*,
Wishes to keep others under its wings.
A small state without overstepping its boundary *(pu kuo)*,
Wishes to offer service to others.
Now both are granted their proper wishes,
It is fitting that a large state takes the low *(hsia)* place.

General Comment

Contrary to the remarks of some commentators (Chan, 1963b: 208), this chapter is not on international intrigue but international peace and cooperation. It tells how a large state may gain the allegiance of a small one, and how a small state may prosper next to a large one. This symbiosis or mutual enchancement of large and small states provides another illustration, this time in the international arena, of the complementarity of opposites discussed in chapters 2.2, 27.3, 66.1, and others. Whether a state is large or small successful diplomacy consists of lowering itself. The character *hsia* (the low or downflowing), in chapter 8 the characteristic of water and of Tao, appears nine times in this chapter, showing that the vision of international peace presented in this chapter is an integral part of the overall religious vision of Tao as the feminine, which is low-lying.

Detailed Comment

1. The Ho-shang Kung commentary explains the first line this way: "He who rules a large state ought to consider himself to be situated downstream." In Confucianism the downstream position *(hsia liu)* is repudiated by the gentleman as the place of evil *(Analects,* 17: 24 and 19: 20). While acknowledging that the downstream position is disdained by all (ch. 8), the *Tao Te Ching* regards it as the commanding position (ch. 66). All rivers flow downward, to gather and converge downstream. The downstream is also the place of the female, lying low in stillness to win the male for the stirrings of new life (ch. 15).

2. The relationship between a large state and a small state is like the relationship between the female and male. If a large state plays the role of the female by lying low, it gains the allegiance of the small state. On the other hand, if a small state courts a large state like a male courting a female, it wins the acceptance of a large state. Thus it is a mutual acquisition—by being either low-lying (female) to receive tributes or by lowering (male) to offer tributes.

3. *Pu kuo,* to not transgress beyond the safe boundary of nature so as to avoid harm, is an important idea in chapter 64.5. There is a way even international relations do not overstep the safe boundary of nature. A large state naturally overpowers a small state. To make this harmless the large state plays the role of the female, winning by being receptive. A small state, naturally overpowered by a large state, maintains its existence by playing the role of the courting male. If relationships between large and small states can be like the relationship between female and male, a mutually enhancing experience producing peace and harmony will exist.

62

---

1. To all beings Tao is the hidden secret *(ao):*
To the good persons it is their treasure *(pao),*
To the not good it is that by which they are preserved *(pao).*

2. Beautiful speech can go to the market.
Respectable conduct can be bestowed on others.

Those who are not good,
Why discard them?

3. Therefore on crowning the Son of Heaven,
On appointing the Three Ducal Ministers *(kung)*,
Although there are tributes of jade,
Preceding teams of four horses,
It is better to kneel *(tso)* and present this Tao.

4. Why did the ancients honor this Tao?
One does not say that they did it for the purpose of gain,
Rather they wish to be free from offenses *(tsui)*.
Therefore they were the honored under heaven.

General Comment

This is an encomium to Tao as the preserver of all beings. A good ruler with his
eyes fixed on Tao rejects no one.

Detailed Comment

1. When Feuerbach speaks of religion as "the solemn unveiling of a man's hidden
treasures" (1957: 13), is he not echoing these lines?
    Ao also means the southwest corner of the house. Duyvendak (1954) con-
nects this location to the ancient fertility cult of the Chinese:

> The south-west corner of the house is the place where the grain is
> stored. It is where the wife slept, who borrowed her fecundity from it,
> and in return bestowed her own. By her side lay the master of the house,
> whose place, during the day, is at the east side of the house. At night
> therefore his position is reversed. So the south-west corner suggests: the
> most important thing in a place where one would least expect it; the
> category *yang* where one would expect *yin*. It is therefore a very
> suggestive image of the Way, with its constant and often unexpected
> alternation of these two aspects of development.
>
> (Cf. also Granet, 1930: 172)

The Wang Pi and most other texts have *ao* as the last character of the first
line. The Ma-wang Tui silk manuscripts has *chu*, to pour into, as the last
character, changing the meaning of the first line to: "Tao is that into which all
beings pour." I consider the Wang Pi text superior. *Ao* (secret) not only rhymes

with *pao* (treasure), and *pao* (preserved), the last characters of the second and third lines, it also explains why it is the treasure of the good person and that by which the bad person is preserved. As the hidden secret *(ao)* of all beings Tao is immanent in all beings. A being exists by virtue of containing this hidden secret. The good person is aware that Tao is his treasure. Yet even though the bad person is not with Tao and does not know Tao, it is Tao that protects and preserves him.

2. Although there are those who speak well in public or outshine others in good deeds, we must not accept only these and reject others. Tao does not distinguish or separate between the good (those who excel others) and the not good (those who do not excel), but accepts and saves all (chs. 27.2 and 49.2). We must do the same if we are to imitate Tao. Tzu-chang among the disciples of Confucius understood the position here:

> The disciples of Tzu-hsia asked Tzu-chang about intercourse with others. Tzu-chang said, What does Tzu-hsia tell you? They replied saying, Tzu-hsia says:
> Go with those with whom it is proper to go; Keep at a distance those whom it is proper to keep at a distance.
> Tzu-chang said, That is different from what I have been told:
> A gentleman reverences those that excel, but "finds room" for all; He commends the good and pities the incapable.
> Do I myself greatly excel others? In that case I shall certainly find room for everyone. Am I myself inferior to others? In that case, it would be others who would keep me at a distance. So that the question of keeping others at a distance does not arise.
>
> *(Analects,* 19: 3, Waley: 224–225)

3. The goal of the *Tao Te Ching* is indeed the kingdom of Tao on earth. In the legitimation of political power, the presentation of the truth of Tao takes precedence over all the other rituals.

4. To distinguish the good and the not good, to discard the not good for the good, is to commit an offense *(tsui)* against Tao. That human actions must not incur any offense against the holy lest there is blame is also a common warning in the *I-ching:*

> The meaning of the yielding is that it is not favorable for it to be far away. The important thing, however, is to remain *without blame;* its expression consists in being yielding and central.
>
> (R. Wilhelm, 1950: 350–351)

The tao of this book is great. It omits none of the hundred things. It is concerned about beginning and end, and it is encompassed in the words *"without blame"*

(Ibid.: 353)

63

1. Do *(wei)* when there is nothing to do *(wu-wei),*
Manage affairs *(shih)* when there are none to manage,
Know *(chih)* by not knowing.
Regard the great as small, the much as little.
Repay injury *(yüan)* with *te.*

2. Plan the difficult while it is easy.
Accomplish *(wei)* the great when it is small.
Difficult affairs of the world,
Must be done while they are easy.
Great affairs of the world,
Must be done while they are small.
The sage never does anything great,
Therefore he can accomplish the great.

3. He who makes promises lightly seldom keeps his words.
He who takes much to be easy finds much to be difficult.
Therefore even the sage takes things to be difficult,
So that in the end they are not difficult.

General Comment

This and the next two chapters are on *te* as the small or incipient state of things (ch. 55) when they are pliant and full of rejuvenating power. Once events become full grown they become intractable. The key to the future is keeping watch over the initial state of things. If the ruler pays attention to that crucial moment, he would have nothing to do, i.e., things would be so well ordered he would need do nothing.

Detailed Comment

1. The third line in the Wang Pi and Ho-shang Kung texts reads "taste the tasteless" *(wei wu wei)*. Kao Heng points out that as quoted in some classical texts this line reads "know by not knowing" *(chih pu chih)*, appearing also in chapter 71.1 (translated as "from knowing to not knowing"). The character "to taste" *(wei)* could have been a copying error from the character "to know" *(chih)*. I have decided in favor of "know by not knowing," which is organically linked with the first two lines on doing and managing: through the intentionality of knowing *(chih)* we launch into actions *(wei)* and projects *(shih)*.

The last line "repay injury with *te,*" traditionally understood to mean "repay injury with virtue," requires a long comment. Confucius was critical of such a position. His question was: "If one requites injury with virtue, how is one to requite virtue?" Confucius believed that we ought to repay injury, an injustice, not with virtue but with justice *(Analects* 14: 36). Moral evils are to be addressed by the moral law.

For Paul Carus (1945: 182) the statement "repay injury with virtue" means that the *Tao Te Ching* teaches the same ethics of forgiveness taught by Jesus (Matt. 5: 43–48) and so anticipated Christianity.

For a proper understanding of this line we must understand that in the *Tao Te Ching te* does not mean virtue. *Te* is the pristine condition of nature unburdened with distinctions between good and evil (E. M. Chen, 1973b). Within the moral sphere distinguishing good from evil there can be no resolution of the problem of evil. Only when humans transcend virtue to the level of nature prior to the distinctions between good and evil can they be free from evil. Injury is unavoidable within the moral sphere; moral evil is the price paid for moral distinctions.

To "repay injury with *te*" means to return injury the way nature returns injury. Nature is not conscious of goodness, nor does it design retaliation. *Yüan,* injury or wrong, also means rancor (ch. 79). Armed with the distinctions between right and wrong humans bear rancor against injuries, but nature bears no rancor. Nature accepts and suffers injury; it also heals injury such that there is no trace of injury left.

This must be what Jesus means when he commands us to forgive our enemies. The Christian is called to rise above ordinary morality which bears rancor to imitate the perfection of the Father in heaven. To become as perfect as the Father we must forgive and forget that there has been injury at all (Matt. 6: 14–15, 18: 21–22; Lk. 6:37, 11: 4, 17: 3–4; Mk. 11: 25).

Further, *te* is not merely nature as prior to virtue, but is the state when all things are yet small prior to their becoming strong, stiff, and thus injurious to one another. The way to remedy the hard and injurious is to abide by the original state when things are small, tender, forgiving, and full of the power to repair.

Like the four preceding lines, "repay injury with *te*" is a call to return to the state when problems have not arisen because the conditions that produce the problems have not arisen. This is the state when there is nothing to do, nothing to manage, nothing to know; when the great is yet small, the much is yet little; when injuries have not yet appeared since all beings, in their beginning state of *te*, are in union with all.

2, 3. The ruler follows the inner potential of things to their full fruition without much effort on his own part. *Wu-wei* is what accomplishes all. This does not mean that things are easy to accomplish; there is none of the American can-do spirit in the Taoist ruler. While marveling at the ease and grace of nature, the Taoist looks upon almost every project as invariably hard if humans are to attempt to do it consciously by themselves (ch. 24). Humans can do the most by not interfering with nature's processes.

64

---

1. What is at equilibrium is easy *(i)* to maintain;
What has not emerged is easy *(i)* to plan *(mou);*
What is fragile is easy *(i)* to dissolve;
What is minute is easy *(i)* to disperse.
Act *(wei)* when there is yet nothing to do.
Govern *(chih)* when there is yet no disorder *(luan)*

2. A tree whose trunk is of a man's embrace,
Begins from something extremely tiny.
A tower of nine stories high,
Is built from a heap of earth.
A trip of a thousand miles,
Begins right at one's feet.

3. He who acts *(wei)* fails,
He who holds on to loses.
Therefore the sage does not act *(wei)* so he does not fail,
He does not hold on to, so he does not lose.

4. The people in launching their projects,
Often fail when these are near completion.
Had they been as careful at the end as at the beginning,
There would have been no failures.

5. Therefore the sage desires not to desire,
He does not treasure hard-to-get goods;
Learns not to learn,
He recovers the transgressions *(kuo)* of many.
In assisting the self-becoming *(tzu-jan)* of all beings,
He dares not act *(wei)*.

General Comment

The entire chapter can be considered an explication of 63.2: "Plan the difficult while it is easy. Accomplish the great when it is small." Two interpenetrating themes, the idea of *te* as the small or beginning state in nature (1 and 2) and non-action as the way to success (3 and 4), are combined in the last stanza.

Detailed Comment

1. The character *mou* in the second line (ch. 73.2) seems to suggest a legalist's devious tactics *(yin mou);* a ruler should nip oppositions at the earliest detection so as to rid himself of later trouble. There is nothing of the sort here. What is described here is the ease *(i,* the first four lines) with which nature initiates and orders all things. Human beings can do no better than to follow nature's easy way.

    2. The idea is a familiar one: all great monuments have their humble beginnings. The *Doctrine of the Mean,* chapter 15, says: "The way of the superior man may be compared to traveling to a distant place: one must start from the nearest point. It may be compared to ascending a height: one must start from below" (Chan, 1963a: 102). The *Huai-nan Tzu,* Book 16, says: "Stitches become tapestries. Heaps of earth become cities. Whether projects are successes or failures, they all begin from the small" (SPTK, 16/7b).

    3, 4. Once a thing has started, one should let it develop naturally; to interfere in its natural process is to ruin it. This means that one should refrain from acting on things in the intermediary and final stages as well as in the beginning stage.

The story of the farmer in the *Mencius* (2A: 2) is a classic illustration of the tragic consequences of human intervention.

> You must not force it to grow. You must not be like the man from Sung. There was a man from Sung who pulled at his rice plants because he was worried about their failure to grow. Having done so, he went on his way home, not realizing what he had done. "I am worn out today," said he to his family. "I have been helping the rice plants to grow." His wife rushed out to take a look and there the plants were all shriveled up.
>
> (Cf. Lau, 1970: 78)

5. The Taoist ruler believes that his role is strictly a passive one. Success lies in respecting the natural processes of things, while failure is due to wantonness, fueled by desire and learning, against the natural processes of things. In desiring not to desire and learning not to learn (ch. 48) he fulfills all without transgressions (*kuo*, ch. 61.3) or offenses (*tsui*, ch. 62.4), as the *Hsi Tzu*, I, 4 says:

> Resembling heaven and earth, he is not in conflict with them. His wisdom embraces all beings, and his *tao* benefits all under heaven, therefore he does not commit transgressions *(pu kuo)*. . . . His transformative power reaches everywhere between heaven and earth, yet he does not commit transgressions *(pu kuo)*. Through the winding way he fulfills all beings without missing any.
>
> (Cf. R. Wilhelm, 1950: 295–296)

65

---

1. Those in the past who were good at practicing Tao,
Did not want to enlighten *(ming)* the people,
But to keep them in ignorance *(yü)*.

2. People are hard to rule,
Because they know *(chih)* too much.

Therefore, to rule a nation by knowledge,
Is to be the nation's thief.
Not to rule a nation by knowledge,
Is to be the nation's blessing.

3. To know these two is to know heaven's rule *(chi shih)*.
Always knowing heaven's rule,
Is called the dark *(hsüan) te*.

4. The dark *te* clarifies *(ch'ing)* and is far away *(yüan)*.
It reverts *(fan)* with things.
Then there arrives the great harmony.

General Comment

What the preceding chapter (64.5) says—that the sage desires not to desire and learns not to learn—is translated in this chapter into a governmental policy. The Taoist does not agree with those eighteenth-century philosophers who believe progress and peace among humans is promoted by enlightenment of the mind. Like Rousseau, the Taoist is a primitivist who believes that education corrupts natural goodness. The people are better off in a state of no-knowledge, at one with nature's harmony and equilibrium.

Detailed Comment

1. In all other chapters (10, 16, 22, 24, 41, 52, 55), *ming* stands for the mystic light leading us to union with the dark hidden Tao. In this chapter *ming* stands for illumination of a different kind. It is a light that makes us self-conscious and stand apart from others, a light that illuminates the end products of Tao such that we become oblivious to their hidden ground. Given a choice between human knowledge *(chih)* and the ignorance *(yü)* of nature, the Taoist chooses ignorance, which, being unconscious, is life, growth, and peace.

2. Knowledge or consciousness as a movement away from nature leads to externalization, discord, and, finally, death. The sage ruler, by keeping his people in ignorance, preserves the peace and harmony of nature in society (ch. 3.2).

The Taoist policy of keeping the people in ignorance has been branded a devious tactic (ch. 36) used by dictators to manipulate the people in the way they see fit. Nothing is further from the truth here. Tao is not a conscious or intellectual principle. It is Hun-tun or creative Chaos (ch. 25). While knowledge is called *kuo*, going beyond or transgressing against nature (ch. 64.5), ignorance *(yü)* is the original and sacred state of things; to thus to remain in ignorance or return to ignorance is the goal of all beings. The Taoist ruler is not one who knows all that goes on while keeping his people in the dark. Rather, he himself is also in a state of ignorance *(yü)* (ch. 20.4) or Chaos *(hun)* (ch. 15.2). The *Tao Te Ching* believes that the duller the government, the more wholesome its people (ch. 58.1). An all-knowing government as portrayed in George Orwell's *1984* interferes with the freedom and dignity of the people.

3. Two modes of knowing are distinguished, the verbal or spoken 智 and the non-verbal or unspoken 知. The former describes consciousness coming out from nature without return while the latter belongs to a reversive consciousness in dynamic union with the unconscious. The sage keeps himself and his people from the kind of knowledge that departs from nature. However, to be able to do this the sage must know the harmfulness of knowledge. This non-verbal knowing is the knowledge that saves *(hsüan te)*. It is the knowledge of *chi shih*, model or heaven's rule (ch. 10.3).

4. These three lines describing the reversive movement of the dark *te* through the clarifying, far away, and return show that *te* is one with the cyclical movement of Tao given in chapter 25. As that which clarifies *(ch'ing)* and is far away *(yüan)*, the dark *te* points to heaven (chs. 1, 6, and 65). The clarifying process is heaven's preparation for the stirrings of new life on earth (ch. 15.3). After having moved far away, *te* returns *(fan)* from heaven to earth (ch. 40.1). As the nurturing power that does not claim anything, the dark *te* is also the providential power of Tao on earth (chs. 10 and 51).

The goal of human history is the naturalization of humans through reintegration into the cyclical process of nature. If humans join in the cyclical process of nature, they will arrive at "the great harmony." This is also the message of chapter 25.4.

66

---

1. Rivers and seas can be kings of the hundred valleys,
Because they are good at flowing downwards *(hsia)*.
Therefore they can be kings of the hundred valleys.

2. Thus if you desire to be above the people,
Your words must reach down *(hsia)* to them.

If you desire to lead the people,
Your person (*shen,* body) must be behind them.

3. Thus the sage is above,
Yet the people do not feel his weight.
He stays in front,
Yet the people do not suffer any harm.
Thus all gladly praise him untiringly *(pu yen).*

4. Because he does not contend with any,
Therefore no one under heaven can contend with him.

General Comment

This chapter on the relationship between the ruler and the people is directly connected with chapter 61, which is on the relationship among states. The key concept is again *hsia,* low or downward flowing. In domestic affairs as well as in international relations, the ruler is to imitate water by reaching downward to the people, assisting in their own self-unfolding without imposing himself on them.

Detailed Comment

1. This is another example that nature is the seat of spirituality presenting humans with models for spiritual edification. Chapter 8.1 says that water flows downward and dwells "in places disdained by the many, therein it is near Tao." Chapter 32.4 says that "Tao in the world is like the valley streams flowing into rivers and oceans." Through this downward flowing, Tao gives birth to all and is respected by all (Ch. 51.2). In the same way rivers and seas in flowing downward sustain the life of the valleys and so become their kings.
   2. One who occupies a high position (the ruler) must identify with those in the low position (the people). This is the secret of peace between the ruler and ruled. In a democracy the one who rules represents the interest of the ruled. In ancient China, which lacked a representative government, this democratic spirit had to be inculcated in the ruler's person. A good ruler lives the life of the coincidence of opposites; he is both exalted and downward flowing, both leading and following.
   3. The ruler can be a burden and source of harm to his people (ch.60) unless he embodies in himself the downward-flowing quality of rivers and seas. A good ruler has the people's affection. According to chapter 17, however, such government is only the second best because the best government is not praised by its people—it is so withered away that the people hardly know of its existence.
   4. These lines are also found in chapter 22.2.

67

---

1. All under heaven say that my Tao is great,
That it seems useless *(pu hsiao)*.
Because it is great,
Therefore it seems useless.
If it were useful,
It would have long been small.

2. I have three treasures *(pao)*,
To hold and to keep:
The first is motherly love *(tz'u)*,
The second is frugality *(chien)*,
The third is daring not be at the world's front.

3. With motherly love one can be courageous,
With frugality one can be wide reaching,
Daring not be at the world's front,
One can grow to a full vessel *(ch'i)*.

4. Now to discard motherly love, yet to be courageous,
To discard frugality, yet to be wide reaching,
To discard staying behind, yet to be at the front,
One dies!

5. One with motherly love is victorious in battle,
Invulnerable in defense.
When Heaven wills to save a people,
It guards them with motherly love.

General Comment

This is a key chapter on Taoist ethics, which are indistinguishable from politics (Clark). The *Tao Te Ching* regards ethics or politics not so much as the way to happiness as the way to long life, for the state as well as for the individual.

Detailed Comment

1. *Pu hsiao,* literally, not like anything, has acquired the meaning of being useless. Since Tao is above all categorization, it is not like anything, thus it is useless (ch. 41). This is like saying that metaphysics is useless, since unlike accounting, engineering, or medicine it does not have any particular use. Of course, metaphysics is most important in providing the foundation of all that bears any particular use. In the same way Tao is useless because it is so very essential. To be useful in a particular way it would be the small, not the great.

2. The three cardinal virtues according to the *Tao Te Ching* are motherly love, frugality, and daring not be at the world's front.

The first treasure, *tz'u,* has been rendered many ways: "deep love" by Chan, "compassion" by Lau, Chang, and Blakney, "commiseration" by Young and Ames, and "pity" by Waley. In chapters 18 and 19 *tz'u* as the correlative of *hsiao,* filial love, means parental love. Primarily *tz'u* is the love that protects and nurtures, most characteristic of a mother's love.

The second treasure, *chien,* is usually rendered "frugality." *Chien* is organically connected with *p'u,* the original state of nature as the uncarved wood. *Chien* stands for the economy of nature that does not waste anything. When applied to the moral life it stands for the simplicity of desire. There is, however, no hint of asceticism or punishment of the body. For the *Tao Te Ching* the mind, not the body, is the source of discord.

The third treasure, daring not be at the world's front, is the Taoist way to avoid premature death. To be at the world's front is to expose oneself, to render oneself vulnerable to the world's destructive forces, while to remain behind and to be humble is to allow oneself time to fully ripen and bear fruit. This is a treasure whose secret spring is the fear of losing one's life before one's time. This fear of death, out of a love for life, is indeed the key to Taoist wisdom.

All three treasures are conserving and life-sustaining. Motherly love conserves by nurturing and sheltering all beings. Frugality conserves by prolonging the life spans of all beings, and daring not be at the world's front conserves by avoiding the destructive forces that cut short the lives of individuals or states. Each of the three treasures reflects the nature of Tao as the preserver of all (ch. 62.1). Tao is the Mother of the world (ch. 52); Tao is inexhaustible exactly because it is all-saving and does not waste; Tao remains behind, so that it fulfills all. To keep and hold these three treasures constitutes the ruler's imitation of Tao.

3. Here the reasons are given why these three are treasures of the Taoist. Motherly love is the foundation of true courage. The mother instinctively responds with courage to what threatens her young, paying no heed to her own

safety. Such an act of courage is not out of defiance of life. Confucius said: "One who is benevolent *(jen)* has no worries, one who knows *(chih)* is not perplexed, and one who is courageous has no fear" (*Analects* 14: 30). To the Taoist, true courage is born from the fear and dread of death (chs. 69 and 73).

Implied in the second treasure, frugality, is the recognition that nature's resources are finite. The very fecundity of nature and its seemingly inexhaustible supply is due to its frugality. Tao is a principle of plenitude exactly because it is a principle of economy. In a finite universe only the frugal can stretch the resources widely. True generosity is therefore premised on frugality (ch. 59), which is also praised by Confucius (*Analects* 4: 23).

"Daring not be at the world's front" has been interpreted by Wang Pi and Ho-shang Kung to mean that by staying behind to allow oneself full development one becomes a vessel more prominent than others; thereby one is fit to become a ruler or official. This traditional interpretation giving a utilitarian twist misses the spirit of these lines. "Daring not be at the world's front" encapsulates a philosophy that says live and let live. As Tao stays behind and below, nurturing all beings, allowing them to grow and become useful vessels, thus fulfilling them all, the categorical imperative for the ruler is to stay behind, to allow himself and his people the time and opportunity to grow to full vessels.

Translated into today's concerns, *tz'u* is the foundation of a compassionate and humanitarian government. *Chien* sets the policy not to waste or destroy the resources of the world and to ensure that future generations are provided for. Daring not be at the world's front slows down breakneck competitions and antagonistic confrontations to promote peace and growth among peoples and nations.

4. As the three treasures are life conserving, their opposites lead to death. Courage not out of love for life, generosity without frugality, daring be at the front instead of remaining at the rear—these are ways to death.

5. This last section serves as a transition to the next two chapters on military art. Here the first treasure, *tz'u*, is valued as the most important of the three. The deep religious sentiment here is the holy as a salvific power. Tao's love for the world is a love that saves and preserves. The belief is that the state defending itself with *tz'u*, out of compassion for the living and not out of wanton destructiveness, will ward off its attackers and survive. Why? Because it has appropriated the very nature of the everlasting Tao.

68

1. A good captain does not exhibit his martial prowess.
A good warrior does not get himself angry.
A good conqueror of enemies does not instigate a combat.
A good employer of people puts himself below them.

2. This is called the power *(te)* of non-contention.
This is called using the strength of others.
This is called perfection *(chi)* in matching the heaven of old.

General Comment

This chapter applies the three treasures of the preceding chapter to the condition
of both peace and war. It also reveals the secret of Chinese martial arts like the
T'ai-chi Ch'üan.

Detailed Comment

1. These lines show that one who is good at something does not lightly show off
his expertise, an application of the third treasure "dare not be at the front of the
world." Showing off one's own strength and abilities in the case of war invites
death and in the case of peace discourages others from putting forth their best
performance. On the other hand, an humble attitude disposes others to peace
and faithful execution of work.

2. In putting into practice the third treasure the Taoist at the same time
exemplifies in his person the first and second treasures. In saving lives, his own
and others, he embodies *tz'u,* the love that saves, and also *chien,* frugality. Being
humble he allows his people to fully develop and apply their talents. There is thus
no squandering of resources, natural or human. In this way he imitates the
perfection of the heaven of old which accomplishes everything without doing
anything *(wu-wei).*

69

---

1. In engaging in warfare it is said:
I dare not be the host but be the guest,
I dare not advance an inch but retreat a foot.

2. This is called to march without advancing,
To roll up one's sleeves without baring one's arms,
To throw a rope without an enemy,
To carry without a weapon.

3. Of all calamities *(huo)*,
None is greater than underestimating one's enemy.
In underestimating my enemy,
I risk losing my treasure *(pao)*.

4. Therefore when opposing armies are engaged in battle,
The sorrowful party will win.

General Comment

This chapter continues the topic of the two preceding chapters, and together with chapters 30 and 31 belongs to the group on military art. It is on how a Taoist ruler fights, or rather avoids, a war. In military affairs, as in all other affairs, the Taoist ruler follows Tao—he holds life to be the highest value.

Detailed Comment

1. In a war the Taoist does not conduct himself as if in command of the situation. He does not play the host but assumes the role of a guest or stranger, circumspect lest he commit a blunder (ch. 15.2). He would rather retreat than advance, heeding the warning in chapter 67.4 that "to discard staying behind, yet to be at the front" is to court death.

2. "To bare one's arms" and "throw a rope" in lines 2 and 3 are found in chapter 38.4. A pacifist, the Taoist ruler would rather avoid conflict than engage in one. Thus he marches without invading his neighbors, rolls his sleeves up his arms without intention of combat, etc.

3. In case one is forced to fight a defensive war, the counsel is to never

underestimate one's enemy. "Treasure" in the last line may be interpreted as the sacrificial bronze vessels giving rulers legitimacy to state power. In defeat these precious vessels are captured by the enemy, symbolizing the transfer of political power to the conqueror. Ho-shang Kung is not far off in taking "treasure" to mean one's life. Wang Pi interprets treasure *(pao)* as the three treasures (motherly love, frugality, and daring not be at the front of the world) mentioned in chapter 67.2, which are ways of conserving life. In light of what is said in (4), Wang Pi's interpretation carries more weight.

4. Fear of death is conducive to survival. The reluctant and sorrowful fighter who fights to preserve life will emerge the victor. Chapter 67.5 calls *tz'u*, motherly love, the love that brings victory in war. Only one who fights with great sorrow at the loss of life is on the side of heaven and so has the assistance of heaven. The same spirit is reflected in chapter 31.6 which tells us that victory marches are to be conducted as funerals, as mourning for the war dead. *Tz'u*, motherly love, as the treasure of a Taoist, ultimately characterizes Tao as the sorrowful mother.

70

---

1. My words *(yen)* are very easy to understand *(i-chih)*,
Very easy to put into practice *(i-hsing)*.
But no one under heaven can understand *(chih)* them,
No one can put them into practice.

2. Words *(yen)* have their ruler *(chün)*;
Events *(shih)* have their progenitor *(tsung)*.
Because people do not understand *(chih)* this,
Therefore they do not understand me.

3. Those who understand me are rare,
Those who follow *(tsê)* my teaching are (preciously) few *(kuei)*.
Therefore the sage wears hair-cloth,
While carrying jade in his breast.

General Comment

This is one of a group of chapters in which the author laments his teaching's lack of success (ch. 20). He is a lonely man who walks hiding his treasure. People have long been on the wrong path (ch. 58.3) and, forgetful of their origin, they thus do not understand *(chih)* the teaching of the sage.

Detailed Comment

1, 2. *I* means the easy. The message here, that the way is easy to know and easy to practice, is also that of the *I-ching.* The *Hsi Tzu* I, chapter 1, says:

> The Creative (Chien) is easy to know *(i-chih),*
> The Receptive (Kun) is simple to do.
> Easy, therefore easy to know,
> Simple, therefore easy to follow.
>
> (Cf. R. Wilhelm, 1950: 286)

The deepest truth is also the plainest and easiest to know and to carry out, since it is present everywhere. Yet people have so lost touch with the primal truth that they can no longer comprehend or practice it. As a result they look for solutions in the hard and difficult.

3. Kao Heng reads the second line to mean "Those who calumniate me occupy high positions," suggesting that Lao Tzu was not only lonely (ch. 20) but also persecuted, which explains why he left the state of Chou to go into exile in the state of Ch'in, as given in the biography of Lao Tzu by Ssu-ma Ch'ien (*Shih chi,* 63: 1a–3b).

Such a reading is unacceptable. There was no record that Lao Tzu left the state of Chou due to persecution. The chapter's structure also discourages such an interpretation. The first two lines of each stanza share a similar pattern of moving from words *(yen)* to actions *(hsing)*, or from *theoria (yen* and *chih*) to *praxis (shih* and *tse).* Kao Heng's reading would destroy the structural unity of the third stanza with the rest of the chapter.

71

1. From knowing to not knowing *(chih, pu chih),*
This is superior.
From not knowing to knowing *(pu chih, chih),*
This is sickness.
It is by being sick of sickness,
That one is not sick.

2. The sage is not sick.
Because he is sick of sickness,
Therefore he is not sick.

General Comment

The preceding chapter uses *chih,* to know or to understand the simple and easy, five times. In this chapter *chih* is looked upon as either a forward or backward movement. The forward-knowing process is a disease; the backward-unknowing process leads to health.

Detailed Comment

1. Most commentators read the first four lines this way:

To know, yet to think that one does not know, is superior.
To be not knowing, yet to think that one knows, is sickness.

Such a reading would put the *Tao Te Ching* in company with Confucius and Socrates. When Confucius said "When you know say that you know, when you don't know say that you don't know. This is knowledge" (*Analects* 2: 17), he spoke of the need for intellectual honesty. Someone who knows, yet thinks that he does not know, is a humble person; someone who does not know, yet thinks that he knows, deceives himself. Socrates was the wisest of mortals because he knew that he did not know. Others who did not know yet thought that they did know had to be shown that their so-called knowledge was ignorance. Life's goal for both Confucius and Socrates was to attain true knowledge or wisdom.

The *Tao Te Ching*, not regarding the acquisition of knowledge as conducive to union with Tao, cannot join the company of Confucius and Socrates. We must not only know that our knowledge is foolishness, but out of this awakening we must embrace our original foolishness full heartedly and so abandon any search for knowledge. The movement from knowing to not knowing restores us to Tao, but the movement from not knowing to knowing, or from the unconscious to the conscious, is a movement away from Tao. Knowledge, sharpening the divisions among beings, is sickness.

The phrase *chih pu chih* (to know not to know) in the first line echoes *yü pu yü* (to desire not to desire) and *hsüeh pu hsüeh* (to learn not to learn) in chapter 64.5. They are all restorative movements which heal the rift caused by consciousness.

2. While others move from the unknowing state to the knowing state, falling into sickness in the process (ch. 2), the sage returns from knowing to not knowing and thereby does not contract the disease of a consciousness cut off from its root.

72

1. When the people fear no power,
Then great power has indeed arrived.
Do not disturb them in their dwellings,
Do not weary them in their living.
It is because you do not weary *(pu yen)* them,
That they are not wearied of you.

2. Therefore the sage knows himself *(tzu chih)*,
But does not see himself *(tzu chien)*.
He loves himself *(tzu ai)*,
But does not exalt himself *(tzu kuei)*.
Therefore he leaves that and takes this.

General Comment

Ho-shang Kung entitles this chapter "On Loving Oneself" *(ai chi)*. True self-love in the case of the ruler means respecting the integrity of the people.

Detailed Comment

1. The greatest power does not oppress (Ch. 40.1). The best government is hardly noticed by its people (ch. 17.1). A government that intrudes upon the lives of the people, disturbing their habitats and destroying their livelihoods, invites their weariness *(yen)* and rebellion. A government that imitates nature inspires respect and compliance in the same way nature's laws are respected and obeyed. Such a government is not feared, yet its authority is unchallenged. This is the mark of great power.

The second character in line three has *hsia* 狎, to abuse, in the Wang Pi text. The Ho-shang Kung and other texts have *hsia* 狹, narrow. In the Ma-wang Tui texts, version A has *cha* 閘 and version B has *chia* 伊, both closer to the Wang Pi version. *Hsia* is the way a predator treats its prey. A patron of a whorehouse is called a *hsia ke*. Here it describes how a ruthless ruler enters a person's house to search and abuse its residents.

2. The enlightened ruler is as self-effacing as Tao. To see oneself is to stand apart from others (chs. 22.2 and 33.1), an act of pride and alienation.

73

1. One who is courageous out of daring *(kan)* is killed.
One who is courageous out of not daring lives.
Of these two, this is beneficial while that is harmful.
What heaven hates, who knows the reason?
Therefore even the sage takes it to be difficult.

2. The way of heaven:
Without contending *(cheng)*, it is yet good at winning,
Without speaking, it is yet good in responding,
Without being beckoned, it yet comes of its own accord,
Unhurried, it is yet good at planning *(mou)*.
The net of heaven is vast,
Widely spaced, yet missing nothing.

General Comment

This chapter shows great religious fervor. It marvels at the inscrutable ways of heaven, then ends with a declaration of faith in heaven's wonderful ways.

This chapter shares its central theme—that heaven helps one who fights courageously out of not daring—with chapter 67, which says that only one who loves *(tz'u)* like a parent is capable of courage and that only such courage leads to survival, and chapter 69, which says that in a war only he who is sorrowful wins. As such this is another chapter on military art, or on how to fight with heaven on one's side.

Detailed Comment

1. In believing that heaven saves those who are courageous not out of daring *(kan),* but out of not daring, the *Tao Te Ching*'s position contrasts with that of Hegel who says:

> And it is solely by risking life that freedom is obtained; only thus is it tried and proved that the essential nature of self-consciousness is not bare existence, is not the merely immediate form in which it at first make its appearance, is not its mere absorption in the expanse of life. . . . Through death, doubtless, there has arisen the certainty that both did stake their life, and held it lightly both in their own case and in the case of the other. . . .
>
> (1955: 233)

For Hegel the willingness to stake life and hold it lightly is an act of freedom by which self-consciousness proves its independence from life. From the Taoist viewpoint, to be courageous with daring *(kan),* an act of *hubris,* invites the hatred of heaven. Only that courage born of a holy reverence for and a humble submission to heaven as the source of life wins heaven's benediction (ch. 67.4 and 64.5). Chapter 30.3 tells us that *kuo,* the determination to fight in the face of death, is a courage that saves life, while *kan,* the daring of the strong who hold life lightly, is a courage that courts death. The courage of a Taoist is courage for nature and life, while the courage admired by Hegel and Socrates, who defined philosophy as the practice of death *(Phaedo,* 64), is the courage of thought in defiance of nature and life.

The last line does not appear in the Tang dynasty stone inscription (Kao Heng: 142), nor in the recently unearthed Ma-wang Tui texts. Both Wang Pi and Ho-shang Kung, however, have commented on it.

2. Wang Pi, Ho-shang Kung, and others have interpreted lines 2–5 as how things respond to heaven; thus, heaven does not contend and yet everything

proclaims its victory; heaven does not speak and yet all things respond to it; heaven does not beckon yet all things return to it on their own; heaven is unhurried, yet all affairs are well planned. I hold that these lines are not meant to describe how creatures respond to heaven, but to declare the providence of heaven on earth. In a most mysterious way heaven, without contending, speaking, being beckoned, or hurrying—which are human ways—wins, responds, arrives, and plans all in the most perfect manner. By these lines the Taoist declares his profound admiration and total trust in heaven. Heaven oversees all, thus all is well.

74

1. The people do not fear death,
Why threaten them with death?
Suppose the people always fear death,
One who does strange things *(ch'i)*,
I shall seize and kill,
Then who dares [to do strange things]?

2. Killing is carried out by the executioner.
To replace the executioner and kill,
Is like chopping wood in place of the master carpenter.
To chop wood in place of the master carpenter,
Rarely one does not hurt one's own hand.

General Comment

This chapter is against tyranny in government. As in the preceding chapter, it declares that ultimate power over life and death rests with heaven.

Detailed Comment

1. There are two reasons why people do not fear death. One is the development of consciousness leading to an awareness of values deemed higher than life; thus,

to realize these values people are willing to repudiate their lives. Some examples: Confucius's saying "A resolute person and a person of humanity *(jen)* will never seek to prolong life by injuring humanity, but would rather sacrifice life to fulfill humanity" *(Analects* 15: 8); Hegel's statement quoted in the preceding chapter that self-consciousness in affirming its freedom is willing to stake its life; and Patrick Henry's famous dictum "give me liberty, or give me death." To the Taoist these statements are wrong. There are no values higher than life. Since knowledge gives people the false sense that there are values higher than life, rulers must not mislead their people onto the path of knowledge. In the ideal Taoist state both ruler and people have forsaken the path of knowledge for the simplicity of nature. Such people love life and fear death.

A second reason why people do not fear death, stated here, is a government so tyrannical that the people can no longer live in peace. To the extent that they can no longer love life, they no longer fear death. We shall see in the next chapter that to those who look upon life as no better than death the death penalty is ineffective as a deterrent. A well-informed and efficient government always mobilizing its people produces disgruntled citizens, while a dull government making no demands on the people produces contented citizens (ch. 58). Knowledge is thus again the root cause of unrest in both government and people. When the ruler models his government on nature, disturbing the people neither in their dwellings nor livelihood (ch. 72), they will love life and fear death.

The structure of the last four lines here parallels the last two lines of chapter 3.2. Chapter 3 says that if the ruler keeps the people in the simplicity of nature, those individuals who wander in the path of knowledge will not dare to cause trouble. In this chapter the same message is put forth in much stronger terms. If the people love life and fear death, the ruler can then make execution the law of the land for those who do strange *(ch'i)* things. The conviction, of course, is that when people love life and fear death no one would want to do strange things.

2. What needs to be cultivated in both ruler and people alike is the sense of not daring, which preserves life. When the people fear death, and when the ruler dares not kill, government reaches its optimal condition. The power to kill is vested in heaven alone. A ruler who commits transgressions against the prerogative of heaven invites harm upon himself.

A passage in the *Hsi-tzu* (I, 11) speaks of one worthy to partake of heaven's secret in divination as someone "who in ancient times was wise, deeply aware, spiritual, martial and yet who did not kill *(erh pu sha che fu)."* (R. Wilhelm had neglected to translate these last five important characters. 1950: 317).

75

---

1. People are hungry.
Because their rulers levy too much grain tax,
Therefore they are hungry.

People are hard to rule.
Because their rulers rule by action *(wei)*,
Therefore they are hard to rule.

People take death lightly.
Because they are in thick pursuit of life,
Therefore they take death lightly.

2. One who has nothing to pursue in life,
Is wiser than one who values life.

General Comment

This chapter further determines that all suffering and rebelliousness of the people are due to the actions *(wei)* or overdoings of the rulers.

Detailed Comment

1. An ambitious government launching many grandiose projects must levy heavy taxes, causing the people to go hungry. In conscripting the labor of its citizens to build roads and palaces and in enlarging its army for military hegemony, the government disrupts the livelihoods of its people. As a result they become rebellious and death defying. That the people should hold their life lightly is prompted by a deep desire to go on living. They risk life in the hope that they may preserve it, thus even in risking life, they are "in thick pursuit of life."

2. These lines shift the ground from interactions between government and people to the root cause of why people are defiant of death. Again consciousness is identified as the culprit (ch. 24). To consciously pursue life one no longer enjoys life for its own sake. Life is now merely a means to other goals, hence dispensable. The person "who has nothing to pursue in life" lives his life

as an end in itself. Such a person is wiser than one who treasures life for the sake of other values.

The same point is driven home in chapters 57, 58, 65, 72, and 74.

76

1. At birth a person is soft *(jou)* and yielding *(jo)*,
At death hard *(chien)* and unyielding *(ch'iang)*.
All beings, grass and trees, when alive, are soft and bending,
When dead they are dry and brittle.
Therefore the hard and unyielding are companions of death,
The soft and yielding are companions of life.

2. Hence an unyielding army *(ping)* is destroyed *(mieh)*.
An unyielding tree breaks *(che)*.
The unyielding and great takes its place below,
The soft and yielding takes its place above.

General Comment

This chapter contrasts the conditions of death *(ssu)* with the conditions of life *(sheng)*. It is thus connected with the three preceding chapters, which all touch on death, whether it is on how heaven sends the daring to their deaths (ch. 73), or on why the people do not fear death (chs. 74 and 75). In this chapter death is identified as a condition of being unyielding *(ch'iang)*.

Detailed Comment

1. The contrast is between the pair of opposites *jo* (yielding) and *ch'iang* (unyielding), elsewhere translated as weak and strong. The character *ch'iang* means not only the strong, but also the oppressive and unbending. In the animal kingdom the strong live while the weak perish. Yet the text says throughout that the strong perish while the weak live (chs. 42, 55, and 78). This means that it is talking about life in plants rather than in animals. An animal after all is short lived, but a plant may be said to live indefinitely. In the plant, life dwells in the soft *(jou)* and

yielding *(jo)*. God as the almighty dominating all is modeled on the warrior or animal. Is characterizing Tao as weak and gentle (ch. 40) perhaps a hint that Tao was originally an agricultural deity?

2. The first two lines in the Wang Pi text read: "Hence an unyielding army *(ping* as army) does not win, an unyielding tree is struck down with a weapon *(ping* as weapon)." Kao Heng points out that these lines, as quoted in the *Wen Tzu,* the *Huai-nan Tzu,* and the *Lieh Tzu,* read: "Hence an unyielding army is destroyed *(mieh),* an unyielding tree breaks *(che)"* (1956: 145). This rhymed reading is clearly more ancient than and superior to the Wang Pi version.

Wang Pi's comment on the last two lines—comparing the unyielding and great to the trunk and root of the tree, and the soft and yielding to the branches and leaves that grow above—may not be appropriate. Tao, gentle and yielding (ch. 40), is the root of all beings (ch. 6). Inasmuch as the root and trunk supply food for the branches and leaves, and thus are very much the seat of life, they are not to be compared to the unyielding and great that are the companions of death. In making this analogy perhaps Wang Pi was thinking of chapter 36.2: "Sharp implements of a state must not be put on exhibit." As long as sharp weapons are hidden like the roots, they are not agents of death. In the same way, when the great and strong take the place below, there is no destruction. The same message is given in chapter 61.

77

1. The way of heaven,
Is it not like stretching a bow?
What is high up is pressed down,
What is low down is lifted up;
What has surplus *(yu yü)* is reduced,
What is deficient *(pu tsu)* is supplemented.

2. The way of heaven,
It reduces those who have surpluses,
To supplement those who are deficient.
The human way is just not so.

It reduces those who are deficient,
To offer those who have surpluses.
Who can offer his surpluses to the world?
Only a person of Tao.

3. Therefore the sage works *(wei)* without holding on to,
Accomplishes without claiming credit.
Is it not because he does not want to show off his merits?

General Comment

Heaven promotes equality (ch. 32.2), whereas humans are the cause of inequality in the world.

Detailed Comment

1. *Matthew* 25: 29 says: "To him that hath shall be given, but from him that hath not shall be taken even that which he hath." Such a view is the basis of Protestant ethics and represents the capitalist spirit. The *Doctrine of the Mean* (ch. 17) also says: "Heaven in its production of things necessarily assists according to the inner endowments of things. Thus a tree that is well established is nurtured, that is about to fall is overthrown" (Cf. Chan, 1963a: 102). The point here, however, is not how heaven promotes and brings to completion what is already in process in the tendencies of things. Here heaven is the reversive power in nature which, like a pendulum, swings back and forth so that the process is unending. Nature avoids irreversible extremes. Heaven's way is the natural self-balancing act in all beings.

2. What is the source of inequality in the world? Rousseau attributes it to the development of individual reason or cunning (209). Marx traces it to the institution of private property.

If we take note of the rigid hierarchy of the animal kingdom, the early societies' division into master and slave, Plato's classification of citizens into gold, silver, copper, and iron, and India's caste system seem but extensions of nature's inequality into the social world. Yet the *Tao Te Ching*'s position is this: Nature being dynamic and self-balancing, what is strong and dominant today becomes weak and submissive tomorrow in the natural realm. Human laws, however, interfere with nature's self-correcting rhythms. Inequalities and imbalances in human society, once legitimized by laws and institutions, do not revert on their own; the rich become richer and the poor poorer. Only a person of Tao, in tune with the self-balancing process of nature, offers surpluses to the deficient.

3. In these concluding lines, as in chapters 73, 74, and 76, the author

meditates on the relationship between humans and heaven. Since heaven presses down one who is puffed up and lifts up one who is depressed, the sage is humble. Like heaven he does not hold on to what he has accomplished (ch. 9.2).

78

1. Nothing under heaven
Is softer *(jou)* and weaker *(jo)* than water,
Yet nothing can compare with it
In attacking the hard *(chien)* and strong *(ch'iang)*.
Nothing can change *(i)* place with it.

That the weak overcomes the strong,
And the soft overcomes the hard,
No one under heaven does not know *(chih)*,
Though none can put it into practice.

2. Therefore a sage said:
"One who receives the filth of a state,
Is called the Master of the Altar of the Soil and Grain;
One who shoulders the evils of a state,
Becomes the king under heaven."
Straightforward words *(yen)* appear to be their reverse.

General Comment

This chapter continues the theme from chapters 76 to 79 that yielding is the secret to life, victory, peace, and harmony as well as to true rulership.

Detailed Comment

1. The same idea is expressed in chapter 43.1. The Taoist path to holiness requires no transcendence of the natural realm. By merely observing the activities of ordinary things like water (ch. 8), one is shown the deepest secret of the universe.
    2. The lord of all is the one who receives the filth of the state; in Christianity

Christ bears the burden of our sins. Confucianism also teaches that the ruler is the redeemer and mediator who bears the burden of sin for his people. The *Shu ching* says that the Shang dynasty ruler T'ang (acceded 1766 B.C.) prayed: "O Most August and Sovereign God. . . . If I have sinned, let it not concern the people; if the people have sinned, let the sin rest on me" (*Analects* 20: 3. Cf. Legge, 1971: 73).

The last line is another example of oppositional logic at work, that the most exalted is also the most humble. For other examples, see chapters 7 and 34.

79

1. In reconciling a great injury *(yüan)*,
There is sure to have some injury left.
How can this be good?

2. Therefore the sage holds the left tally,
He does not blame others.
One who has *te* is in charge of the tally,
One who has no *te* is in charge of the tax law.

3. The Tao of heaven has no partiality *(ch'in)*,
It is always with the good people.

General Comment

This chapter culminates the discussions in the preceding chapters by reflecting on the truly good as all-giving and forgiving. Stanzas (1) and (2) also furnish the best explanation for the last line in chapter 63(1): "Repay injury *(yüan)* with *te*."

Detailed Comment

1. There is a deep message apart from the straightforward meaning of these lines. If one remains on the level of distinction between good and evil, no amount of reconciliation between two sides can completely bury the sense of injury. The Japanese had paid nothing for their crime of slaughtering millions of Chinese.

Still, no amount of German restitution can remove the hurt the Holocaust victims suffered. Paul Edwards says: "It would most certainly be wrong for Jewish children to forgive their Nazi exterminators." In the same way no amount of reparation can obliterate the wrongs the Japanese committed. As long as we *remember* the wrong, the injury and rancor will be there. Is there then no freedom from pain and resentment in the minds of the victims? Are they then condemned to remembering and reliving the injuries, never attaining the peace of heaven? "How can this be good?" asks the *Tao Te Ching*.

According to the *Tao Te Ching* there can be no salvation in the realm of ethics that demands justice. When we "repay injury with justice" (*Analects* 14: 36), as Confucius demands, there is no forgiveness of injury. The wronged party, though vindicated, is still tormented by the wrong. But the religious person rises beyond justice to healing, a healing which comes only if we can rise above the distinction between good and evil, to the forgiveness and forgetfulness found in nature *(te)*. This is why chapter 63.1 tells us to "repay injury *(yüan)* with *te* (nature)." Only in the blissful oblivion of nature *(te)*, which sleeps and forgets that there had been any injuries at all, can there be real healing from injury.

2. The left tally is the debtor's tally, "the sign of inferiority in an agreement" (Lin Yutang, 1942: 308). The sage, being humble, acknowledges that he is the debtor. He has *te* (the goodness of nature). The tax collector, always remembering how much the people owe him, has no *te*. Rulers who levy too much grain tax cause the people to go hungry (ch. 75). The Bible tells us even the tax collector can be saved.

3. In these two lines the difficulty presented in chapter 5.1 that "heaven and earth are not humane *(pu jen)*" and "the sage is not humane *(pu jen)*" is solved. *Jen* as benevolence or humanity is the Confucian ideal of love, a love that extends to all humans. The *Tao Te Ching*, in claiming that heaven, earth, and the sage are not humane, denies that humans possess the highest standard of goodness or that they are most deserving of love. The highest goodness transcends the partiality for humans *(jen)* toward the love *(te)* for all beings, human or non-human.

But then, what does it mean that the Tao of heaven "is always with the good people"? Does this mean heaven is partial to the good? Not so. The Tao of heaven "is always with the good people" because they, having transcended the bifurcation of good and not good, the human and non-human, are always with the Tao of heaven. The *Shu-ching (Book of History)* says: "High Heaven has no partiality, it always assists those who have (the goodness of) *te*. People's hearts have no constancy *(ch'ang)*, they always remember those who are kind" (Cf. Legge, 1971: 189). Chapter 23.2 says that "one who follows Tao identifies with Tao" and that "one who identifies with Tao is glad to be with Tao." Since the good are always with heaven, heaven is also always with them.

80

---

1. A small state with few people.
Let the implements *(ch'ih)* for ten and hundred men be unused,
Let the people fear death such that they do not move far away.
Although there are boats and carriages,
There are no places to ride them to.
Although there are weapons and armours,
There are no occasions to display them.
Let the people again tie ropes and use them (as memory aids).

2. Let them enjoy their food,
Consider their clothing beautiful,
Be contented with their dwellings,
And happy with their customs.
The neighbouring states overlooking one another,
The dogs' barkings and cocks' crowings are heard from other states,
Yet till they are old and dying the people do not visit one another.

General Comment

In this next to last chapter we are presented the ideal Taoist state when human society blends in seamlessly with the society of nature. What we witness here is not the beginning of human institutions but their withering away. The ideal Taoist state represents the result of humankind's about-face from the destructive forces that have been gathering momentum since the dawn of civilization. We are offered here a way to "long life and enduring vision" (ch. 59) for societies and states.

Detailed Comment

1. To keep the pulse of human society synchronized with the rhythm of nature, the *Tao Te Ching* subscribes to Schumacher's motto—small is beautiful—as well as to an economics of no growth.

The character for machines, *chi,* 機 does not appear in the text. What we have here is *ch'i* 器, an implement (chs. 11, 28, 29, 31, 36, and 41). Implements for ten and hundred men *(shih pai chih ch'i)* are machines. According to Yü Yu, they refer to military weapons requiring ten and a hundred soldiers for their operation (Kao Heng: 150–151). This is the only reference to machines in the text, and includes the advice that they be unemployed.

Machines have been hailed as a great blessing liberating humankind from the drudgeries of labor, thus making possible the abolishing of slavery. Taoism's contribution to the development of Chinese science and technology, through the monumental works of Joseph Needham, has been well documented. In the texts of the *Tao Te Ching* and the *Chuang Tzu,* however, we don't detect a pro-science attitude. Taoism sees a deep danger in the invention and use of machines. As concrete embodiments of the spirit of conquest, machines are direct results of human struggle and scheming *(chi)* against nature, and they indirectly promote struggle and scheming among humans. The *Chuang Tzu,* chapter 12, relates the meeting of Tzu-kung, a disciple of Confucius representing the spirit of progress, with an old gardener preparing his fields for planting with great hardship. Upon Tzu-kung's suggestion that he use labor-saving machines, the old man flushes with anger:

> I've heard my teacher say, where there are machines, there are bound to be machine worries; where there are machine worries, there are bound to be machine hearts. With a machine heart in your breast, you've spoiled what was pure and simple; and without the pure and simple, the life of the spirit knows no rest. Where the life of the spirit knows no rest, the Way will cease to buoy you up. It's not that I don't know about your machine—I would be ashamed to use it!

> (Watson: 134–136)

The Taoist state is a retrenchment from civilization. It represents humanity's decision to pull back from unmitigated growth—political, economic, scientific, technological, or military. Wars have been fought not just for self-preservation. Humans have always marched to war and their deaths armed with the sense of moral righteousness (chs. 2, 18, and 38). Since in the Taoist state the people return to no knowledge, no desire, and no action, they are not roused to conflict or war and so there are no occasions for the deployment of military weapons. The spirit of adventure and greed, and the restlessness of body, mind, and soul, what goaded humans of another age to risk their lives to conquer strange lands and accomplish new feats are all things of the past in the Taoist state. It offers a sharp contrast to the United States where the average citizen, according to Vance Packard, moves about fourteen times in his life. In the Taoist state boats and carriages have outlived their usefulness. Humans have not only outgrown their need for civilization, they are now like plants so firmly rooted in the soil that to move about would be to court death. Computers also have no use in the Taoist state. Life is so simple that no complicated memory aids are needed. The people return to using knotted cords to assist in their remembering and simple reckoning.

2. This does not mean that life is dull in the Taoist state. On the contrary, it seems that only in the Taoist state does Marx's statement "the cultivation of the five senses is the work of all previous history" (1963: 161) become an accomplished fact. Only when humans are no longer goaded by the restlessness that comes with the consciousness of new values are they contented with the food they eat, the clothes they wear, the houses they live in, and the festivals they celebrate. The keynote of the Taoist state is contentedness *(chih tsu)* (chs. 33, 44, and 46), the foundation of happiness.

Once humans return to nature their relationships with one another also undergo a fundamental change. People need to form alliances with one another when they are confronted with a common enemy. Dictators know how to create common enemies and national emergencies to distract and unite the people. In the Taoist state, where the peace of nature reigns, humans are contented with their lot and no longer seek out each other on false pretenses. As beasts and plants do not seek out one another, there is also little traffic among the people. The barking of their dogs and the crowing of their cocks puncture the silence of nature, but people find no need to associate with one another. Human relations now return to the peace and oblivion of nature. Chapter 6 of the *Chuang Tzu* puts it this way:

> When the spring is dry and the fish find themselves on land, they spit moisture at one another and smear one another with froth. It would be better if they forget one another in rivers and lakes. Rather than denounce Chieh or praise Yao, it would be better if both are forgotten in the transformation of Tao.
>
> (Cf. Watson: 80)

81

1. Truthful *(hsin)* words *(yen)* are not beautiful,
Beautiful *(mei)* words are not truthful.
The good *(shan)* does not distinguish,

One who distinguishes *(pien)* is not good.
One who knows *(chih)* does not accumulate knowledge,
One who accumulates knowledge *(po)* does not know.

2. The sage does not hoard.
Having worked *(wei)* for his fellow beings,
The more he possesses.
Having donated himself to his fellow beings,
The more abundant he becomes.

3. The way of heaven,
It benefits *(li)*, but does not harm.
The way of the sage,
He works *(wei)*, but does not contend.

General Comment

This concluding chapter reiterates the faith in Tao as the benevolent power in
the world and in the sage as exemplifying the spirit of peace in the world.

Detailed Comment

1. Here we have three pairs of opposites representing two ways of life. Truthful
(hsin) words, representing unembellished *(p'u,* the uncarved wood, chs. 28 and
32) nature are the opposite of beautiful appearances *(mei)* which contain no
authenticity (ch. 2.1). Goodness *(shan)* which accepts both the good and the not
good (ch. 49.2) is the opposite of clear distinction *(pien,* ch. 45) between good
and evil, with every good burdened by evil. Speechless knowing *(chih)* of the
unitive ground (ch. 56.1) is the opposite of wide learning *(po)* of many things
without their unity (ch. 47). In each case the original and simple stand for the
authentic, the embellished, and the accumulated represent the inauthentic.

2. The sage abides in the authentic. He does not join in the foray of those
who amass wealth and power (chs. 9 and 20). Like the creative Goodness which
pours out and gives without end (ch. 34), the sage offers himself as a donation
to the world.

3. Notwithstanding the statement in chapter 5.1 that heaven and earth are
unkind, the firm belief throughout the *Tao Te Ching* is that heaven is providential. Imitating heaven the sage works to fulfill all beings, not to dominate or harm
them.

BIBLIOGRAPHY

Altizer, Thomas J. J. 1966. *The Gospel of Christian Atheism.* Philadelphia: The Westminster Press.

Aquinas, St. Thomas. 1945. *Summa Contra Gentiles (SCG). Basic Writings of Saint Thomas Aquinas.* Edited by Anton C. Pegis. 2 vols. New York: Random House.

———. 1945. *Summa Theologica (ST). Basic Writings of Saint Thomas Aquinas.* Edited by Anton C. Pegis. 2 vols. New York: Random House.

———. *The Soul.* 1949. Translated by J. P. Rowan. St. Louis: B. Herder.

Aristotle. 1941. *Basic Writings.* New York: Random House.

Bahm, Archie J. 1958. trans. *Tao Teh King.* New York: Frederick Ungar.

Bergson, Henri. 1912 [1929]. *Matter and Memory.* Translated by N. M. Paul and W. S. Palmer. New York: Macmillan.

Blakney, Raymond B. 1955. *The Way of Life.* New York: Mentor.

Bodde, Derk. 1961. "Myths of Ancient China." *Mythologies of the Ancient World.* Edited by S. N. Kramer. Garden City, N.Y.: Doubleday.

Boltz, Judith M. 1987. *A Survey of Taoist Literature, Tenth to Seventeenth Centuries.* Berkeley: University of California Press.

Bonhoffer, Dietrich. 1959. *Ethics.* New York: Macmillan.

———. 1963. *Letters and Papers from Prison.* New York: Macmillan.

Brown, Norman O. 1959. *Life Against Death.* Middletown, Conn: Wesleyan University Press.

Buchanan, James. 1983. "Creation and Cosmos: The Symbolics of Proclamation and Participation." *Cosmology and Theology.* Edited by Tracy, David, and Nicholas Lash. New York: The Seabury Press.

Butler, Dom Cuthbert. 1966. *Western Mysticism.* New York: Harper & Row.

Carus, Paul. 1900–1901. "The Authenticity of the *Tao Teh King.*" *The Monist*: 11: 574–601.

————. 1909 [1945]. trans. *The Canon of Reason and Virtue*. Chicago: Open Court.

Chan, Wing-tsit. 1963a. ed. and trans. *A Source Book in Chinese Philosophy*. Princeton: Princeton University Press.

————. 1963b. trans. *The Way of Lao Tzu*. New York: Bobbs-Merrill.

————. 1963c. trans. *The Platform Scripture, The Basic Classic of Zen Buddhism*. New York: St. John's University Press.

————. 1975a. "Chu Hsi's Appraisal of Lao Tzu." *Philosophy East and West*: 25/2:131–144.

————. 1975b. "Chu Hsi's Criticism of Lao Tzu and on His Relationship to the Neo-Confucian Concept of 'Production and Reproduction.'" *Tsing Hua Journal of Chinese Studies*, New Series (1975): XI/1 & 2: 89–104.

Chang, Chung-yüan. 1963 [1970]. *Creativity and Taoism*. New York: The Julian Press, Harper & Row.

Chang, Kwang-chih. 1964. *The Archaeology of Ancient China*. New Haven: Yale University Press.

Chavannes, Edouard. 1905. trans. *Les memoires historiques de Se-ma Ts'ien*. Vol. 5. Paris: Leroux.

Ch'en, Chu. 1934. *Chu Lao Tzu* (Commentary on the *Lao Tzu*). Shanghai: Commercial Press.

Chen, Ellen M. 1973a. "Is There a Doctrine of Physical Immortality in the *Tao Te Ching?*" *History of Religions*, February.

————. 1973b. "The Concept of Nature in Chinese Taoism." *Philosophy East and West*, October.

————. 1975. "The Dialectic of *Chih* (Reason) and *Tao* (Nature) in the *Han Fei Tzu.*" *Journal of Chinese Philosophy* 2 (1975): 2: 1–21.

Ch'en, Hao. n.d. *Li-chi chi-shuo* (Collected Discussions on the *Li-chi*), in *Ssu-shu wu-ching*. 3 vols. Shanghai: World Publishing Co.

Ch'en, Kuo-fu. 1963. *Tao-tsang yüan-liu k'ao* (Studies in the Evolution of the Taoist Canon). Peking: Chung Hua Book Co.

Chen, Shih-hsiang. 1957. "On the Historical and Religious Significance of the Tun-Huang Manuscript of *Lao-Tzu*, Book I, with Commentaries by 'Hsiang Erh'." *Tsing Hua Journal of Chinese Studies*, New Series I, 2: 41–62.

Chiang, Hsi-ch'ang. 1937 [1971]. *Lao Tzu chiao-ku* (Lao Tzu Collated and Explained). Shanghai: Commercial Press; Taipei: Ming Lun Press.

Chiang Hsia-an. 1931 [1975]. ed. *Hsien-Ch'in ching-chi k'ao* (Textual Criticism on Pre-Ch'in Classics). Shanghai: Commercial Press; Taipei: Ho Lo Pictorials and Book Co.

Chiao, Hung. 1962. *Lao Tzu i* (Wings to the *Lao Tzu*). Taipei: Kuang Wen Book Co.

Ch'ien, Mu. 1957. *Chuang-Lao t'ung-pien* (General Discussions on Lao Tzu and Chuang Tzu). Kowloon: New Asia Research Institute.

————. 1971. *Chu-tzu hsin hsueh an*. 5 vols. Taipei: San Ming Book Co.

Ch'ing, Hsi-t'ai. 1980. *Chung-kuo tao-chiao ssu-hsiang shih kang* (Outline of a History of Thought in Chinese Religious Taoism). Chengdu: Jen Min Press.

Chu, Ch'ien-chih. 1958 [1971]. *Lao Tzu chiao-shih* (*Lao Tzu* Collated and Explained). Shanghai, Taipei reprint: Ming Lun Press.

Clark, John P. 1983. "On Taoism and Politics." *The Journal of Chinese Philosophy*, (1983): 10: 65–88.

Comte, Auguste. 1974. *The Positive Philosophy*. New York: AMS Press.

Conze, Edward. 1959. *Buddhist Scriptures*. Baltimore: Penguin Classics.

———. 1964. *Buddhist Texts Through the Ages*. New York: Harper & Row.

Couling, Samuel. 1917 [1965]. ed. *Encyclopaedia Sinica*. Taipei reprint: Chinese Materials and Research Aids Center.

Cox, Harvey. 1965. *The Secular City*. New York: Macmillan.

Creel, Herrlee G. 1929. *Sinism, A Study of the Evolution of the Chinese World-View*. Chicago: Open Court.

———. 1970. *What is Taoism*. Chicago: University of Chicago Press.

Cua, A.S. 1978. *Dimensions of Moral Creativity*. University Park, Pa. and London: Pennsylvania State University Press.

———. 1985. *Ethical Argumentation: A Study of Hsün Tzu's Moral Epistemology*. Honolulu: University Press of Hawaii.

Dawson, Christopher. 1929. *Progress & Religion, An Historical Enquiry*. New York: Sheed and Ward.

DeBary, W. T. 1963. ed. *Sources of Chinese Tradition*. New York: Columbia University Press.

de Groot, J. J. M. 1969. *The Religious System of China*. 6 vols. New York: Paragon Book Gallery. Taipei reprint: Ch'eng Wen Publishing Company.

Demiéville, Paul. 1948. "Le Miroir spirituel." *Sinologica* I/2: 112–37.

Dewey, John. 1929. *The Quest for Certainty*. New York: G. P. Putnam's Sons.

Dondeyne, A. 1958. *Contemporary European Thought and Christian Faith*. Pittsburgh: Duquesne University Press.

Dubs, Homer H. 1941–1944. "The Date and Circumstances of Lao-dz." *Journal of American Oriental Society*, 61 (1941): 215–221; 62 (1944):8–13, 300–304; 64 (1944): 24–27.

Dupre, Louis. 1969. "Themes in Contemporary Philosophy of Religion." *The New Scholasticism*, 43/4: 577–601.

Durkeim, Emile. 1915. *The Elementary Forms of the Religious Life*. Translated by Joseph Ward Swain. London: George Allen & Unwin.

Duyvendak, J. J. L. 1954. *Tao Te Ching*. London: John Murray.

———. 1928 [1963]. trans. *The Book of Lord Shang*. London: Arthur Probsthain; Chicago: University of Chicago Press.

Eberhard, Wolfram. 1968. *The Local Cultures of South and East China*. Translated by Alide Eberhard. Leiden: E. J. Brill.

Edwards, Paul. 1968. "Difficulties in the Idea of God." *The Idea of God.* Edited by Edward Madden, et al. Springfield, Ill: Charles C. Thomas.

Eliade, Mircea. 1959. "Methodological Remarks on the Study of Religious Symbolism." *History of Religions.* Chicago: University of Chicago Press.

———. 1964. "The Quest for the 'Origins' of Religion." *History of Religions,* 4: 154–169.

———. 1971. *The Forge and the Crucible.* New York: Harper Torchbook.

Englebert, Omer. 1965 [1979]. *St. Francis of Assisi: A Biography.* Ann Arbor: Servant Books.

Erkes, Eduard. 1950. *Lao Tzs (With Ho Shang-Kung's Commentary).* Switzerland: Ascona.

Feuerbach, Ludwig. 1957. *The Essence of Christianity.* New York: Harper & Row.

Findlay, J. N. 1948–1949. "Can God's Existence be Disproved?" *Mind* (April 1957): 176–183; (July 1958): 352–354.

Fingarette, Herbert. 1972. *Confucius—The Secular as Sacred.* New York: Harper & Row.

Forke, A. 1925. *The World-Conception of the Chinese.* London: Probsthain.

Frazer, James George. 1935 [1963]. *The Golden Bough, The Magic Art.* Abridged Ed. Vol. 1. New York: Macmillan.

Freud, Sigmund. 1918. *Totem and Taboo.* New York: Dodd, Mead and Co.

Fu, Ch'in-chia. *Chung-kuo tao chiao shih* (History of Chinese Taoist Religion). Taipei reprint: Commercial Press, 1967.

Fu, I. *Chiao-ting ku-pen Lao Tzu* (Ancient Text of the *Lao Tzu*).

Fung, Yu-lan. 1952–1953. *A History of Chinese Philosophy.* Translated by Derk Bodde. 2 vols. Princeton: Princeton University Press.

———, Jen, Chi-yu et al. 1959 [1972]. *Lao-tzu che hsueh t'ao lun chi* (Collection of Discussions on the *Lao Tzu*). Hong Kong: Ch'ung Wen Book Co.

Gebser, Gean. 1985. *The Ever-Present Origin.* Athens, Ohio: Ohio University Press.

Gersh, S. E. 1973. *A Study of Spiritual Motion in the Philosophy of Proclus.* Leiden: E. J. Brill.

Giles, Herbert A. 1901 [1958]. *History of Chinese Literature.* London: W. Heinemann; New York: Grove Press.

———. 1905 [1969]. *Religions of Ancient China.* New York reprint: Books for Libraries Press.

———. 1915. *Confucianism and its Rivals.* London: Williams & Norgate.

Girardot, N. J. 1983. *Myth and Meaning in Early Taoism.* Berkeley: University of California Press.

Graham, A. C. 1960. trans. *The Book of Lieh-tzu.* London: John Murray.

Granet, Marcel. 1922 [1975]. *The Religion of the Chinese People.* Translated by Maurice Freedman. New York: Harper & Row.

———. 1926 [1959]. *Danses et Legendes de la Chine ancienne.* Paris reprint: University of France.

———. 1930 [1957]. *Chinese Civilization.* London: Routledge & Kegan Paul; New York: Alfred A. Knopf, Barnes & Noble.

———. 1932. *Festivals and Songs of Ancient China.* Translated by E. D. Edwards. New York: E. P. Dutton & Co.

Grava, Arnolds. 1963. "Tao: An Age-Old Concept in its Modern Perspective." *Philosophy East and West,* October: 235–250.

Griffith, Gwilym O. 1946. *Interpreters of Reality, A Comment on Heracleitus, Lao-tse and the Christian Faith.* London: Lutterworth Press; Chicago: A. R. Allenson.

Hall, David L. 1978. "Process and Anarchy—A Taoist Vision of Creativity." *Philosophy East and West* 28.

———. 1982. *The Uncertain Phoenix, Adventures Toward a Post-Cultural Sensibility.* New York: Fordham University Press.

Han-shan Te-ch'ing. 1979. *Tao te ching ming chu hsuan chi* (Selected Collection of Famous Commentaries on the *Tao Te ching*). Edited by Hsiao T'ien-shih, et al. Taipei: Chung kuo tzu hsueh ming chu chi ch'eng.

Han, Ying. 1952. *Han Shih Wai Chuan, Han Ying's Illustrations of the Didactic Application of the Classic of Songs.* Translated by J. R. Hightower. Cambridge, Mass.: Harvard University Press.

Han, Yu. *Ch'ang-li hsien-sheng wen-chi.* SPTK edition.

Harper, Donald J. 1978–1979. "The Han Cosmic Board *(Shih)." Early China* 4: 1–10.

Hawkes, David. 1959. *Ch'u Tz'u: The Songs of the South.* Oxford: Clarendon Press.

Hegel, G. W. F. 1953. *Reason in History.* New York: The Liberal Arts Press.

———. 1955. *The Phenomenology of Mind.* New York: Macmillan.

Heidegger, Martin. 1977. *Basic Writings.* Edited by D. F. Krell. New York: Harper & Row.

Hendry, George Stuart. 1980. *The Theology of Nature.* Philadelphia: The Westminster Press.

Henricks, Robert G. 1978–1979. "A Note on the Question of Chapter Division in the Ma-wang Tui Manuscripts of the Lao-Tzu." *Early China* (1978–1979): 4: 49–51.

Ho, Ch'i-min. 1967. *Wei Chin ssu hsiang yu t'an feng* (Philosophy and Pure Talk in *Wei* and *Chin* Dynasties). Taipei: China Committee for Publication Aid and Prize Awards.

Ho, Ping-ti. 1975. *The Cradle of the East.* Chicago: University of Chicago Press.

Ho-shang Kung. 1950. *Lao Tzu chu: Ho-shang-kung's Commentary on Lao-tse.* Translated by Eduard Erkes. Ascona, Switzerland: Artibus Asiae Publishers.

Hobbes, Thomas. 1965. *Leviathan.* Edited by Michael Oakeshott. Oxford: Basil Blackwell.

Hou, Wai-lu. 1944. *Chung-kuo ku-tai ssu-hsiang hsueh-shuo shih* (History of Ancient Chinese Thought and Theories). Chunking: Wen-feng.

———. 1979. *Chung-kuo ku tai she-hui shih lun* (On A History of Ancient Chinese Society). Hong Kong: San Lien Book Co.

Hsiao T'ien-shih et al. 1977–1979. *Tao te ching ming chu hsuan chi* (Selected Collection of Famous Commentaries on the *Tao Te ching*). Taipei: Chung kuo tzu hsueh ming chu chi ch'eng.

Hsü, Fu-kuan. 1975. "Pai-shu *Lao-tzu* so fan-ying ch'u-te jo-kan wen-t'i" (Some Problems Reflected by the Silk Manuscripts of *Lao Tzu*). *Ming Pao Yueh-k'an* (Ming Pao Monthly). (June): 114:97.

Hsü, Hsü-sheng. 1962. *Chung-kuo ku shih ti chuan shuo shih tai* (The Legendary Period of Ancient Chinese History). 2nd ed. Peking: Science Publishing Co.

Hsü, Shen. 1969. *Shuo wen chieh tzu.* Taipei Commercial Press.

Hsün Tzu. 1963. *Hsün Tzu, Basic Writings.* Translated by Burton Watson. New York: Columbia University Press.

Hu, Shih. 1919 [1938]. *Chung-kuo che-hsueh shih ta-kang* (Outline of the History of Chinese Philosophy). Shanghai, Hong Kong reprint: Commercial Press.

————. 1928 [1966]. *Development of the Logical Method in Ancient China.* Shanghai: Oriental Book Co.; New York: Paragon House.

————. 1931. "Religion and Philosophy in Chinese History." *Symposium on Chinese Culture.* Edited by Sophia H. Chen Zen. Shanghai: Institute of Pacific Relations.

————. 1934 [1963]. "Religion in Chinese Life." *The Chinese Renaissance.* Chicago: University of Chicago Press; New York: Paragon House. 80–81.

————. 1935 [1953]. *Shuo ju* (On the Literati). *Hu Shih wen-ts'un.* Vol. 4:1–81. Taipei: Far East Pictorial and Book Co.

————. 1937. "A Criticism of Some Recent Methods used in Dating Lao Tzu." *Harvard Journal of Asiatic Studies.* 2: 373–397.

————. 1962. *Huai-nan wang shu* (On the *Huai-nan Tzu*). Taipei: Commercial Press.

Huai-nan Tzu. 1935 [1966]. *Tao, The Great Luminant.* Translated by Evan Morgan. Shanghai: Kelly and Walsh; Taipei reprint: Ch'eng-Wen Publishing Co.

Hurvitz, Leon. 1961. "Recent Japanese Study of Lao-tzu: Kimura Eiichi's *Roshi no shin Kenkyu.*" *Monumenta Serica.* 20: 311–367.

Izutsu, Toshihiko. 1983. *Sufism and Taoism.* Berkeley, Calif.: University of California Press.

James, E. O. 1961. *Comparative Religion.* New York: Barnes & Noble.

Jan, Yun-hua. 1978. "The Silk Manuscripts on Taoism." *T'oung Pao.* 63/1: 65–84.

Jao, Tsung-i. 1956. *Lao Tzu hsiang-erh chu chiao chien* (A Study of the Hsiang-erh Commentary on the *Lao-tzu*). Hong Kong: Tong Nam., 1956.

Jaspers, Karl. 1962. *The Great Philosophers.* 2 vols. Edited by Hannah Arendt. Translated by Ralph Manheim. New York: Harcourt, Brace & World.

John of the Cross. 1961. *Spiritual Canticle.* 3rd ed. Translated by E. Allison Peers. New York: Doubleday Image Books.

Kaltenmark, Max. 1969. *Lao Tzu and Taoism.* Translated by Roger Greaves. Stanford, Calif.: Stanford University Press.

————. 1979. "The Ideology of the *T'ai-p'ing Ching.*" *Facets of Taoism.* Edited by Holmes Welch and Anna Seidel. New Haven: Yale University Press.

Kao, Heng. 1956. *Ch'ung-ting Lao Tzu cheng-ku* (Revised Collation of the *Lao Tzu*). Peking: Chung-hua Press.

———— and Ch'ih Hsi-chao. 1974. "Shih-t'an Ma-wang-tui Han-mu chung-te pai-shu *Lao-tzu*" (Notes on the Silk Manuscript Text of *Laotzu* Found in the Han Tomb No. 3 at Ma-wang-tui, Changsha). *Wen Wu* (Cultural Relics). 11: 1–7.

Karlgren, Bernhard. 1932. "The Poetical Parts in Lao-tsi." *Goteborgs Hogskolas Arsskrift.* Goteborg. 37: 1–45.

Kimura, Eiichi. 1959. "A New Study on Lao-tzu." *Philosophical Studies of Japan.* I: 85–104.

Ko, Hung. *Pao P'u Tzu, Nei-P'ien* (Inner Chapters). See James Ware.

Ku, Chieh-kang. 1916–1940 [1927–1941]. ed. *Ku-shih pien* (Discussions on Ancient History). 7 vols. Peiping: Pu She; Hong Kong: T'ai P'ing Book Co.

Kuan Chung. 1954. *Kuan-Tzu.* Translated by T'an Po-fu and Wen Kung-wen. Carbondale, Ill.: Lewis Maverick.

————. 1965. *Kuan-Tzu.* Translated by W. Allyn Rickett. Hong Kong: Hong Kong University Press.

Kuan, Feng and Lin, Yu-shih. 1971. "Third Discussion of lao Tzu's Philosophy." *Chinese Studies in Philosophy.* 2: 158–186.

Kuo, Mo-jo. 1945 [1962]. *Ch'ing-t'ung shih-tai* (The Bronze Age). Chungking, Peking reprint: Science Publishing.

Lach, Donald. 1945. "Leibniz and China." *Journal of the History of Ideas.* 6: 436–455.

Lagerway, John. 1987. *Taoist Ritual in Chinese Society and History.* New York: Macmillan.

Lang, Andrew. 1898 [1968]. *The Making of Religion.* New York: AMS Press.

Lao Tzu che-hsueh t'ao-lun chi (Symposium on the Philosophy of Lao Tzu). 1959 [1972]. Hong Kong: Ch'ung Wen Book Co.

Laszlo, Ervin. 1983. *Systems Science & World Order.* New York: Pergamon Press.

Lau, D. C. 1958. "The Treatment of Opposites in *Lao Tzu.*" *Bulletin of the School of Oriental and African Studies.* 21/2: 344–360.

————. 1963. trans. *Lao Tzu Tao Te Ching.* Baltimore: Penguin Books.

————. 1970. trans. *Mencius.* Baltimore: Penguin Books.

Legge, James. 1960. trans. *The Chinese Classics.* 5 vols. Hong Kong reprint: Hong Kong University Press.

————. 1885 [1967]. trans. *The Li Ki.* 2 vols. Oxford: The Clarendon Press; New Hyde Park, New York: University Books.

————. 1891. trans. *The Texts of Taoism.* Oxford: The Clarendon Press.

————. 1971. trans. *Shu Ching.* Modernized by Clae Waltham. Chicago: Henry Regnery Co.

Lévi-Strauss, Claude. 1966. *The Savage Mind.* Chicago: University of Chicago Press.

Liang, Ch'i-chiao. n.d. *Chung-kuo ku-tai ssu-ch'ao* (Thought Currents in Ancient China). *Yin-ping-shih ch'ung chu* (Collected Works of Yin-ping Study). No. 5. Shanghai: Commercial Press.

————. 1923. *Ku-shu chen-wei chi ch'i nien-tai* (Authenticity of Ancient Texts and Their Dates). *Yin-ping-shih ho-chi* (Collection of Literary Works of Yin-ping Study). Shanghai and Taipei: Chung Hua Book Co.

Liao, W. K. 1939 [1960]. trans. *The Complete Works of Han Fei Tzu.* 2 vols. London: Arthur Probsthain.

Lieh Tzu. 1960. *The Book of Lieh Tzu.* Trans. A.C. Graham. London: Murray.

Lin, Paul J. 1977. *A Translation of Lao Tzu's Tao Te Ching and Wang Pi's Commentary.* Ann Arbor: Center for Chinese Studies, University of Michigan.

Lin Tung-chi. 1947. "The Chinese Mind: Its Taoist Substratum." *Journal of the History of Ideas.* 8: 259–273.

Lin, Yutang. 1942. *The Wisdom of Lao Tzu.* New York: Modern Library.

————. 1943. *The Wisdom of Confucius.* New York: Modern Library.

Liu, Hsiang. *Lieh-hsien chuan* (Biographies of the Many Immortals). SPTK.

————. *Shuo-yüan* (Collection of Discourses). SPTK.

Liu, I-cheng. 1948–1952. *Chung-kuo wen-hua-shih* (History of Chinese Culture). 3 vols. Taipei: Cheng Chung Book Co.

Lo, Ken-tse. 1958 [1967]. *Chu-tzu k'ao-so* (Inquiries on Ancient Philosophers). Peking and Hong Kong: Hsueh Lin Book Co.

Lokuang, Stanislas. 1957. *Ju-chia hsing-shang-hsueh* (Confucian Metaphysics). Taipei: Chung Hua Publishing Committee.

Lorenz, Konrad. 1967. *On Aggression.* New York: Bantam.

Lovejoy, Arthur O. 1936. *The Great Chain of Being.* Cambridge, Mass.: Harvard University Press.

Lovelock, J. E. 1979. *Gaia: A New Look at Life on Earth.* New York: Oxford University Press.

Lü-shih ch'un-ch'iu (Mr. Lü's Spring and Autumn Annals). SPTK

Lu, Te-ming. 1965. *Lao Tzu yin-i* (Pronunciations and Meanings of the *Lao Tzu*). Taipei: I Wen Press.

————. 1967. *Ching-tien shih-wen* (Explanation of Words in the Classics). Taipei: Commercial Press.

Lucretius. 1969. *The Way Things Are (De Rerum Natura).* Translated by Rolfe Humphries. Bloomington, Ind.: Indiana University Press.

Lung, Hui. 1975. "A Philological Study of the Lost Ancient Treatise found at the Head of the Manuscript of the *Lao Tzu* (Text B) Unearthed at Ma-Wang-Tui." *Kao ku hsueh pao.* 2: 23–31.

Ma, Hsü lun. 1956 [1964]. *Lao Tzu chiao ku* (*Lao Tzu* Collated and Explained). Peking and Hong Kong: T'ai P'ing Book Co.

Ma, Kuo-han. 1967. ed. *Yü han shan fang chi i shu* (Lost Texts Edited in House in Yu-han Mountain). 6 vols. Taipei: Wen Hai Press.

"Ma-wang-tui Han-mu ch'u-t'u Lao-tzu shih-wen" (Transcriptions of the Two Copies of the *Lao-tzu* Found in the Ma-wang-tui Han Tomb). 1974. *Wen Wu.* (November): 8–20.

Ma-wang-tui Han-mu po-shu (The Silk Manuscripts of the Han Tomb of Ma-wang-tui). 1975. 8 vols. Peking: Wen-wu.

"Ma-wang-tui san-hao Han-mu po-hua tao-yin-t'u te ch'u-pu yen-chiu" (A Preliminary Study of the Diagram of Breathing Exercises on Silk in No. 3 of the Han Tombs Unearthed at Ma-wang-tui). 1975b. *Wen-wu.* 6: 6–13.

Maclagan, P. J. 1926. *Chinese Religious Ideas.* London: Student Christian Movement.

Macnicol, Nicol. 1959. ed. *Hindu Scriptures.* New York: E. P. Dutton & Co.

Marx, Karl. 1963. *The Economic and Philosophical Manuscripts. Karl Marx: Early Writings.* Translated and Edited by T. B. Bottomore. New York: McGraw-Hill.

———. 1977. *Selected Writings.* Edited by David McLellan. London: Oxford University Press.

Marx, Werner. 1971. *Heidegger and Tradition.* Evanston, Ill.: Northwestern University Press.

Maspero, Henri. 1981. *Taoism and Chinese Religion.* Translated by Frank A. Kierman, Jr. Amherst, Mass.: University of Massachusetts Press.

Ming-huang, Emperor Hsuan Tsung. *Tao-te ching chu* (Commentary on the Classic of Tao and Te). See Hsias T'ien-shih, Vol. 2.

Moltmann, Jurgen. 1977. *The Future of Creation.* Philadelphia: Fortress Press.

Morgan, Evan. 1933 [1966]. *Tao, the Great Luminant: Essays from the Huai-nan Tzu.* Shanghai, Taipei Reprint: Ch'eng-Wen Publishing Co.

Murray, John Courtney. 1964. *The Problem of God.* New Haven: Yale University Press.

Nakayama, Shigeru and Nathan Sivin. 1973. *Chinese Science, Explorations of an Ancient Tradition.* Cambridge, Mass.: MIT Press.

Needham, Joseph. 1954–1988. *Science and Civilization in China.* 6 Vols. Cambridge, England: University Press.

Needham, Rodney. 1973. ed. *Right and Left: Essays on Dual Symbolic Classification.* Chicago: University of Chicago Press.

Neumann, Erich. 1954. *The Origins and History of Consciousness.* Princeton: Princeton University Press.

———. 1955. *The Great Mother.* Princeton: Princeton University Press.

Northrop, F. S. C. 1946. *The Meeting of East and West.* New York: Macmillan.

Novak, Michael. 1979. *Capitalism and Socialism: A Theological Inquiry.* Washington, D. C.: American Enterprise Institute for Public Policy Research.

———. 1981. *Toward a Theology of the Corporation.* Washington, D. C.: American Enterprise Institute for Public Policy Research.

Ofuchi, Ninji. 1941. "Taiheikyo no shiso ni tsuite" (The Philosophy in the *Peace Sutra*). *Toyogakuho.* 28/4: 145–168.

Ogilvy, James. 1979. *Many Dimensional Man*. New York: Harper & Row.

Orwell, George. 1949. *1984*. New York: Harcourt, Brace.

Packard, Vance. 1972. *A Nation of Strangers*. New York: David Makey.

Pan, Ku. *Han shu* (History of the Former Han Dynasty). PNP.

Pelikan, Jaroslav. 1971. *The Christian Tradition, A History of the Development of Doctrine*. Vol. 1: *The Emergence of the Catholic Tradition (100–600)*. Chicago: University of Chicago Press.

Plato. 1937. *The Dialogues of Plato*. Translated by B. Jowett. 2 vols. New York: Random House.

Plotinus. 1917–1930. *The Enneads*. Translated by Stephen MacKenna. London: Faber and Faber.

Porket, Manfred. 1974. *The Theoretical Foundations of Chinese Medicine*. Cambridge, Mass.: MIT Press.

Prigogine, Ilya. 1980. *From Being to Becoming: Time and Complexity in the Physical Sciences*. San Francisco: W. H. Freeman and Co.

Rifkin, Jeremy. 1984. *Algeny*. New York: Penguin.

Robinet, Isabelle. 1979. "Metamorphosis and Deliverance from the Corpse in Taoism." *History of Religions*. 19/1: 37–70.

———. 1977. *Les Commentaires du Tao To King Jusqu'un VII siecle*. Paris: College de France.

Rouner, Leroy S. 1984. ed. *On Nature*. South Bend, Ind.: Notre Dame University Press.

Rousseau, Jean Jacques. 1950. *The Social Contract and Discourses*. Translated by G. D. H. Cole. New York: E. P. Dutton.

Royce, Josiah. 1967. *The Problem of Christianity*. New York: Archon Books.

Rump, Ariade and Wing-tsit Chan. 1979. trans. *Commentary on the Lao Tzu by Wang Pi*. Honolulu: University Press of Hawaii.

Russell, Bertrand. 1922. *The Problem of China*. New York: Century Co.

De Santillana, Giorgio and Hertha von Dechend. 1969. *Hamlet's Mill: An Essay on Myth and the Frame of Time*. Boston: Gambit.

Sartre, Jean-Paul. 1949 [1964]. *Nausea*. Translated by Lloyd Alexander. Norfolk, Conn.: New Directions.

———. 1955. *No Exit and Three Other Plays*. New York: Vintage Books.

Saso, Michael. 1972. *Taoism and the Rite of Cosmic Renewal*. Pullman, Wash.: Washington State University Press.

———. 1978. *The Teachings of Taoist Master Chuang*. New Haven: Yale University Press.

Schipper, Kristopher M. 1978. "The Taoist Body." *History of Religions*. 17/3 & 4: 355–386.

Schumacher, E. F. 1973. *Small is Beautiful: Economics as if People Mattered*. New York: Harper & Row.

Seidel, Anna K. 1969. *La Divinisation de Lao tseu dans le taoisme des Han*. Paris: Ecole Francaise d'Extreme-Orient.

————. 1969–1970. "The Image of the Perfect Ruler in Early Taoist Messianism: Lao-Tzu and Li Hung." *History of Religions.* 9/2 & 3: 216–247.

Shiner, Larry E. 1966. *The Secularization of History: An Introduction to the Theology of Friedrich Gogarten.* Nashville: Abingdon Press.

Shryock, John K. 1966. *The Origin and Development of the State Cult of Confucius.* New York: Paragon House.

Sivin, Nathan. 1968. *Chinese Alchemy: Preliminary Studies.* Cambridge, Mass.: Harvard University Press.

————. 1978. "On the Word 'Taoist' as a Source of Perplexity." *History of Religions.* 17: 303–330.

Smith, Huston. 1967. *Forgotten Truth.* New York: Harper & Row.

Soothill, W. E. 1937. trans. *Analects.* London: Oxford University Press.

Spencer, Herbert. 1885. *Principles of Sociology.* 3 vols. New York: D. Appleton & Co.

Ssu-ma, Ch'ien. 1905. *Shih chi* (Records of the Historian). *Les memoires historiques de Se-Ma Ts'ien.* Trans. Edouard Chavannes. Vol. 5. Paris: Leroux.

Stace, Walter T. 1960. *The Teaching of the Mystics.* New York, Mentor Books.

Strauss, Leo. 1953. *Natural Right and History.* Chicago: University of Chicago Press.

Strickmann, Michel. 1974. "History of Taoism." *Encyclopaedia Britannica.* 15th Ed. vol. 17: 1044–1055.

Su, Ch'e. 1965. *Lao Tzu chu* (Commentary on the *Lao Tzu*). Taipei: I Wen Press.

Sun, K'o-k'uan. 1977. *Han Yüan tao lun.* Taipei: Lien Ching Publishing Co.

SSU-PU Ts'ung-k'an. 1967. Collected Works of the Four Libraries. 2nd Edition. Tapei: Commercial Press.

Suzuki, D. T. 1956. *Zen Buddhism.* Edited by William Barrett. Garden City, N. Y.: Doubleday Anchor Books.

Swimme, Brian. 1985. *The Universe is a Green Dragon.* Santa Fe, N. M.: Bear & Co.

T'ai-p'ing yü-lan (Imperial Collection of the T'ai-p'ing Period).

Takeuchi Yoshio. 1931 [1975]. *"Lao Tzu yuan-ssu"* (The Origin of the *Lao Tzu*). *Hsien-Ch'in ching-chi k'ao* (Textual Criticism on Pre-Ch'in Classics). Translated by Chiang Hsia-yen. Shanghai: Commercial Press.

Tan, Qi Xiang. 1982. ed. *The Historical Atlas of China.* 6 vols. Shanghai: Cartographic Publishing House.

T'an Chieh-fu. 1924. "Erh Lao yen chiu" (A Study on the Two Laos). *Ku shih pien.* Edited by Ku Chieh-kang. Vol. 4: 505–508.

T'ang, Chun-i. 1968 [1974]. *Chung kuo che hsueh yuan lun, yuan hsin p'ien* (On the Origin of Chinese Philosophy: On the Origin of the Concept of Human Nature). Hong Kong: New Asia Research Institute.

T'ang, Lan. 1975. "Ma-wang-tui ch'u-t'u Lao Tzu i-pen chuan-ch'ien ku-i-shu te yen-chiu—chien-lun ch'i yu Han-ch'u Ju-Fa tou-cheng te kuan-hsi" (A Study of the Lost Ancient Texts Preceding Version B of the *Lao Tzu* Unearthed at Ma-wang-tui with Comments on Their Relation to the Struggle Between Confucians and Legalists in Early Han). *K'ao-ku hsueh-pao*, (Acta Archaeologica Sinica). 1: 7–38.

———. 1975. "Ma-wang-tui po-shu Ch'ueh-ku-shih-ch'i p'ien k'ao" (An Examination of the Treatise Entitled "Abstaining from Cereals and Inhaling Air" in the Silk Manuscripts of Ma-wang-tui). *Wen-wu*. 6: 14–15.

T'ang, Yung-t'ung. 1972. *Wei Chin hsuan hsueh lun kao* (Metaphysical Speculation in Wei and Chin Dynasties). Taipei: Lu Shan Press.

Thompson, Laurence G. 1972. *The Chinese Way in Religion*. Belmont, Calif: Dickenson.

Tillich, Paul. 1959. *Theology of Culture*. London: Oxford University Press.

Ts'ui, Shu. 1924 [1936]. *Chu-Ssu k'ao-hsin lu* (Inquiry into the True Facts Concerning Confucius). *Ts'ui Tung-pi i-shu* (Surviving Works of Ts'ui Shu). Shanghai: East Asia Library Press.

Tu, Wei-ming. 1979. "The 'Thought of Huang-Lao': A Reflection on the Lao Tzu and Huang Ti Texts in the Silk Manuscripts of Ma-wang-tui." *Journal of Asian Studies*. XXXIX/1: 95–110.

Tylor, Edward Burnett. 1871 [1958]. *Religion in Primitive Culture*. New York: Harper & Row.

Waley, Arthur. 1937 [1960]. trans. *The Book of Songs*. New York: Grove Press.

———. 1938. trans. *Analects*. New York: Random House, Vintage Books.

———. 1943 [1958]. trans. *The Way and Its Power*. London: George Allen & Unwin; New York: Grove Press.

———. 1946. *Three Ways of Thought in Ancient China*. London: George Allen & Unwin.

Walker, Richard Louis. 1953. *The Multi-State System of Ancient China*. Hamden, Conn.: Shoe String Press.

Wang, An-Shih. *Lao Tzu chu* (Commentary on the *Lao Tzu*). Fragments in the *Wen-hsien t'ung-k'ao* (General Collection of Literary Works and Documents).

Wang Chung. *Lao Tzu k'ao-i* (Inquiry into Discrepancies About Lao Tzu). Supplement to the *Shu-hsueh* (Notes from Studies). SPTK.

Wang, Hsiao-po and Leo S. Chang. 1986. *The Philosophical Foundations of Han Fei's Political Theory*. Honolulu: University of Hawaii Press.

Wang, Huai. 1969. *Lao Tzu t'an i*. Taipei: Commercial Press.

Wang, Ming. 1960. ed. *Tai-p'ing ching ho-chiao* (A Reconstruction of the Canon of Supreme Peace). Peking: Chung-hua Press.

Wang, Pi. 1979. *Lao Tzu chu* (Commentary on the *Lao Tzu*). Translated by Ariade Rump and Wing-tsit Chan. Honolulu: University Press of Hawaii.

Ware, James R. 1966. trans. *Alchemy, Medicine, Religion in the China of A.D. 320: The Nei P'ien of Ko Hung (Pao-p'u tzu)*. Cambridge, Mass.: MIT Press.

Watson, Burton. 1963. trans. *Mo-Tzu, Basic Writings*. New York: Columbia University Press.

———. 1963. trans. *Hsün Tzu, Basic Writings*. New York: Columbia University Press.

————. 1968. trans. *The Complete Works of Chuang Tzu*. New York: Columbia University Press.

Weber, Max. 1951. *The Religion of China*. Translated by Hans H. Gerth. New York: Free Press.

————. 1958. *Protestant Ethics and the Rise of Capitalism*. New York: Charles Scribner's Sons.

Wei, Yuan. 1955. *Lao Tzu pen-i* (Original Meaning of the *Lao Tzu*). Taipei: World Book Co.

Welch, Holmes. 1957 [1965]. *Taoism, The Parting of the Way*. Boston: Beacon Press.

———— and Anna Seidel. 1979. *Facets of Taoism. Essays in Chinese Religion*. New Haven: Yale University Press.

Wheelwright, Philip. 1966. ed. *The Presocratics*. New York: Odyssey Press.

White, Lynn Jr. 1967. "The Historical Roots of Our Ecologic Crisis." *Science*. 155: 1203–1207.

Whitehead, Alfred North. 1925. *Science and the Modern World*. New York: Macmillan.

————. 1926. *Religion in the Making*. New York: Macmillan.

————. 1967. *Adventures of Ideas*. New York: Free Press.

————. 1969. *Process and Reality*. New York: Free Press.

Wilhelm, Hellmut. 1960. *Change: Eight Lectures on the I Ching*. New York: Harper Torchbooks.

Wilhelm, Richard. 1950 [1967]. trans. *The I-ching*. Princeton: Princeton University Press.

————. 1986. trans. *Tao Te Ching: The Book of Meaning and Life*. London: Arkana.

Wu, Ching-hsiung. 1965. *Chinese Humanism and Christian Spirituality*. New York: St. John's University Press.

Wu, Ching-yu. 1965. *Lao Tzu i su-chu* (Textual Commentary on the *Lao Tzu*). Kao Hsiung: Ta Chung Book Co.

Yang, Chia-lo. 1953. "Lao Tzu hsin-chuan" (A New Biography of Lao Tzu). *The Works of Lao Tzyy*. Translated by Cheng Lin. Taipei: World Book Co.

Yang, Lien-sheng. 1969. *Excursions in Sinology*. Cambridge, Mass.: Harvard University Press.

Yang, Yung-kuo. 1952 [1973]. *Chung-kuo ku-tai ssu-hsiang shih* (History of Ancient Chinese Thought). Peking: Jen Min Press.

Yen, Ling-fen. 1957. *Chung-wai Lao Tzu chu-shu mu-lu* (Bibliography on the *Lao Tzu* in Chinese and Foreign Languages). Taipei: Chung Hwa Ch'ung Shu Committee.

————. 1959 [1966]. *Lao-Chuang yen-chiu* (Studies on the *Lao Tzu* and the *Chuang Tzu*). Taipei: Chung Hua Book Co.

————. 1965. *Wu chiu pei chai Lao-tzu chi cheng ch'u pien* (First Edition of Collections on *Lao Tzu* in Wu chiu pei House). 160 vols. Taipei: I Wen Press.

Yen, Tsun. *Lao Tzu chih-kuei* (Essential Principles of the *Lao Tzu*). Fragments.

Yü, David C. 1981. "The Creation Myth and Its Symbolism in Classical Taoism."
    Philosophy East and West. 31: 479–500.
Yüan, K'e. 1951 [1957]. *Chung-kuo ku tai shen hua* (Ancient Chinese Myths).
    Shanghai: Commercial Press.
Zampaglione, Gerardo. 1973. *The Idea of Peace in Antiquity.* Translated by Richard
    Dunn. South Bend, Ind.: University of Notre Dame Press.

CHINESE GLOSSARY
(With Pinyin spelling, when different, in parentheses)

ai 哀,愛

an 安

an p'ing t'ai (an ping tai) 安平太

ao 奧

ch'a (cha) 察

chan (zhan) 湛

chan hsi ssu jo (huo) ts'un (zhan xi si ruo cun) 湛兮似若(或)存

ch'an (shan) 禪

Chan kuo ts'e (Zhanguo ce) 戰國策

chang (zhang) 長

chang erh pu tsai (zhang er bu zai) 長而不宰

ch'ang (chang) 常, 長

ch'ang chiu (chang jiu) 長久

ch'ang hsin (chang xin) 常心

ch'ang ming (chang ming) 常名

ch'ang sheng chiu shih chih tao (chang sheng jiu shi zhi dao)
　長生久視之道

ch'ang Tao (chang Dao) 常道

ch'ang te (chang de) 常德

chao (zhao) 兆,昭

che (zhe) 者,折

chen (zhen) 眞

chen-jen (zhen ren) 眞人

ch'en (chen) 臣

Ch'en Chu (Chen zhu). *Chu Lao Tzu (Zhu Lao Zi)* 陳柱,注老子

Ch'en Hao (Chen Hao). *Li-chi chi-shuo (Li-ji ji-shuo)* 陳澔,禮記集說

247

Ch'en Kuo-fu (Chen Guo-fu). *Tao tsang yuan liu k'ao* (*Dao zong yuan liu kao*) 陳國符,道藏源流攷

Ch'en Meng-chia (Chen Meng-jia) 陳夢家

cheng (*zheng*) 爭,政,正

Cheng Hsuan (Zheng Xuan) 鄭玄

cheng ming (*zheng ming*) 正名

cheng shan chih (*zheng shan zhi*) 正善治

Cheng-t'ung Tao-tsang (*Zheng-tong Dao-zong*) 正統道藏

cheng yen jo fan (*zheng yan ruo fan*) 正言若反

ch'eng (*cheng*) 成, 逞

ch'eng chi szu 成其私

chi (*ji*) 及,已,紀,積,極,幾,機,既

chi shih or *chieh shih* (*ji shi*) 稽式

ch'i (*qi*) 器,其,谿,奇,氣,齊

chia (*jia*) 家

Chiang Hsi-ch'ang (Jiang Xi-chang). *Lao Tzu chiao-ku* (*Lao Zi kiao gu*) 蔣錫昌,老子校詁

Chiang Hsia-an (Jiang Xia-an). (*Hsien-Ch'in ching-chi k'ao* (*Hsien-Qin jing ji kao*) 江俠菴,先秦經籍考

ch'iang (*qiang*) 強

ch'iang liang (*qiang liang*) 強梁

chiao (*jiao*) 噭,徼

Chiao Hung (Jiao Hong). *Lao Tzu i* (*Lao Zi yi*) 焦竑,老子翼

ch'iao (*qiao*) 巧

chieh-jan (*jie ran*) 介然

chien (*jian*) 堅,間,見,儉,健

chien chih yü ch'ang wu yu (*jian zhi yu chang wu you*) 建之於常無有

chien yen (*jian yan*) 建言

ch'ien (*qian*) 乾,前,謙

Ch'ien Mu (Qian Mu). *Chuang-Lao t'ung-pien* (*Zhuang-Lao tong bian*). *Chu-tzu hsin hsüeh an* (*Zhu-zi xin xue an*) 錢穆,莊老通辯,諸子新學案

ch'ien shih (*qian shi*) 前識

chih (*zhi*) 知,智,志,致,治,止,之,執,直

chih chien (*zhi jian*) 至堅

chih chih (*zhi zhi*) 知止

chih jou (*zhi rou*) 至柔

chih shan (*zhi shan*) 至善

chih pu chih (*zhi bu zhi*) 知不知

chih te chih shih (*zhi de zhi shi*) 至德之世

chih tsu (*zhi zu*) 知足

ch'ih (*chi*) 持

ch'ih ch'eng (*chi cheng*) 馳騁

chin (*jin*) 今

chin chih yu (jin zhi you) 今之有

Chin-yü (Jin-yu) 晉語

ch'in (qin) 親, 勤

ching (jing) 精, 矜, 靜, 鏡, 經, 景

ching ch'i (jing qi) 精氣

ching tso (jing zuo) 靜坐

Ching-t'u Tsung (Jing-tu Zong) 淨土宗

ch'ing (qing) 輕, 清, 馨

ch'ing ching (qing jing) 清靜

Ch'ing Hsi-t'ai (Qing Xi-tai). *Chung-kuo tao chiao ssu hsiang shih kang (Zhongguo dao jiao si xiang shi gang)* 卿希泰, 中國道教思想史綱

chiu (jiu) 久, 咎, 救

chiu shih (jiu shi) 久視

Ch'iu (Qiu) 丘

ch'iu sheng chih hou (qiu shang zhi hou) 求生之厚

cho (zhuo) 濁

chou (zhou) 周

chou hsing erh pu tai (zhou xing er bu dai) 周行而不殆

Chou shu (Zhou shu) 周書

Chou Tun-i (Zhou Dun-yi). *T'ung-shu (Tong shu)* 周敦頤, 通書

chu (zhu) 主, 居, 注

Chu Ch'ien-chih (Zhu Qian-zhi). *Lao Tzu chiao-shih (Lao Zi jiao shi)* 朱謙之, 老子校釋

Chu Hsi (Zhu Xi) 朱熹

chu-tzu pe-chia (zhu-zhi bai-jia) 諸子百家

ch'u (chu) 芻, 出, 處

ch'u kou (chu guo) 芻狗

Ch'u tz'u (Chu ci) 楚辭

chü (ju) 居

chü shan ti (ju shan di) 居善地

ch'ü (qu) 屈, 去

Ch'ü Fu (Qu Fu) 曲阜

Ch'ü Yüan (Qu Yuan) 屈原

chüan (juan) 卷

ch'üan (quan) 拳

Chuang Tzu, Chuang Chou (Zhuang Zi or Zhuang Zhou) 莊子, 莊周

chüeh (jue) 絕

ch'üeh (que) 缺

chün (qun) 均, 君

chün tzu (qun zi) 君子

The Ch'un-ch'iu (The Chun-qiu) 春秋

chung (zhong) 重, 中, 終, 盅

chung chi te (zhong ji de) 重積德

chung fu (*zhong fu*) 衆甫

chung fu fu (*zhong fu fu*) 衆父父

chung jen (*zhong ren*) 衆人

ch'ung (*chong*) 寵, 冲

ch'ung ch'i i wei ho (*chong qi yi wei he*) 沖氣以爲和

Ch'ung-hsü Tao-te chen-ching (*Chong-xu Dao-de zhen-jing*) 沖虛道德眞經

erh (*er*) 耳, 二, 而, 兒

erh min hao chin (*er min hao jin*) 而民好徑

erh pu sha che fu (*er bu sha zhe fu*) 而不殺者夫

erh wu pu wei (*er wu bu wei*) 而無不爲

fa 法, 伐

fan 反

fang 方

fang shih (*fang shi*) 方士

fei 非

fu 甫, 勿, 父, 腹, 復, 負, 福

Fu Ch'in-chia (Fu Qin-jia). *Chung-kuo tao chiao shih* (*Zhongguo dao jiao shi*) 傅勤家, 中國道教史

Fu-hsi (Fu-xi) **優義**

Fu I (Fu Yi). *Chiao-ting ku-pen Lao Tzu* (*Jiao-ding gu-ben Lao zi*) 傅奕, 校定古本老子

Fung Yu-lan (Feng You-lan) and Jen Chi-yü (Ren Ji-yu). *Lao-tzu che hsueh t'ao lun chi* (*Lao-zi zhe xue tao lun ji*) 馮友蘭, 任繼愈, 老子哲學討論集

hai 害, 海, 孩

Han Fei Tzu (Han Fei Zi) 韓非子

Han Ku Kuan (Han Gu Guan) 涵谷關

Han-shan Te-ch'ing (Han-shan De-qing) 寒山德清

Han shu 漢書

Han Wu Ti (Han Wu Di) 漢武帝

Han Ying. *Han shih wai chuan* (*Han shi wai juan*) 韓嬰, 韓詩外傳

Hang Yü (Hang Yu). *Ch'ang-li hsien-sheng wen-chi* (*Chang-li xian-sheng wen-ji*) 韓愈, 昌黎先生文集

hao 好

hao yao or *t'o yo* (*tou yo*) 槖籥

heh (*hei*) 黑

ho (*he*) 和

Ho Ch'i-ming (He Qi-ming). *Wei Chin ssu hsiang yu t'an feng* (*Wei jin si xiang yu tan feng*) 何啓明, 魏晉思想與談風

Ho-shang Kung (He-shang Kung). *Lao Tzu chu* (*Lao Zi zhu*) 河上公, 老子注

hou 後, 厚

Hou Han shu 後漢書

Hou Wai-lu. *Chung-kuo ku-tai ssu-hsiang hsüeh-shuo shih* (*Zhongguo gu-dai si-xiang xue-shuo shi*). *Chung-kuo ku tai she-hui shih lun* (*Zhongguo gu-dai she-hui shi-lun*) 矦外盧, 中國古代思想學説史, 中國古代社會史論

hsi (*xi*) 觀, 希, 習

Hsi-tz'u (*Xi-ci*) 繫辭

hsia (*xia*) 下, 狎, 狹

hsia liu (*xia liu*) 下流

hsiang (*xiang*) 象, 相, 鄉

Hsiang-erh (Xiang-er) 想爾

hsiao (*xiao*) 小, 肖, 孝

Hsiao ching (*Xiao jing*) 孝經

Hsiao T'ien-shih (Xiao Tian-shi). *Tao te ching ming chu hsüan chi* (*Dao de jing ming zhu xuan ji*) 蕭天石, 道德經名著選集

hsien (*xian*) 賢, 仙, 先

hsien hua (*xian hua*) 仙化

hsin (*xin*) 信, 伸, 心, 新

hsin hsüeh (*xin xue*) 心學

hsin shan yüan (*xin shan yuan*) 心善淵

hsin-tsai (*xin zai*) 心齋

hsing (*xing*) 行, 性, 刑, 姓, 形

hsing cheng (*xing zheng*) 姓爭

hsing erh hsia (*xing er xia*) 形而下

hsing erh shang (*xing er shang*) 形而上

hsing ming (*xing ming*) 刑名

hsiu (*xiu*) 修

hsiung (*xiong*) 凶

hsü (*xu*) 虛, 畜

hsü-chi (*xu ji*) 虛極

Hsü Fu-kuan (Xu Fu-guan) 徐復觀

Hsü Hsü-sheng (Xu Xu-sheng). *Chung-kuo ku shih ti ch'uan shuo shih tai* (*Zhongguo gu shi di chuan shuo shi dai*) 徐旭生, 中國古史的傳説時代

Hsü Shen (Xu Shen). *Shuo wen chieh tzu* (*Shuo wen jie zi*) 許慎, 説文解字

hsüan or *yüan* (*xuan* or *yuan*) 玄, 元

hsüan chih yu hsüan (*xuan zhi you xuan*) 玄之又玄

hsüan hsüeh (*xuan xue*) 玄學

hsüan lan (*xuan lan*) 玄覽

hsüan p'in (*xuan pin*) 玄牝

hsüan t'ien (*xuan tian*) 玄天

hsüan t'ung (*xuan tong*) 玄同

hsüeh (*xue*) 學

hsüeh pu hsüeh (*xue bu xue*) 學不學

Hsün Tzu (Xun Zi) 荀子

hu huang 惚恍

Hu Shih (Hu Shi). *Shuo ju* (*Shuo ru*). *Huai-nan wang shu* 胡適, 説儒, 淮南王書

hua 化

Huai-nan tzu (*Huai-nan ji*) 淮南子

huan 渙, 還, 患

Huan Yüan 環淵

huang 恍, 荒, 慌

Huang Lao 黃老

Huang-ti shu (*Huang-di shu*) 黃帝書

Huang-ti ssu-ching (*Huang-di si jing*) 黃帝四經

Huang Tzu (Huang Zi) 黃子

hui 慧

Hui Neng 慧能

hun 混, 昏, 魂

hun-t'un or *hun ch'eng* (*hun-tun* or *hun cheng*) 混沌, 混成

huo 或, 貨, 禍

i (*yi*) 易, 異, 一, 義, 溢, 益, 夷, 遺

i che (*yi zhe*) 一者

i ch'i sheng sheng chih hou (*yi qi sheng sheng zhi hou*) 以其生生之厚

I-Lao t'ung yen (*Yi-Lao tong yan*) 易老通言

I-wei ch'ien-tso-tu (*Yi-wei qian-zuo-du*) 易緯乾鑿度

I-ching (*Yi-jing*) 易經

I Shen-ting (Yi Shen-ding) 易順鼎

jan (*ran*) 然, 燃

jan erh (*ran er*) 然而

jan hou (*ran hou*) 然後

Jao Tsung-i (Rao Zong-yi). *Lao Tzu hsiang-erh chu chiao chien* (*Lao Zi xiang-er zhu jiao jian*) 饒宗頤, 老子想爾注校箋

jen (*ren*) 仁, 人, 忍

jeng (*reng*) 扔

jo (*ruo*) 若, 弱

jou (*rou*) 柔

ju (*ru*) 辱, 儒, 入

jung 榮

kai (*gai*) 改

Kai-chih fu-chih (*gai-zhi fu-zhi*) 蓋之覆之

kan (*gan*) 敢

k'an (*kan*) 坎

Kao Heng (Gao Heng). *Ch'ung-ting Lao Tzu cheng-ku* (*Chong-ding Lao Zi zheng-gu*). With Ch'ih Hsi-chao (Chi Xi-zhao) "Shih-t'an Ma-wang-tui Han-mu chung-te pai-shu *Lao-tzu*." *Wen Wu*. 高亨, 重訂老子正詁

k'e (*ke*) 客, 咳

ken (*gen*) 根

ko (*ge*) 割

Ko Hsüan (Ge Xuan) 葛玄

Ko Hung (Ge Hong). *Pao P'u Tzu (Bao Pu Zi)* 葛洪, 抱樸子

k'o (ke) 可

k'o yü (ke yu) 可欲

kou (gou) 狗

ku (gu) 固, 古, 谷

ku shen 谷神

Ku Chieh-kang (Gu Jie-gang). *Ku-shih pien (Gu-shi bian)* 顧頡剛, 古史辨

ku chih tao (gu zhi dao) 古之道

Kua tz'u (Gua zi) 卦辭

kuan (guan) 觀

Kuan Chung (Guan Zhong). *Kuan Tzu (Guan Zi)* 管仲, 管子

Kuan-ling-yin (Guan-ling-yin), Kuan Yin 關令尹, 關尹

kuang (guang) 光, 廣

kuang te (guang de) 廣德

kuei (gui) 歸, 貴, 鬼

Kuei Tsang (Gui Zang) 歸藏

k'un (kun) 坤

kung (gong) 公, 功

k'ung (kong) 空, 孔

kuo (guo) 過, 果, 國

Kuo Hsiang (Guo Xiang) 郭象

Kuo Mo-jo (Guo Mo-ruo). *Ch'ing-t'ung shih-tai (Qing-tong shi-dai)* 郭沫若, 青銅時代

Kuo-yü (Guo-yu) 國語

lan 覽

Lao Lai-tzu (Lao Lai-zi) 老萊子

Lao Tan (Lao Dan) 老聃

Lao Tzu (Lao Zi) 老子

lei 類

li 利, 離, 禮, 理

Li chi (Li ji) 禮記

li yun 禮運

Liang Ch'i-ch'ao (Liang Qi-chao). *Chung-kuo ku-tai ssu-ch'ao (Zhongguo gu-dai si-cao)* 梁啓超, 中國古代思潮

Lieh Tzu (Lie Zi) 列子

Liu Hsiang (Liu Xiang). *Lieh-hsien chüan (Lie-xian zhüan). Shuo-yüan* 劉向, 列仙傳, 說苑

Liu I-cheng (Liu Yi-zheng). *Chung-kuo wen-hua-shih (Zhongguo wen-hua-shi)* 柳詒徵, 中國文化史

Lo Ken-tse (Lo Gen-ze). *Chu-tzu k'ao-so (Zhu-zi kao-suo)* 羅根澤, 諸子考索

Lokuang (Loguang). *Ju-chia hsing-shang-hsüeh (Ru-jia xing-shang-xue)* 羅光, 儒家形上學

Lu Hsiang-shan (Lu Xiang-shan). 陸象山, 象山全集

Lü-shih ch'un-chiu (*Lu-shi chun-qiu*) 呂氏春秋

Lü Szu-mien (Lu Si-mian) 呂思勉

Lu Te-ming (Lu De-ming). *Lao Tzu yin-i* (*Lao Zi yin-yi*). *Ching-tien shih-wen* (*Jing-dian shi-wen*) 陸德明, 老子音義, 經典釋文

luan 亂

Ma Hsü-lun (Ma Xu-lun). *Lao Tzu chiao ku* (*Lao Zi jiao-gu*) 馬敍倫, 老子校詁

Ma Kuo-han (Ma Guo-han). *Yü han shan fang chi i shu* (*Yu han shan fong ji yi shu*) 馬國翰, 玉函山房輯佚書

"Ma-wang-tui Han-mu ch'u-t'u *Lao-tzu* shih-wen." *Wen Wu.* 馬王堆漢墓出土老子釋文

Ma-wang-tui Han-mu po-shu. 馬王堆漢墓帛書

"Ma-wang-tui san-hao Han-mu po-hua tao-yin-t'u te ch'u-pu yen-chiu." 馬王堆三號漢墓帛畫導引圖的初步研究

mei 美

men 門, 悶

miao 妙

mieh (*mie*) 減

mien mien jo ts'un (*mian mian ruo cun*) 緜緜若存

min 民

ming 名, 命, 明

ming ching (*ming jing*) 明鏡

mo chih ling (*mo jhi ling*) 莫之令

mo neng ch'en (*mo neng chen*) 莫能臣

Mo Ti (Mo Di) 墨翟

mo shen pu tai (*mo shen bu dai*) 沒身不殆

mou 牡謀

mu 母

na 訥

nan 男, 難

nan te chih huo (*nan de zhi huo*) 難得之貨

nei 內

neng 能

neng wei tz'u (*neng wei ci*) 能爲雌

neng wu tz'u (*neng wu ci*) 能無雌

nu 女

o (*wu*) 惡

p'a (*pa*) 怕

Pan Ku 班固

pao (*bao*) 抱, 保, 寶

pao i (*bao yi*) 抱

pen (*ben*) 本

pi (*bi*) 敝

pien (*bian*) 辮

pin (*bin*) 賓

p'in (*pin*) 牝

ping (*bing*) 兵

po (*bo*) 博

po, pai, pe (*bo, bai*) 白

p'o (*po*) 魄, 泊

pu (*bu*) 不

pu-k'o ming 不可名

pu ming-yu 不名有

pu tai (*bu dai*) 不殆

pu tzu sheng (*bu zi sheng*) 不自生

pu wei shih (*bu wei shi*) 不爲始

pu yü i ching (*bu yu yi jing*) 不欲以靜

p'u (*pu*) 樸

san 三

se 嗇

shan 善

shan wei shih che (*shan wei shi zhe*) 善爲士者

shang 上, 商, 尙

shang chiang chün (*shang jiang jun*) 上將軍

shang hsien (*shang xian*) 尙賢

shen 神, 深, 伸, 身

shen ch'i (*shen qi*) 神器

sheng 生, 聖, 勝, 聲

sheng jen (*sheng ren*) 聖人

shih (*shi*) 失, 逝, 始, 事, 式, 食, 勢, 是, 視, 十, 史, 士

Shih chi (*Shi ji*) 史記

Shih Huang Ti (Shi Huang Di) 始皇帝

shih pai chih ch'i (*shi bai zhi qi*) 十佰之器

shih-ta ching or *Shih-liu ching* (*shi da jing* or *shi liu jing*) 十大經, 十六經

shih yu san (*shi you san*) 十有三

shou 守, 首

shu 數, 速

Shu ching (*Shu jing*) 書經

shui 水

shui hsing (*shui xing*) 贅行

Shuo kua (*Shuo gua*) 說卦

Shuo Wen 說文

ssu, (*sz*), *szu* (*si*) 死, 私

ssu erh pu-wang (*si er bu-wang*) 死而不亡

Ssu K'u Chuan Shu (*si ku quan shu*) 四庫全書

Ssu-ma Ch'ien (Si-ma Qian). 司馬遷, 史記

Ssu Pu Pei Yao (SPPY) 四部備要

Ssu Pu Ts'ung K'an (SPTK) 四部叢刊

Ssu-shu wu-ching (*Si-shu wu-jing*) 四書五經

su 素,俗

Su Ch'e (Su Che). *Lao Tzu chu* (*Lao Zi zhu*) 蘇轍, 老子注

sun 損

Sun K'o-k'uan (Sun Ke-kuan). *Han Yüan tao lun* (*Han Yuan dao lun*) 孫克寬, 寒原道論

ta (*da*) 大

ta shun (*da shun*) 大順

tai (*dai*) 殆

T'ai Chi (Tai Ji) 太極

T'ai-p'ing yü-lan (*Tai-ping yu-lan*) 太平御覽

T'ai-shih Tan (Tai-shi Dan) 太史儋

Tan Qi Xiang 譚其驤

T'an Chieh-fu (Tan Jie-fu). *"Erh Lao yen chiu"* (*"Er Lao yan jiu"*) 譚戒甫, 二老研究

T'ang Chün-i (Tan Jun-yi). *Chung kuo che hsüeh yüan lun, yüan hsin p'ien* (*Zhong-guo zhe xue yuan lun, yuan xin pian*) 唐君毅, 中國哲學原論, 原性篇

T'ang Lan. "Ma-wang-tui ch'u-t'u *Lao Tzu* i-pen chuan-ch'ien ku-i-shu te yen-chiu— chien-lun ch'i yu Han-ch'u Ju-Fa tou-cheng te kuan-hsi." *K'ao-ku hsueh-pao.* 唐蘭, 馬王堆出土老子乙本卷前古佚書的研究兼論 其與漢初儒法鬥爭的關係, 考古學報

"Ma-wang-tui po-shu Ch'ueh-ku-shih-ch'i p'ien k'ao." *Wen wu.* 馬王堆帛書絕穀食氣篇考, 文物

T'ang Yun-t'ung (Tang Yun-tong). *Wei Chin hsüan hsüeh lun kao* 湯用彤, 魏晉玄學論稿

Tao (Dao) 道

te (*de*) 德,得

t'eh (*te*) 忐

ti (*di*) 帝, 蒂, 地

t'ien (*tian*) 天

t'ien hsia (*tian xia*) 天下

ting (*ding*) 定

t'ing chih tu chih (*Ting zhi du zhi*) 亭之毒之

to (*duo*) 多

t'o yo (*tou yo*) or *hao yao* 橐籥

tsai ying p'o pao i (*zai ying po bao yi*) 戴營魄抱一

tsao (*zao*) 躁

tse (*ze*) 則

Ts'eng-tzu wen (*Zeng-zi wen*) 曾子問

Tso ch'iu-ming (Zuo qiu ming). *Tso Chuan* (*Zuo Zhuang*) 左邱明, 左傳

tso (*zuo*) 坐

tsou (*zou*) 走

tsu (*zu*) 足

ts'u (*chu*) 出

tsui (*zui*) 罪

Ts'ui Shu (Cui Shu). *Chu-Ssu k'ao-hsin lu* (*Zhu-si kao-xin lu*)
   崔述, 洙泗考信錄

tsung (*zong*) 宗

ts'un (*cun*) 存

tu (*du*) 獨

Tu Erh-wei (Du Er-wei) 杜而未

Tu Fu (Du Fu) 杜甫

t'u (*tu*) 徒, 土

tui (*dui*) 兌

t'ui (*tui*) 退

t'un (*tun*) 沌

tung (*dong*) 動

t'ung (*tong*) 通, 同

T'ung-shu (*Tong-shu*) 通書

tz'a (*ca*) 察

tzu (*zi*) 自, 字, 子, 滋, 輜

tzu chang (*zi zhang*) 滋彰

Tzu-chang (Zi-zhang) 子張

tzu ch'i (*zi qi*) 滋起

tzu chien (*zi jian*) 自見

tzu chung (*zi zhong*) 輜重

Tzu-hsia (Zi-xia) 子夏

tzu hua (*zi hua*) 自化

tzu hun (*zi hun*) 滋昏

tzu jan (*zi ran*) 自然

tzu ku chi chin (*zi gu ji jin*) 自古及今

Tzu-kung (Zi-gong) 子貢

Tzu-lu (Zi-lu) 子路

tz'u (*ci*) 雌, 慈, 辭

wan wu 萬物

wang 王, 亡, 忘

Wang An-shih (Wang An-shi). *Lao Tzu chu* (*Lao Zi zhu*) 王安石, 老子注

Wang Chung (Wang Zhong). *Lao Tzu k'ao-i* (*Lao Zi kao-yi*) 汪中, 老子考異

Wang Huai. *Lao Tzu t'an i* (*Lao Zi tan yi*) 王淮, 老子探義

Wang Ming. *Tai-p'ing ching ho-chiao* (*Tai-ping jing he-jiao*) 王明, 太平經合校

Wang Pi (Wang Bi). *Lao Tzu chu* (*Lao Zi zhu*) 王弼, 老子注

Wang Yang-ming 王陽明

wei 爲, 畏, 僞, 未, 微, 惟

wei miao yüan t'ung (*wei miao yuan tong*) 微妙元通

wei ming　微明

wei sheng chih ching (*wei sheng zhi jing*) 衛生之經

wei yang　未央

Wei Yüan. *Lao Tzu pen-i* (*Lao Zi ben-yi*) 魏源, 老子本義

wen 文

Wen Tzu (*Wen Zi*) 文子

Wen Wu 文物

wu　無, 舞, 巫, 物, 五

wu chi (*wu ji*)　無極

wu chih (*wu zhi*)　無止, 無知

Wu Ching-yü (Wu Jing-yu). *Lao Tzu i su-cheng* (*Lao Zi yi su-zheng*)
　　吳靜宇, 老子義疏證

wu ch'ing (*wu qing*)　無情

wu hou ju yu chien (*wu hou ru you jian*)　無厚入有間

wu-hsing (*wu xing*)　五行

wu so kuei (*wu suo gue*)?　無所歸

wu wei　無爲

wu wei erh wu pu wei (*wu wei er wu bu wei*)　無爲而無不爲

wu yü i ching (*wu yu yi jing*)　無欲以靜

wu yu ju wu chien (*wu you ru wu jian*)　無有入無間

yang　陽, 央

Yang Chia-lo (Yang jia-lo). "Lao Tzu hsin-chuan" ("Lao Zi xin chuan")
　　楊家駱, 老子新傳

yang chih fu chih (*yang zhi fu zhi*)　養之覆之

Yang Chu (Yang Zhu) 楊朱

Yang Tzu-chü (Yang Zi-ju) 楊子居

Yang Yung-kuo (Yang Yong-guo). *Chung-kuo ku-tai ssu-hsiang shih* (*Zhongguo gu-dai si-xiang shi*) 楊榮國, 中國古代思想史

yao 爻

Yao tz'u (*Yao ci*) 爻辭

yeh (*ye*) 亦

yen (*yan*) 言, 厭

yen-ch'u (*yan chu*) 燕處

Yen Ling-feng (Yan Ling-feng). *Chung-wai Lao Tzu chu-shu mu-lu* (*Zhong-wai Lao Zi ju-shu mu lu*). *Lao-Chuang yen-chiu* (*Lao-Zhaung yan-jiu*). 嚴靈峯, 中外老子著述目錄, 老莊研究

yen shan hsin (*yan shan xin*) 言善信

Yen Tsun (Yan Zun). *Lao Tzu chih-kuei* (*Lao Zi chi-gui*) 嚴遵, 老子指歸

yin 音, 陰, 殷

yin mou　陰謀

ying　盈, 嬰, 營

ying erh (*yin er*)　嬰兒

ying p'o (*ying po*) 營魄

yu (*you*) 有, 尤, 由

yu chih (*you zhi*) 有之

yu yü (*you yu*) 有餘

yu wu hun ch'eng (*you wu hun cheng*) 有物混成

yü (*yu*) 欲, 餘, 愈, 予, 與, 愚, 域

yü pu yü (*yu bu yu*) 欲不欲

yü shan jen (*yu shan ren*) 與善仁

yü shih (*yu shi*) 餘食

yüan 遠, 冤, 元, 淵

Yüan K'e (Yuan Ke). *Chung-kuo ku tai shen hua* (*Ghongguo gu dai shen hua*) 袁柯, 中國古代神話

yüan t'ung (*yuan tong*) 元同

yueh (*yue*) 閱

yün 韻, 運

yung (*yong*) 容, 用, 榮, 勇

INDEX

Tao Te Ching: A New Translation and Commentary by Ellen M. Chen

Acquisition, desire for, 162, 165, 166
Adam and Eve, 180
Ai (love or care), 123
Analects of Confucius, 20, 92, 114,
    162, 190, 201, 210, 215, 220, 226,
    227
Ancestor worship, 25
Ancient Text of the Lao Tzu Collected
    (Chiao-ting ku-pen Lao Tzu), 44
Animal postures, health-inducing, 187
Animism, 24
An Yang, excavations at, 14
Ao:
    hidden secret, 198–99
    south-west corner of the house, 198
Archeological excavation in China, 4,
    14, 54
Aristotle, 29, 31, 57, 69–70, 87, 100,
    109, 117, 123
Atheism, 31–32, 35
Augustine, St., 145, 167, 179
Axial period, religions of the, 27–31

Belly, symbol of the, 85
Bergson, Henri, 52

Blakney, Raymond B., 209
Bodhidharma, 157
Body, 72, 73, 179
    love of the, and misfortunes, 86–89
Bonhoffer, Dietrich, 33
Book of Changes, 108
Book of Chou (Chou shu), 19, 141–42
Book of History (Shu-ching), 112, 227
Book of Mountains and Seas (Shan Hai
    Ching), 71
Book of Odes, 176
Book of Rites (Li-chi), 8–9, 20, 104,
    131, 158
Book of the Yellow Emperor (Huang Ti
    shu), 19, 19*n.*, 54, 69
Breath control techniques, 79, 80, 187
Brown, Norman O., 125*n.*
Buchanan, James, 39–40
Buddha, 157
Buddhism, 28, 29, 30, 70, 115, 151,
    168

Campbell, Joseph, 121
Capitalism, 34–36, 38, 224
Carus, Paul, 5, 201

Catholics, 37
Ch'a (clearsightedness), 105
Chan:
dark, 62
hidden, 63
Chan, Wing-tsit, 76n., 83, 93, 103n.,
125n., 209
Chang (to grow [in years]), 177
Ch'ang:
always, 53
constancy, 227
everlasting, 52, 53–54, 71, 94, 178
Chang Chung-yüan, 209
Change, 91
Ch'ang hsin (set mind), 171
Ch'ang te (everlasting creative power),
125
Ch'ang Ts'ung, 19
Ch'ang-wu (Everlasting Non-Being), 54
Ch'ang-yu (Everlasting Being), 54
*Chan-kuo ts'e (Strategies of the
Warring States)*, 13, 19, 141
Chao (beginning of distinction), 104
Che (to break), 223
Ch'en (minister), 120n.
Cheng:
contend, 69
equilibrium, 164
normal condition, 190
rectification, 190
Ch'eng (existence), 117
Ch'eng ch'i szu (fulfillment of the self),
73
Ch'en Hao, 132
Chi:
near, 75
scheming, 229
Ch'i:
abnormal condition or state of war,
190
air or breath, 159, 187
implement, machine, 228–29
strange things, 220
surprise tactics, 190
vessels, 126, 156
vital energy, 137

Chia (family), 183
Ch'iang:
military power, 128, 129
unyielding, 222
violence, 136
Ching Hsi-ch'ang, 4, 103n., 151, 164
Chiao (manifest and great), 53
Ch'iao (ingenuity), 102
Chiao Hung, 136
*Chiao-ting ku-pen Lao Tzu (Ancient
Text of the Lao Tzu Collated)*, 44
Chien (frugality), 194, 209, 210, 211
Chien Mu, 5, 21
Ch'ien shih (foreknowledge), 149
Chih:
consciousness of self, 144
knowledge, 60, 97, 136, 165, 182,
201, 205, 210, 215–16, 231
will, 58, 70, 137
Ch'ih ch'eng (to gallop on horseback),
161
Ch'ih Hsi-chao, 102n.
Chih pu chih (know by not knowing),
201, 216
Chih tsu (contentedness), 230
Children:
becoming like, 172, 174, 187
infants, 125, 185–87, 194
Ch'in (close relatives), 189
Chin chih yu (world of now), 90
Ching:
to boast, 129
clarity, 93
germ or life seed, 108, 151, 186
quietude or tranquility, 96, 145, 164,
191, 194
semen, 70, 186
Ching, Emperor, 43
Ch'ing (clarify), 206
Ch'ing-ching (tranquility), 18
Ch'ing Dynasty, 4
Chiu shih:
enduring vision, 193
fixed staring, 193
heaven's rule, 206
Cho (murkiness or turpidity), 92

Chou (to move round and round), 152
Chou dynasty, 4
Chou shu (Book of Chu), 19, 141–42
Christ, 152, 157, 166, 171, 201, 226
Christian Atheism, 35
Christianity, 28, 29, 30, 31, 35, 201,
    225–26
  material acquisitions and, 166
  Messiah in, 152–53
  relationship between God and the
    world in, 179
  theology of nature and, 39
Chu (to pour into), 198
Ch'ü (winding or bending), 129
Chuang Tzu, 9, 10–11, 12, 13, 16–18,
    19, 21, 22, 26, 67, 68, 77–78, 88,
    89–90, 93, 100, 106, 109, 115–16,
    121, 134, 142, 148, 151, 152, 155,
    156, 158, 161, 165, 173–74, 180,
    186, 187, 229, 230
Chüeh (to eliminate), 102*n.*
Chu Hsi, 70, 141
Ch'ui Su, 5
Ch'u kou (straw dogs), 66
Chün:
  evenly, 134, 134*n.*
  semen, 122
  ruler, 120*n.*, 122
Chung:
  center, 68
  heavy, 121
Ch'ung:
  to agitate, 62
  dynamic, 159
  the empty, 61, 62, 63
Ch'ung ch'i (dynamic airs of breath),
    159
Chung fu (origins of the many), 109
Chung jen (multitudes), 104
Chün tzu (gentlemen), 73
Ch'u Tz'u (Ch'u Yüan), 79–80
Ch'u Yüan, 79
Collection of Discourses (Shuo-Yüan),
    19, 160
Commentary on the Chuang Tzu (Kuo
    Hsiang), 57

Commentary on the Decision, 111,
    152
Communism, 34, 35–36, 38
Comte, Auguste, 33, 36
Confucianism, 9, 20, 33, 70, 75, 144,
    183, 190, 197, 226
  beliefs of, in contrast with Taoism,
    162, 184, 201
  learning in, 106
  love in, 171
  religion and, x, 28
  rivalry between Taoism and, 15–18,
    40–41
  Taoism's outgrowth from, 20–21,
    107–108
Confucius, 11, 29, 75, 114, 160, 210
  Analects of, 20, 92, 114, 162, 190,
    201, 210, 215, 220, 226, 227
  Lao Tzu and, 4, 6–10, 13, 15–18,
    19, 20
Contentedness, 230
Cosmogony and cosmology, 157–60
Courage, 209–10, 218
Cox, Harvey, 31, 32
Cyclical movement of nature, 94, 117,
    119, 206

Daring not be at the world's front, 209,
    210, 211, 220
Darwin, Charles, 26–27, 35, 145
Death, 173–74, 218
  as condition of being unyielding,
    222
  dread of, 209, 210, 213, 220
  immortality, 137, 174
  reason for not fearing, 219–20
Deathless, 173
  life of the round, 93–96, 163, 164,
    173–74, 176–77, 181, 192, 206
Death of God Theology, 35
Democracy, 207
Descartes, Rene, 33, 169
Dewey, John, 32
Divination, 149
Doctrine of the Mean, 15, 121, 136–37,
    149, 183, 203, 224

Dubs, Homer H., 5
Dupre, Louis, 28
Durkheim, Emile, 26
Duyvendak, J. J. L., 5, 22, 52, 57n.,
    59, 68, 70–71, 79, 83, 93n., 98,
    115, 118, 127, 160, 169

Earth, 120–21
    see also Heaven and earth
Eberhard, Wolfram, 16
Eckhart, Meister, 157
Eliade, Mircea, 67–68
Enlightenment, 205
Erigena, Johannes Scotus, 153
Erkes, E., 77
Essential Principles of the Lao Tzu
    (Lao Tzu chih-kuei), 44
Ethics, 72, 150, 151, 158, 177, 208–10
    of survival, 111
    see also Politics
Experience of worldly things,
    knowledge and, 166–68
Eyes, symbol of the, 85

Fa:
    follow, imitate, 119
    to show off, 129
Fame, 162
Fan (to return to the world), 152, 153,
    206
Female:
    -male relationship, 197
    priority of the, 69–71, 78–79, 125
Fertility cults, ancient, 67, 70, 198
Feuerbach, Ludwig, 33, 41, 198
Findlay, J. N., 28
Fingarette, Herbert, 147
Forgiveness, ethics of, 171, 201,
    226–27
Four Texts of the Yellow Emperor, 108,
    113
Francis of Assisi, St., 39, 74
Frazer, James George, 25, 132
Freedom on non-being, 161
Freud, Sigmund, 26–27, 30, 80, 132

Frugality, 194, 209, 210, 211
Fu:
    the father, 160
    to recover, repeat, or return, 152
Fu I, 44, 61
Fung Yu-lan, 5

Garden of Eden, 180
Gebser, Jean, 90
Genesis, 127
Germany, 227
Ghosts, 195
Giles, Herbert A., x
Gogarten, Friedrich, 33
Goodness, 75–76, 122, 123, 170–72, 231
Government, 177, 195, 225–26, 231
    ambitious, 221
    the best, 97–99, 217
    holding on to power, 183
    ideal Taoist state, 228–30
    long life of the state, 183–84,
        193–94
    of nature, 97, 98–99, 205, 220
    passive, 161, 180–81, 190–92, 204
    paying attention to the incipient
        state of things, 200–201, 202
    by reaching downward to people, 207
    tyranny, 219, 220
    see also Politics
Granet, Marcel, 16, 67, 104–105, 106
Great Learning, The, 184

Hai (child who has not yet smiled),
    104–105
Han dynasty, 190
Han Fei Tzu, 19, 22
Han Fei Tzu, 18, 19, 20, 44, 46, 64,
    120n., 121, 123, 136, 141, 142,
    143, 173, 174, 183, 184, 194
Han-shan Te-ch'ing, 169, 186
Han shih wai chun, 7
Han Shu (History of the Former Han
    Dynasty), 12–13, 43
Han Yü, 9
Harper, Donald J., 80

Heaven, 17, 18, 218–19, 224–25, 231
    high religions and, 27–28, 29, 37
Heaven and earth, 65–66, 67, 71, 72,
    73, 114, 153, 158
Hebrews, 37
Hegel, Georg Wilhelm Friedrich, 36,
    66, 169, 180, 218, 220
Heh (black), 155–56
Heidegger, Martin, x
Hendry, George S., 41–42
Henry, Patrick, 220
Hesiod, 110
Hinduism, 28, 29
History, 67
Ho (harmony), 158, 186, 187
Hobbes, Thomas, 162, 165
Homeopathic magic, 25
Ho-shang Kung text, 44, 45, 46
    Chapter 1, 51, 52, 53
    Chapter 2, 55, 57
    Chapter 4, 63
    Chapter 6, 70, 71
    Chapter 9, 77
    Chapter 10, 77*n.*, 78, 80, 81
    Chapter 13, 86*n.*, 87
    Chapter 15, 91
    Chapter 16, 95
    Chapter 21, 109
    Chapter 22, 111
    Chapter 26, 120*n.*, 122
    Chapter 29, 127
    Chapter 33, 136
    Chapter 35, 139
    Chapter 39, 151
    Chapter 40, 153
    Chapter 42, 159
    Chapter 45, 163, 164
    Chapter 49, 172
    Chapter 51, 176
    Chapter 52, 180
    Chapter 53, 182
    Chapter 59, 193
    Chapter 61, 197
    Chapter 63, 201
    Chapter 67, 210
    Chapter 69, 213
    Chapter 72, 216, 217
    Chapter 73, 218
Hou Wai-lu, 58
Hsi (hardly), 156
Hsia:
    to abuse, 217
    low or down-flowing, 196, 207
Hsia ke (whorehouse patron), 217
Hsia liu (downstream position), 197
Hsiang:
    elephant, 64
    image, 63, 64, 108, 119
    village, 183
*Hsiang Erh Commentary on the Tao Te
    Ching,* 108
Hsiao (filial piety), 100
Hsia shih (inferior person), 154
Hsien (able, wise, prudent), 58–59
Hsien jen (worthy person), 58
Hsin:
    coming forth, 17
    faith, 172
    human heart, 56
    mind, 59, 187
    trust or growth of power, 98,
        108–109, 158, 172
    truthful, 231
Hsin tsai ("fasting the mind"), 60,
    187
Hsi Tzu, 91, 119, 204, 214, 220
Hsu (empty), 159
Hsüan (dark and mysterious), 54–55,
    70, 91, 206
Hsüan lan (dark vision), 81
Hsuan p'in (dark mare), 69, 70, 71
Hsüan Tsung, Emperor, 43
Hsu-chi (pole of emptiness), 95
Hsüeh pu hsueh (to learn not to learn),
    216
Hsü Fu-kuan, 44
Hsün Tzu, 10, 17, 18, 20, 22, 81, 144,
    147–48
Hua (natural transformations), 144
Huai-nan Tzu, 23, 88, 192, 203, 223

Huan:
 dissolving, 92
 returning, 129, 152
Huang:
 wilderness, 103*n.*, 104
 yellow, 54
Huang Lao (Yellow Emperor) school,
 11
Huang Ti (Yellow Emperor), 54,
 112–13
Huang Tzu, 43
Huan Yüan, 11
Hu-huang (evasive), 107
Hui Neng, 80
Humanity (humane), 65, 67, 102, 104,
 146, 147, 148, 149, 220, 227
Hun:
 to blend, chaotic, or nebulous, 117
 nebulous, chaos, 172, 206
 soul, 70, 79
Hun-ch'eng (something nebulous), 158,
 172
Huntun (cosmogenic deity), 117
Hun-tun (chaos), 107, 180, 205
Hu Shih, 4, 9, 18, 20, 23, 28

I:
 easy, 203, 214
 to increase, 160
 righteousness, 73, 100, 102, 146,
 147, 148, 149
 use, 106
I-ching (Book of Changes), 54, 70, 71,
 81, 91, 92, 95, 108–109, 111, 117,
 118, 125, 149, 152, 158, 179, 199,
 214
 *Shuo kua (Discussion of the
 Trigrams),* 85, 134*n.*, 179–80
I ch'i sheng sheng chih hou (because
 the intense life-producing activity),
 174
Ignorance, 205–206, 215
Immortality, 137, 174
Inequality, 224
Infants, *see* Children
Injury, to repay, 201, 226–27

"Inquiry On the Way, An," 9
International relations, 196–97, 207
I Shen-ting, 93*n.*, 151
Islam, 37
I-wei ch'ien-tso-tu, 93

James, E. O., 24
Japan, 226, 227
Jaspers, Karl, 27
Jen:
 benevolent, 210
 humane, humanity, 65, 67, 102, 104,
 146, 147, 148, 149, 220, 227
 rulers, 182, 192
Jesus, 152, 157, 166, 171, 201, 226
Jews, 227
Jo:
 dark, 155
 weak, 153
 yielding, 222, 223
John of the Cross, St., 156
Jo ts'un (seems to exist), 71
Jou (soft), 222
Ju:
 defilement, disgrace, 156
 literati, 9–10
 obscure or ignoble, 125
 spotted, 155
Judaism, 29
Jung (illustrious), 125

Kai chih fu chih (to cover and bury),
 176
Kaltenmark, Max, 14, 79
Kan (daring), 218
Kao Heng texts, 4, 68
 Chapter 1, 52
 Chapter 3, 59
 Chapter 4, 61–62
 Chapter 15, 92, 92*n.*
 Chapter 17, 97
 Chapter 20, 102*n.*
 Chapter 21, 106*n.*
 Chapter 25, 118, 119
 Chapter 30, 129
 Chapter 41, 156

Chapter 63, 201
Chapter 70, 214
Chapter 76, 223
Karlgren, Bernhard, 19
Karma, 129
Katha Upanishad, 28
Keats, John, 29
Kimura Eiichi, 5, 21
Knowledge, 60, 97, 136, 165, 166–68,
205–206, 210, 215–16, 220
see also Learning
Ku:
to nourish, 70
valley, 70
Kuan:
to observe, 54, 95, 184
Taoist temple or palace, 121–22
Kuang (bright light of day), 155
Kuan-ling-yin (keeper of the pass), 4
Kuan Yin, 10–11
Ku chih tao (Tao of old), 90
Kuei:
to honor or exalt, 123
to return, 113, 152
Kuei Tsang (To Return and Become
Hidden), 71
Kumarajiva, 168–69
Kuan-tzu, 184, 184*n*.
Kung:
duke, 96
public, 96
K'ung:
Confucius' surname, 107–108
empty, 106*n*.
vast, 106*n*.
Kuo:
resolute, 129, 218
the state, 183
transgressions, 204, 205
Kuo Hsiang, 57
Kuo Mo-jo, 5, 11, 18

Lan:
contemplation, 80
heaven plate, 80
mirror, 80

Lang, Andrew, 26
Lao Lai Tzu (old master Lai), 4, 12–
14
Lao Tan, *see* Lao Tzu
Lao Tzu (Lao Tan), 147, 156, 191, 214
as author of *Tao Te Ching*, 4–22
birthplace of, 6
Confucious and, 4, 6–10, 13, 15–18,
19, 20
descendants of, 12
how *Tao Te Ching* came to be
written, 10–12
name of, 6
occupation of, 6
other identities of, 12–15
rivalry between Confucius and
Taoism and teachings of, 15–18
Lao Tzu, see Tao Te Ching
Lao Tzu chih-kuei (Essential Principles
of the Lao Tzu), 44
Laplace, 32
Lau, D. C., 209
Learning, 169–70
see also Knowledge
Legalism, 121, 123, 124, 141, 142
Legge, James, 5
Lei (knotty), 155
Leibniz, Gottfried, Wilhelm, 108
Leviathan (Hobbes), 162
Lévi-Strauss, Claude, 40
Li:
to benefit, 83
departing, 125
principle, 168
ritual, 6–10, 73, 132, 146, 147–48,
149
separation, 85, 125
sorrow and mourning, 133
Liang Ch'i-Ch'ao, 5, 15
Li-chi (Book of Rites), 8, 9, 20, 104,
131, 158
Lieh Hsien Chuan (Liu Hsiang), 14
Lieh-nü Chuan (Biographies of Famous
Women), 13
Lieh Tzu, 11
Lieh Tzu, 69, 223

Life of the round, 93–96, 163, 164,
    173–74, 176–77, 181, 192, 206
Lin Yutang, 4
Liu Hsiang, 13, 14, 19, 160
Liu I-cheng, 16
Liu Ssu-p'ei, 115
Local cult theory, 16
Lorenz, Konrad, 37–38
Love:
    Christian teachings, 171
    Confucian teachings, 171
    female, 125
    motherly, 209–10, 211, 213, 218
    parental, 100, 209
    self-, 216
Lovejoy, Arthur O., 30
Lo Yun-hsien, 103n.
Lucretius, 31
Lu Hsi-sheng, 140
Lü-shih ch'un-ch'iu (Mr. Lu's Spring
    and Autumn Annals), 8, 11, 18,
    19, 80n., 100, 177

Machines, 228–30
Maclagan, P. J., 5
Magic, 25, 30
Ma Hsü-lun, 4, 57n., 151, 160, 164,
    169
Malinda, King, story of, 151
Mana (power), 195
Martial arts, 211
Marx, Karl, 35, 36, 41, 112, 224, 230
Marxists, 56, 57
Matthew, 171, 201, 224
Ma-wang Tui, 113
Ma-wang Tui texts, 44, 45, 46, 187
    Chapter 1, 52, 53
    Chapter 2, 55, 57
    Chapter, 4, 63
    Chapter 10, 78n., 80
    Chapter 14, 89
    Chapter 18, 99n.
    Chapter 21, 107n.
    Chapter 24, 115
    Chapter 26, 120n.
    Chapter 31, 131

Chapter 42, 157, 158
Chapter 62, 198
Chapter 72, 217
Chapter 73, 218
Mei (the beautiful), 56, 231
Men (dull-witted), 105
Mencius, 5, 20
Mencius, 16, 204
Messiah, 152–53
Miao:
    hidden, 53
    mysterious, 91
Mieh (to destroy), 223
Military art, see Warfare
Military school, 190
Ming:
    destiny, 96
    enlightenment, 123, 136, 181
    illuminating, 155, 178, 205
Mr. Lu's Spring and Autumn Annals
    (Lü-shih ch'un-ch'iu), 8, 11, 18,
    19, 80n., 100, 177
Mo chih ling (without being
    commanded), 134
Moltmann, Jurgen, 39
Mo neng ch'en (nothing under heaven
    can subjugate it), 134
Monotheism, 26, 28
Motherly love, 209–10, 211, 213, 218
Mo Ti, 5, 11
Mou (to plan), 203
Mu (mother), 71, 179
Murray, John Courtney, 32

Natural opposites, 57, 58, 123
Nature, 28, 29–31, 33, 35–36, 145–49,
    167, 171, 175–77, 207, 227
    Chinese view of, 33–34
    Christianity and theology of, 39
    cyclical movement of, 94, 117, 119,
        206
    frugality and preservation of, 210
    government of, 97, 98–99, 205, 220
    Judeo-Christian view of, 127
    sacredness of, 133
    science and, 32

as self-balancing, 224
Taoism and, 41–42, 127
te, 114, 146, 171, 175–77, 184, 193, 201
virtue and, 99–100, 201–202
way to restore people to harmony of, 101
Needham, Joseph, 54, 229
Neo-Platonism, 179
Neumann, Erich, 67
Nicomachean Ethics, 87
Nietzsche, Friedrich Wilhelm, 30, 40, 187
1984 (Orwell), 206
Nirvana, 28, 37
No action, 18, 41, 52, 60, 127, 142, 144, 147, 167, 169, 170, 187, 191, 202, 211
Non-contention, 110–13, 114
Nuclear warfare, xi, 36, 38, 129

O (the ugly), 56
Old age, 185, 187
Ontology, fundamental, 89, 117, 150, 152
Opposites, 56–57, 61, 104, 123, 125, 136, 154, 159, 163, 222, 226, 231
in international relations, 196
Orwell, George, 206
Outline of the History of Chinese Philosophy (Hu Shih), 23

Pacifism, 212
Packard, Vance, 229
Pao:
preserved, 199
treasure, 199, 213
Pao i (to embrace the one), 112
Parmenides, 7–8, 28
Peace, x, xi, 24, 128, 131, 139, 144, 145, 160, 165
complementarity of opposite states and, 196–97
vision of, 40–43
Pen (foundation), 120n.
Phaedo (Plato), 165

Pien (eloquence), 163
P'in:
mare, 70
stillness, passivity, 70–71
Ping:
army, 223
weapon, 223
P'ing t'ai (peace), 139
Pinyin system, 47–48
Plato, 28, 29, 30, 109, 121, 137, 138, 224
Allegory of the Cave, 81
Phaedo, 165
Symposium, 165
Plotonius, 95, 105, 168
Po:
whiteness, 155
wide learning, 231
P'o:
bland, 104
soul, 70, 79
Politics, 150, 151, 208
cyclical process and, 142
see also Ethics; Government
Polytheism, 26
Predestination, 123
Protestant ethic, 224
Proudhon, Pierre Joseph, 182
Pu (the not), 89, 146
P'u (uncarved wood), 125, 126, 134, 136, 144, 181, 209, 231
Pu cheng (non-contention), 75, 110, 112–13
Pu ching (show off), 112
Pu fa (does not boast), 112
Pu hsiao:
not like anything, 209
useless, 209
Pu hsin (untrustworthy), 98
Pu-k'o ming (impossible to name), 52
Pu ku (not worthy), 151
Pu kuo:
not oversteppings its boundary, 197
transgressions, 204
Pu ming-yu (having no name), 52
Pu tai (without becoming exhausted), 96, 97

Pu-tsu (inadequacies), 102
Pu̲ tsu sheng (live for self), 73
Pu tz'u (he does not decline them), 57
Pu wei shih (he does not initiate them), 57
Pu ying:
  not exhausted, 62
  not filled to the fill, 61
Pu yü i ching (not desiring there is thus quietude), 143*n.*
Pythagoreans, 28

Records of the Historian (Shih chi) (Ssu-ma Ch'ien), 4, 6–18, 43, 191
Religion(s):
  of the axial period, 27–31
  Confucianism and, x, 28
  for or against life, 36–40
  function and role of early, 24–27
  humans becoming gods on earth, 31–34
  pseudo-, 34–36
  Tao Te Ching as religious text, x, 22–43
  vision of peace in, 40–43
  see also individual religions
Reversion, 152–53, 176, 179, 206
Rituals, 6–10, 73, 132, 146, 147–48, 149
Round, life of the, 93–96, 163, 164, 173–74, 176–77, 181, 192, 206
Rousseau, Jean Jacques, 205, 224
Royce, Josiah, 38
Ruler/mystic, psychology of the, 188–89
Russell, Bertrand, 40

Sage ruler, 22, 101, 192
  see also Government; Politics
Saint, 22
Sartre, Jean-Paul, 38, 40, 161, 187
Schafer, E. H., 180
Schmidt, Wilhelm, 26
Schumacher, E. F., 228
Science, 30, 31–32, 33, 167
  in China, 33, 34, 229

Se (sparing), 193–94
Secularization, 32–33
Self-equilibrium, 16, 191
Selflessness, 73–77
Self-love, 216
Self-preservation, 110
Self-renewal, 93
Self-transformation, 18, 144, 185
Senses, 84
  overstimulation of, 84
Sensual pleasures, 140
Sermon on the Mount, 111
Shamanism, 67–68, 195
Shan:
  the good, 75, 122, 123, 231
  superior, high, 155
Shang hsien (honoring the worthy), 58
Shan Hai Ching (Book of Mountains and Seas), 71
Shen:
  body, 72, 73, 179
  to expand, grow, or advance forward, 108–109
  the individual, 183
  spirit, 70, 161
Shen ch'i:
  the people, 127
  spirit vessel, 127
Sheng:
  life, 220
  to overcome, to win, 164
  sage ruler, 101
Sheng jen (sage ruler, saint), 22
Sheng sheng (production and reproduction), 70
Shen Hsui, 80
Shih:
  circumstances, 176
  loss of original endowment of nature, 114, 115, 146, 148, 149
  moving away, 63
  origin, 179
  projects, 201
Shih chi (Records of the Historian) (Ssu-ma Ch'ien), 4, 6–18, 43, 191, 214

Shih-yu-san:
   four limbs and nine orifices, 173, 174
   one-third, 173
   ten-with-three, 173, 174
Shou (to abide by), 134
Shu:
   number or counting, 68
   speed or quickness, 68
Shu-ching (Book of History), 227
Shui hsing (moral actions superfluous
      to activity of natural beings), 115
Shuo Kua (Discussion of the Trigrams),
      85, 134n., 179–80
Shuo Wen, 62, 63, 104, 193
Shuo-yüan (Collection of Discourses),
      19, 60
Sinism, 16
Socrates, 8, 28, 215, 218
Spencer, Herbert, 25–26, 35
Spirits, 195
Spiritual Canticle, 156
Ssu (death), 222
Ssu-ma Ch'ien, 4, 6–18, 43, 191, 214
Ssu-ma T'an, 21
Stace, Walter, 89
Su Ch'e, 66
Su jen (worldly people), 104
Sun (to decrease), 160
Sung Dynasty, 4
Suzuki, O. T., 115
Swimme, Brian, 43
Symposium, Plato's 159
Szu:
   private self, 72, 96
   self-awareness, 102

Ta (great), 155, 156
Tai (destruction), 162
T'ai-chi (Supreme Ultimate), 96, 118,
      158
T'ai-chi Ch'uan, 211
T'ai p'ing (peace), x
T'ai-shih Tan (grand historian Tan), 4
Takeuchi Yoshio, 19
T'ang Chün'i, 18
Tan of Chou, 12, 14

Tao, 40, 51–231
Taoism, 5, 9, 28, 33, 34
   contrasting beliefs of Confucianism
      and, 162, 184, 201
   nature and, 41–42, 43
   as outgrowth from Confucianism,
      20–21, 107–108
   religious, 13n.–14n., 34, 70, 87,
      125n., 159, 187
   rivalry between Confucianism and,
      15–18, 40–41
   version of everlasting life, 40
Tao Te Ching:
   date and authorship of, 4–22
   division into parts and chapters,
      45–46
   how it came to be written, 10–12
   need for a new translation, 47
   oldest texts of, 44–45
   as religious text, x, 22–43
   title of, 43
   transliteration of the Chinese, 47–48
   various arrangements of the text,
      46–47
Tao-yin (circulating the Tao), 187,
      187n.
Te:
   communal wealth, 184
   consciousness and, 146–47
   heavy with accumulated, 194
   high, 146–47, 155
   as life force, 195
   low, 146–47
   moral perfection, 184
   nature, 114, 146, 171, 175–77, 184,
      193, 201
   as the small or incipient state of
      things, 200–201, 203
   the state prior to desire or action, 185
   virtue, 107–108, 201
"Te Classic," 146
Theogony (Hesiod), 110
Thomas Aquinas, 29, 31–32, 167, 169
Ti:
   fruit or the bud, 63
   God, 63, 64

T'ien (heaven), 17, 161
T'ien hsia (world), 17, 127, 178, 183
T'ien men (heaven's gate), 81
Tillich, Paul, 37
Time, 90
Totemism, 26
  taboo and, 26–27
T'o yo:
  bellows, 67–68
  musicial instrument, 68
  reproduction by male and female, 68
Tranquility, 18, 164, 191, 194
Transcendence, x, 27, 40, 42
Treasures, three cardinal, 209–10, 211, 213
Tree and its root, symbol of, 95
Tsai (power to judge and execute), 177
Tsao (agitated), 164
Tse (thus, then), 111
Tso chuan (Tso's Commentary on the Spring and Autumn Annals), 10, 36–37, 37
Tsui (offenses), 199, 204
Ts'ui Shu, 4, 5
Tsung (ancestor), 62
Tui (aperture), 179–80
T'ung (penetrating or passing through), 91, 96
Tylor, Edward B., 24, 25, 26
Tzu (self), 72
Tz'u:
  benevolence and compassion of the creative being, 132–33, 209, 210
  female, 125
  motherly love, 209–10, 211, 213, 218
  parental love, 100, 209
Tzu-chang, 199
Tzu-cheng (self-equilibrium), 18, 191
Tzu chung (baggage wagon), 143
Tzu-hua (self-transformation), 18, 144, 185
Tzu-jan:
  natural path, 189
  self-becoming, creativity, 119
  spontaneity, 136

Tzu-kung, 75, 229
Tzu sheng (the self), 136

Universal brotherhood, 29
Urgrund, 63
Value consciousness, 180
Value opposites, 56–57, 58, 104, 123
Virtue, 107–108
  nature and, 99–100, 201–202
Viscera, five, 70

Wade-Giles system, 47–48
Waley, Arthur, 40, 76n., 79, 83, 151, 193
Wang:
  forgetfulness, 186
  without being forgotten, 137
Wang An-shih, 62
Wang Chung, 4, 5
Wang Huai, 63
Wang Pi, 65–66
Wang Pi text, 44, 45, 46, 56, 69
  Chapter 1, 52, 53
  Chapter 2, 55, 56
  Chapter 3, 58–59
  Chapter 4, 61, 62, 63
  Chapter 5, 68
  Chapter 7, 73
  Chapter 8, 75
  Chapter 9, 76n.
  Chapter 10, 77n.
  Chapter 11, 85
  Chapter 13, 86n.
  Chapter 15, 91, 93
  Chapter 16, 95, 96
  Chapter 17, 98
  Chapter 18, 100, 101
  Chapter 20, 106
  Chapter 21, 106n., 107n., 109, 110
  Chapter 22, 114
  Chapter 25, 118–19
  Chapter 26, 120n.
  Chapter 31, 131
  Chapter 33, 135, 137, 139
  Chapter 36, 142
  Chapter 37, 143n.

Chapter 38, 146
Chapter 39, 151
Chapter 40, 153
Chapter 41, 155, 156
Chapter 47, 167–68
Chapter 51, 176
Chapter 53, 182
Chapter 55, 186, 187
Chapter 56, 189
Chapter 62, 198
Chapter 63, 201
Chapter 67, 210
Chapter 69, 213
Chapter 72, 217
Chapter 73, 218
Chapter 76, 223
Warfare, 128–33, 148, 165, 166,
    212–13, 218, 229
  daring not to be at the world's front,
    209, 210, 211
  martial arts, 211
  nuclear, xi, 36, 38, 129
  weaponry, 143, 223
Warring States Period, 5, 21
Warrior syndrome, religion and, x,
    36–38
Watson, Burton, 155n.
Wealth, 162, 165, 184, 231
Weaponry, 143, 223
  nuclear warfare, xi, 36, 38, 129
  see also Warfare
Wei:
  action, 60, 127, 144, 145, 184, 201
  artificiality, 100
  small or subtle, 91
Weil, Simone, 168
Wei wu wei (taste the tasteless), 201
Wei yang:
  down, 103n., 104
  limitless, 103n.
  no place of belonging, 103n.
Wei Yüan, 40, 65
Wei Yüan text, 45
Wen (cover up), 102
Wen, King, story of, 123–24
Wen Tzu, 223

White, Lynn, Jr., 39
Whitehead, Alfred North, 38, 63, 153,
    176
Wilhelm, Hellmut, 85
Wilhelm, Richard, 131n., 220
Wittgenstein, Ludwig Josef Johann,
    68
Wu:
  nonbeing, nothing, 52–53, 54, 63,
    75, 82, 158, 159, 177, 179
  as part of duality with yu, 56
  thinghood, 108, 176
Wu chi:
  non-ultimate, 125n.
  without limit, 52, 95, 125, 194
Wu-chih:
  no knowledge, 60
  process of nihilation, 83
Wu-ch'in (without partiality), 52
Wu hou ju yu chien (that which has
    no thickness penetrates that which
    has crevices), 161
Wu-ming (nameless), 52, 179
Wu so kuei (without a home), 105
Wu szu (selflessness), 73
Wu-wei (no action), 18, 41, 52, 60,
    127, 142, 144, 147, 167, 169, 170,
    187, 191, 202, 211
Wu yu (non-being), 161
Wu-yü (desireless), 52, 60
Wu yu i ching (without desire there is
    thus quietude), 143n.

Yang, 93, 158
  active, 99
  as co-creative force with yin, 158–59
Yang Chia-lo, 8
Yang Chu, 5, 11, 20
Yang Yung-kuo, 5
Yen:
  speech, 68, 98
  weariness, 217
Yen-ch'u (sumptuous apartments),
    122
Yen Ling-feng, 52, 53
Yen Tsun text, 44, 45

Yin, 93
  as co-creative force with *yang,*
    158–59
  passive, 69
  voice, 156
Ying:
  the full, 61, 62
  soul, 79
Ying erh (return of the infant), 125
Yin mou (devious tactics), 143, 203
Yoga, 193
Yu:
  being, having, 52–53, 54, 63, 75, 82,
    90, 107, 117, 153, 158, 177, 179
  as part of duality with *wu,* 56
Yü:
  desire, 60, 102, 144, 145, 165–66
  ignorance, 205
  space, 90

Yüan:
  far away, 206
  fathomless, 62
  injury or wrong, 201, 227
  original or primal principle, 54–55,
    91
Yüan te (dark virtue), 81
Yu-chih (coming to be), 83
Yüeh (survey), 109
Yu-ming (named), 52, 179
Yung:
  to describe or give the features, 92
  glory, honor, 156
  to use, usefulness, 61, 62, 71, 82, 83
Yü pu yü (to desire not to desire),
    216
Yü shih (excess food), 115
Yü te (excess nature), 115–16
Yu yü (to have extra), 105